THE
2003 ANNUAL:
Volume 1
Training

(The Fortieth Annual)

JOSSEY-BASS/PFEIFFER
A Wiley Imprint
www.pfeiffer.com

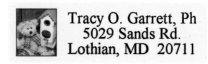
THE
2003 ANNUAL:
Volume 1
Training

(The Fortieth Annual)

Edited by Elaine Biech

JOSSEY-BASS/PFEIFFER
A Wiley Imprint
www.pfeiffer.com

Published by Jossey-Bass/Pfeiffer
A Wiley Imprint
989 Market Street, San Francisco, CA94103-1741   www.pfeiffer.com

Looseleaf ISBN:0-7879-6261-9
Paperback ISBN 0-7879-6264-3
ISSN 1046-333X

Jossey-Bass/Pfeiffer books and products are available through most bookstores. To contact Jossey-Bass/Pfeiffer directly call our Customer Care Department within the U.S. at 800-274-4434, outside the U.S. at 317-572-3985 or fax 317-572-4002.

Jossey-Bass/Pfeiffer also publishes its books in a variety of electronic formats. Some content that appears in print may not be available in electronic books.

Printed in the United States of America

Acquiring Editor: Martin Delahoussaye
Director of Development: Kathleen Dolan Davies
Developmental Editors: Susan Rachmeler and Rebecca Taff
Senior Production Editor: Dawn Kilgore
Manufacturing Supervisor: Becky Carreño

Printing   10   9   8   7   6   5   4   3   2   1

PREFACE

The *2003 Annual: Volume 1, Training*, is the fortieth volume in the *Annual* series, a collection of practical materials written for trainers, consultants, and performance-improvement technologists. This source for experiential learning activities, resource for instruments, and reference for cutting-edge articles has inspired human resource development (HRD) professionals for thirty-two years.

The *Annuals* are published as a set of two: Volume 1, Training, and Volume 2, Consulting. Materials in the training volume focus on skill building and knowledge enhancement. The training volume also features articles that enhance the skills and professional development of trainers. Materials in the consulting volume focus on intervention techniques and organizational systems. The consulting volume also features articles that enhance the skills and professional development of consultants.

Whether you are a trainer, a consultant, a facilitator, or a bit of each, you will find tools and techniques between the *Annual* covers. Trainers, are you looking for ideas to train members of a new department? Design a new training program? Refresh training that is a mainstay in your organization? Incorporate e-learning into your programs? Check out Volume 1. Consultants, are you searching for just the right team-building intervention? New concepts for coaching executives? Resources to send to your clients? A new approach to address communication? You will find it in Volume 2. Facilitators, are you seeking evaluation tools for teams? Feedback tools? Experiential activities to enhance learning? You will find answers in both volumes.

Both volumes provide you with the basics, such as conflict management and communication skills. Both volumes challenge you to use new techniques and models such as storytelling and HR partnerships. Both volumes show you how to utilize technology, such as evaluating e-learning and online communication, throughout your efforts. And both volumes introduce cutting-edge topics such as measuring online learning readiness and retaining high-performance employees.

As you might expect, there is some overlap between the two volumes. Therefore, it is sometimes difficult for an editor to determine which volume is the better location for each submission. And indeed, often submissions could be placed in either. As you search for resources, examine both volumes to find materials that will best meet your needs. You will find that, with a slight modification, you will be able to use activities, articles, and instruments from both volumes.

To ensure that you get the most from both of the *Annuals*, be sure that you have a *Reference Guide* to help you identify all the materials available to you. The *Reference Guide* is a giant index to all of the *Annuals* and the *Handbook of Structured Experiences*, Volumes I through X, that helps you locate just what you need based on topics and key words. A print version of the *Reference Guide* is available for volumes through 1999. An online supplement covering the years through 2003 can be found at www.pfeiffer.com/go/supplement.

There are good reasons that the *Annual* series has been around for over thirty years. In addition to the wide variety of topics and implementation levels, the *Annuals* provide materials that are applicable to varying circumstances. You will find instruments for individuals, teams, and organizations; experiential learning activities to round out workshops, team building, or consulting assignments; and articles to assign as pre-reading, to read to increase your own knowledge base, or to use as reference materials in your writing tasks.

Probably the most important reason the *Annuals* are a success is that they are immediately ready to use. All of the materials in the *Annuals* may be duplicated for educational and training purposes. If you need to adapt or modify the materials to tailor them for your audience's needs, go right ahead. We only request that the credit statement found on the copyright page be included on all copies. In addition, if you intend to reproduce the materials in publications for sale or if you wish to use the materials on a large-scale basis (more than one hundred copies in one year), please contact us for prior written permission. Our liberal copyright policy makes it easy and fast for you to use the materials to do your job. Please call us if you have any questions.

Although the *2003 Annuals* are the newest in the series, you will benefit from having the entire series for your use. They are available in paperback and as a three-ring notebook—and the Pfeiffer Library is available on CD-ROM. I personally refer to many of my *Annuals* from the 1980s. They include several classic activities that have become a mainstay in my team-building designs.

But most of all, the *Annuals* have been a valuable resource for over thirty years because the materials come from professionals like you who work in the field as trainers, consultants, facilitators, educators, and performance-improvement technologists. This ensures that the materials have been tried and perfected in real-life settings with actual participants and clients to meet real-world needs. To this end, we encourage you to submit materials to be considered for publication in the *Annual*. At your request we will provide a copy of the guidelines for preparing your materials. We are interested in receiving experiential learning activities (group learning activities based on the five stages of the experiential learning cycle: experiencing, publishing, processing, generalizing, and applying); inventories, questionnaires, and surveys (both paper-

and-pencil as well as electronic rating scales); and presentation and discussion resources (articles that may include theory related to practical application). Contact the Jossey-Bass/Pfeiffer Editorial Department at the address listed on the copyright page for copies of our guidelines for contributors or contact me directly at Box 8249, Norfolk, VA 23503, or by email at pfeifferannual@aol.com. We welcome your comments, ideas, and contributions.

Thank you to the dedicated, friendly, thoughtful people at Jossey-Bass/ Pfeiffer who produced the *2003 Annuals*: Josh Blatter, Kathleen Dolan Davies, Matt Davis, Dawn Kilgore, Susan Rachmeler, Samya Sattar, and Rebecca Taff. Thank you to Beth Drake of ebb associates inc, who organized this huge task and kept various stages of the submissions flowing in the right directions.

Most important, thank you to our authors, who have once again shared their ideas, techniques, and materials so that HRD professionals everywhere may benefit.

Elaine Biech
Editor
June 2002

About Jossey-Bass/Pfeiffer

Jossey-Bass/Pfeiffer is actively engaged in publishing insightful human resource development (HRD) materials. The organization has earned an international reputation as the leading source of practical resources that are immediately useful to today's consultants, trainers, facilitators, and managers in a variety of industries. All materials are designed by practicing professionals who are continually experimenting with new techniques. Thus, readers and users benefit from the fresh and thoughtful approach that underlies Jossey-Bass/Pfeiffer's experientially based materials, books, workbooks, instruments, and other learning resources and programs. This broad range of products is designed to help human resource practitioners increase individual, group, and organizational effectiveness and provide a variety of training and intervention technologies, as well as background in the field.

CONTENTS

---

*See Experiential Learning Activities Categories, p. 6, for an explanation of the numbering system.

INVENTORIES, QUESTIONNAIRES, AND SURVEYS

PRESENTATION AND DISCUSSION RESOURCES

**Topic is "cutting edge."

GENERAL INTRODUCTION
TO THE 2003 ANNUAL

The 2003 Annual: Volume 1, Training is the fortieth volume in the *Annual* series, a collection of practical and useful materials for professionals in the broad area described as human resource development (HRD). The materials are written by and for professionals, including trainers, organization-development and organization-effectiveness consultants, performance-improvement technologists, facilitators, educators, instructional designers, and others.

Each *Annual* has three main sections: experiential learning activities; inventories, questionnaires, and surveys; and presentation and discussion resources. Each published submission is classified in one of the following categories: Individual Development, Communication, Problem Solving, Groups, Teams, Consulting and Facilitating, Leadership, and Organizations. Within each category, pieces are further classified into logical subcategories, which are identified in the introductions to the three sections.

We continue to identify "cutting edge" topics in this *Annual*. This designation highlights topics that present information, concepts, tools, or perspectives that may be recent additions to the profession or that have not previously appeared in the *Annual*.

The series continues to provide an opportunity for HRD professionals who wish to share their experiences, their viewpoints, and their processes with their colleagues. To that end, Jossey-Bass/Pfeiffer publishes guidelines for potential authors. These guidelines are available from the Pfeiffer Editorial Department at Jossey-Bass, Inc., in San Francisco, California.

Materials are selected for the *Annuals* based on the quality of the ideas, applicability to real-world concerns, relevance to current HRD issues, clarity of presentation, and ability to enhance our readers' professional development. In addition, we chose experiential learning activities that will create a high degree of enthusiasm among the participants and add enjoyment to the learning process. As in the past several years, the contents of each *Annual* span a wide range of subject matter, reflecting the range of interests of our readers.

Our contributor list includes a wide selection of experts in the field: in-house practitioners, consultants, and academically based professionals. A list of contributors to the *Annual* can be found at the end of the volume, including their names, affiliations, addresses, telephone numbers, facsimile numbers, and email addresses. Readers will find this list useful if they wish to locate the authors of specific pieces for feedback, comments, or questions. Further information is presented in a brief biographical sketch of each contributor that appears at the conclusion of each article. We publish this information to encourage "networking," which continues to be a valuable mainstay in the field of human resource development.

We are pleased with the high quality of material that is submitted for publication each year and often regret that we have page limitations. In addition, just as we cannot publish every manuscript we receive, you may find that not all published works are equally useful to you. Therefore, we encourage and invite ideas, materials, and suggestions that will help us to make subsequent *Annuals* as useful as possible to all of our readers.

Introduction
to the Experiential Learning Activities Section

Experiential learning activities ensure that lasting learning occurs. They should be selected with a specific learning objective in mind. These objectives are based on the participants' needs and the facilitator's skills. Although the experiential learning activities presented here all vary in goals, group size, time required, and process,[1] they all incorporate one important element: questions that ensure learning has occurred. This discussion, lead by the facilitator, assists participants to process the activity, to internalize the learning, and to relate it to their day-to-day situations. It is this element that creates the unique experience and learning opportunity that only an experiential learning activity can bring to the group process.

Readers have used the *Annuals'* experiential learning activities for years to enhance their training and consulting events. Each learning experience is complete and includes all lecturettes, handout content, and other written material necessary to facilitate the activity. In addition, many include variations of the design that the facilitator might find useful. If the activity does not fit perfectly with your objective, within your time frame, or to your group size, we encourage you to adapt the activity by adding your own variations. You will find additional experiential learning activities listed in the "Experiential Learning Activities Categories" chart that immediately follows this introduction.

The *2003 Annual: Volume 1, Training* includes seventeen activities, in the following categories:

Individual Development: Self-Disclosure

723. Purposeful Spot Game: Creating Winners in Business, by Teri-E Belf

---

[1]It would be redundant to print here a caveat for the use of experiential learning activities, but HRD professionals who are not experienced in the use of this training technology are strongly urged to read the "Introduction" to the *Reference Guide to Handbooks and Annuals* (1999 Edition). This article presents the theory behind the experiential-learning cycle and explains the necessity of adequately completing each phase of the cycle to allow effective learning to occur.

Leadership: Motivation

736. Intrinsic/Extrinsic Motivators: Encouraging Creativity,
    by Elizabeth A. Smith

Leadership: Styles

737. When I Manage, When I Lead: Separating the Functions,
    by Steve Sphar

738. Meet My Leader: Using Analogy to Describe Traits, by Lois B. Hart

Organizations: Vision, Mission, Values, Strategy

739. Lasso Your Vision, Mission, and Values: Building Team Support and
    Commitment, by Cher Holton

Locate other activities in these and other categories in the "Experiential Learning Activities Categories" chart that follows or in the comprehensive *Reference Guide to Handbooks and Annuals*. This guide, which is updated regularly, indexes all of the *Annuals* and all of the *Handbooks of Structured Experiences* that we have published to date. With each revision, the *Reference Guide* becomes a complete, up-to-date, and easy-to-use resource for selecting appropriate materials from all of the *Annuals* and *Handbooks*. A print version of the *Reference Guide* is available for volumes through 1999. An online supplement covering the years through 2003 can be found at www.pfeiffer.com/go/supplement.

EXPERIENTIAL LEARNING ACTIVITIES CATEGORIES

Vol. Page

INDIVIDUAL DEVELOPMENT

Sensory Awareness

	Vol.	Page
Feelings & Defenses (56)	III	31
Lemons (71)	III	94
Growth & Name Fantasy (85)	'72	59
Group Exploration (119)	IV	92
Relaxation & Perceptual Awareness (136)	'74	84
T'ai Chi Chuan (199)	VI	10
Roles Impact Feelings (214)	VI	102
Projections (300)	VIII	30
Mastering the Deadline Demon (593)	'98–1	9
Learning Shifts (643)	'00–1	11
Secret Sponsors (657)	'00–2	11
Spirituality at Work (670)	'01–1	11
What You See (740)	'03–2	11

Self-Disclosure

	Vol.	Page
Johari Window (13)	I	65
Graphics (20)	I	88
Personal Journal (74)	III	109
Make Your Own Bag (90)	'73	13
Growth Cards (109)	IV	30
Expressing Anger (122)	IV	104
Stretching (123)	IV	107
Forced-Choice Identity (129)	'74	20
Boasting (181)	'76	49
The Other You (182)	'76	51
Praise (306)	VIII	61
Introjection (321)	'82	29
Personality Traits (349)	IX	158
Understanding the Need for Approval (438)	'88	21
The Golden Egg Award (448)	'88	89
Adventures at Work (521)	'95–1	9
That's Me (522)	'95–1	17
Knowledge Is Power (631)	'99–2	13
Spirituality at Work (658)	'00–2	15

	Vol.	Page
The Imposter Syndrome (696)	'02–1	11
Internet Impressions (710)	'02–2	11
Purposeful Spot Game (723)	'03–1	11

Sex Roles

	Vol.	Page
Polarization (62)	III	57
Sex-Role Stereotyping (95)	'73	26
Sex-Role Attributes (184)	'76	63
Who Gets Hired? (215)	VI	106
Sexual Assessment (226)	'78	36
Alpha II (248)	VII	19
Sexual Values (249)	VII	24
Sex-Role Attitudes (258)	VII	85
Sexual Values in Organizations (268)	VII	146
Sexual Attraction (272)	'80	26
Sexism in Advertisements (305)	VIII	58
The Promotion (362)	IX	152
Raising Elizabeth (415)	'86	21
The Problem with Men/Women Is .. (437)	'88	9
The Girl and the Sailor (450)	'89	17
Tina Carlan (466)	'90	45

Diversity

	Vol.	Page
Status-Interaction Study (41)	II	85
Peer Perceptions (58)	III	41
Discrimination (63)	III	62
Traditional American Values (94)	'73	23
Growth Group Values (113)	IV	45
The In-Group (124)	IV	112
Leadership Characteristics (127)	'74	13
Group Composition (172)	V	139
Headbands (203)	VI	25
Sherlock (213)	VI	92
Negotiating Differences (217)	VI	114
Young/Old Woman (227)	'78	40

	Vol.	Page
Pygmalion (229)	'78	51
Race from Outer Space (239)	'79	38
Prejudice (247)	VII	15
Physical Characteristics (262)	VII	108
Whom To Choose (267)	VII	141
Data Survey (292)	'81	57
Lifeline (298)	VIII	21
Four Cultures (338)	'83	72
All Iowans Are Naive (344)	IX	14
AIRSOPAC (364)	IX	172
Doctor, Lawyer, Indian Chief (427)	'87	21
Life Raft (462)	'90	17
Zenoland (492)	'92	69
First Impressions (509)	'94	9
Parole Board (510)	'94	17
Fourteen Dimensions (557)	'96–2	9
Adoption (569)	'97–1	9
Globalization (570)	'97–1	19
Generational Pyramids (571)	'97–1	33
People with Disabilities (594)	'98–1	15
Expanding the Scope of Diversity Programs (617)	'99–1	13
Tortuga Place and Your Place (644)	'00–1	15
Unearned Privilege (659)	'00–2	25
What's Your Generation X IQ? (682)	'01–2	11
Cultural Triangle (697)	'02–1	19
Other Perspectives (724)	'03–1	25
Early Memories (741)	'03–2	17

Life/Career Planning

	Vol.	Page
Life Planning (46)	II	101
Banners (233)	'79	9
Wants Bombardment (261)	VII	105
Career Renewal (332)	'83	27
Life Assessment and Planning (378)	'85	15

723. Purposeful Spot Game: Creating Winners in Business

Goals

- To explore the relationship between the self and the whole.
- To create a context for making choices that are congruent personally, professionally, and organizationally.
- To experience making purposeful choices in a partnership or a group setting where multiple or competing goals exist.
- To highlight personal responsibility for making choices.
- To increase awareness of how one operates in a partnership or a group when a personal purpose, agenda, or goal may be contrary to that of the group purpose or goal.
- To learn how to create win-win scenarios in any setting and under any circumstances.

Group Size

Five to one hundred participants.

Time Required

Approximately two and one-half hours.

Materials

- A copy of the Purposeful Spot Game Affirmative Statements List for the facilitator.

- Copies of the Purposeful Spot Game Reflection Handout for all participants.

- Copies of the Purposeful Spot Game Development Plan for all participants.

- Copies of the Purposeful Spot Game Identity and the Infinite I Handout for all participants.

- Music (on tape or CD).

- Tape or CD player.

- Whiteboard or flip-chart easel with paper.

- Felt-tipped markers.

- Pencils for participants.

Physical Setting

Participants need to sit, write, and move about. The room must be large enough for participants to mill around and join hands so that everyone is connected. Some chairs, tables, pillows, and any other obstructions lower than the height of the participants must be inside the circle, and some must be outside the circle. Ensure safety and ensure that nothing of value can be damaged. Auditorium style seating works as well as any number of round or oblong tables.

Preparation

1. Use the Purposeful Spot Game Affirmative Statements List to familiarize yourself with the process of writing affirmative statements.

Process

1. Say to participants, "We will play a game first. Then you will write down your thoughts about the experience. After the game ends, reflections, learning, insights, and applications will be discussed in the large group. At the end you will have the option of playing the game again."

2. Instruct participants to stand and mill around the room and, while milling, to select spots somewhere in the room (or visible from the room) as their own private spots, keeping the location of their chosen spots secret. (Three minutes.)

3. Ask participants to stop milling and hold hands so that all participants together form one large group, whether circle or any other shape.

4. Explain these rules of the game: "From this point on, you may not let go of the hands you are holding. You may not speak. Your task is to take everyone in the group to your private spot. You will begin when the music starts and stop when the music stops." Repeat these instructions slowly and clearly.

5. Before you continue, say, "If anyone in the group has a physical condition that might hinder participation, or if anyone anticipates discomfort in playing this game, I invite you now to step out of the circle silently and stand or sit on the sidelines." Let participants choose for themselves. After you begin, greet latecomers and invite them to stand or sit anywhere and silently observe. (You might write a note on the flip chart for latecomers saying: "If you arrive after the music has begun, find a place to stand or sit and observe what transpires. Your observations will be useful when the music stops.")

6. Allow a moment for those people who choose to leave the circle to do so and for remaining players to readjust their positions and hold hands again. Ask whether there are any questions and repeat the instructions if necessary.

7. Begin the music and instruct them to begin.

8. Only interfere if, in your judgment, safety is about to be compromised. Allow the game to continue until you see evidence that the movement of the group begins to flow instead of appearing erratic, hesitant, jerky, or aggressive. This will take at least ten minutes, likely longer. If there is no evidence of this phenomenon, stop the music after a maximum of twenty-five minutes.

9. Observe what happens. Take notes for discussion.

   ■ Note people pulling and tugging at each other to influence the group's movement and direction.

   ■ Note when people break the rules, for example, by letting go of hands, speaking, or using intense nonverbal gestures.

   ■ Note expressions on participants' faces such as delight, frustration, amusement, anger, and so on.

   ■ Listen for any side talk, whispering, or laughter.

- Pay attention to the movement of the group as a whole as well as to individuals who stand out in some manner, for example, by refusing to move, sitting down, or pulling on others.

(Fifteen to twenty-five minutes.)

10. Ask them to stop and give each participant a copy of the Purposeful Spot Game Reflection Handout and a pencil. Tell everyone to find a place to quietly reflect on the questions and write down their thoughts. Ask them to be sure they jot down their answers to question fifteen. Tell them they have fifteen minutes to complete the handout. (Fifteen minutes.)

11. Bring everyone together again and begin group discussion by saying, "Your choice of a personal spot was analogous to setting a personal goal or having a personal purpose or agenda. In that sense, your task was to share your goal with other members of the group. Let's examine how you behaved when attempting to achieve a personal goal in a group. As you listen to what other people say, remember these guidelines for listening." (Read the following aloud and post them on the flip chart.)

- Any point of view is potentially an accurate one.
- All contributions have value.
- Take this opportunity to learn as much as you can about yourself.
- Be open to the unexpected.
- Listen with your heart.
- Own, even treasure, your personal needs.
- Come from a state of wonder (One-der).

(Five minutes.)

12. Begin the reflection process by asking any of the questions from the Purposeful Spot Game Reflection Handout. Encourage participants to share what they learned about themselves. Capture their insights as affirmative statements for all to see on the flip chart. Title this list "Guidelines for Living." Use only participants' own words, but convert them into affirmative statements, written in the present tense, positively stated, and personalized, that is, using the terms "I," "me," "my," and "myself." Use the Purposeful Spot Game Affirmative Statements List to remind yourself of the wording of affirmative statements, but do not share the list with the participants. They will generate their own insights. Your role is to translate their insights into affirmations.

13. Post people's insights, interspersing your observations and those of any other observers. (Thirty minutes.)

14. Close the discussion and then share the following story: "A college student who played this game selected a spot on her own body as her personal spot. She came to realize that, wherever she moved, the whole group was always at her spot because all hands remained connected. She experienced continual success effortlessly."

15. Now introduce the concept of encompassment (Belf, 2002). Say, "The concept of encompassment is transferable to any experience with another person or group, although in the definition I am about to read the author is referring to a coach working with a client. Encompassment is the practice of going with emergent energy instead of denying or resisting. The word *compass,* representing the whole circle, lies within *encompassment.* In coaching, encompassment means drawing a circle around you and the client so you both reside in the same circle. When you encompass a client, rapport and respect strengthen. Encompassment can happen through verbal language, physical gestures, or the sounds of silence, as we saw by playing our game." Ask for comments about the concept of encompassment. (Ten minutes.)

16. Continue by saying, "In order to be winners in any game we play, we must be purposeful, downgrade what is not purposeful to the background, let go of attachment to results, trust that what happens is for the highest good of ourselves and all others concerned; be in the present moment, available, connected to ourselves, each other, and the whole, able to choose our responses in a state of wonder and curiosity; and be of service. If we are grateful for all of this, then we all 'win.'" Ask for comments about how a sense of purpose, encompassment, and personal goals are connected and post them on the flip chart. (Fifteen minutes.)

17. Next, ask participants to reflect on the applicability of the principles that have been posted to their personal and professional lives. Ask this question: "How might you behave differently in your next group [team, community] meeting as a result of what you have learned about yourself today?" Give everyone copies of the Purposeful Spot Game Development Plan and give them ten minutes to answer the questions. (Twelve minutes.)

18. After they have had ten minutes to work on their development plans, lead a discussion of their answers and how they plan to change their lives

as a result of what they have learned about themselves and setting and sharing goals. (Fifteen minutes.)

19. Ask those who would like to play the game again or those who observed last time and would like to play now to stand up. Have them choose personal spots again and form a loose circle by joining hands. Remind them to apply what they have learned to how they play the game this time. Encourage experimentation, trying out new behavior, taking risks, and being their authentic selves.

20. Repeat the rules, begin the music, and observe. Note that this game could be over very quickly and you can expect within the first minute to see the group functioning as a whole. Allow a few rounds of this experience to reinforce the learning. (Five to eight minutes.)

21. Bring everyone together for a wrap-up discussion. Ask participants to what extent they "encompassed" the whole picture this time on a scale of 1 to 10. Have them compare the two experiences. Present your own observations about any differences between the first and second rounds. Discuss and list the reasons why there was a change on the flip chart. (Ten minutes.)

22. To move toward closure, say, "In summary, I'd like to read some excerpts, paraphrased only slightly, from the book, *Simply Live It UP.* I will give you a copy of this handout as you leave, so listen, rather than try to take notes." Then read from the Purposeful Spot Game Identity and the Infinite I Handout and summarize its meaning through discussion. (Ten minutes.)

23. Thank the participants for coming and daring to play the game. Give everyone copies of the Purposeful Spot Game Identity and the Infinite I Handout as they leave.

24. Congratulate yourself for having facilitated an extremely powerful and meaningful exercise. Take a moment and list what you have learned too.

Variations

- Use an overhead projector for larger groups.
- Play this game outdoors.

References

Belf, T. (2002). *Coaching with spirit: Allowing success to emerge.* San Francisco, CA: Jossey-Bass/Pfeiffer.

Belf, T., & Ward, C. (1997). *Simply live it up: Brief solutions.* Bethesda, MD: Purposeful Press.

Submitted by Teri-E Belf.

Teri-E Belf, M.A., C.A.G.S., M.C.C., *is a purposeful, inspired coaching leader, author, and speaker, cited in the* International Who's Who of Entrepreneurs. *She shares her sixteen years of certified coaching and eighteen years of HRD management experience in her workshops, articles, and books, among them,* Simply Live It UP: Brief Solutions *(Purposeful Press, 1997), the* Facilitating Life Purpose Manual *(self-published, 2001), and* Coaching with Spirit: Allowing Success to Emerge *(Jossey-Bass/Pfeiffer, 2002).*

PURPOSEFUL SPOT GAME AFFIRMATIVE STATEMENTS LIST

I use the support of others.

I remember that things change.

I compromise so all can win.

I am clear about my purpose.

I stay focused and concentrate.

I recognize that I have and make choices.

My power comes from within, not outside.

I always have a backup plan.

I wait and am patient.

I can be playful, aggressive, and determined at the same time.

I go with the flow.

I realize everything that happens is okay, regardless.

I know where I am at all times.

I'm always in the process of accomplishing.

I now have ways of changing and creating that are assertive and not destructive.

I see how we are connected, instead of separate.

Purposeful Spot Game Reflection Handout

Instructions: Please reflect on the following questions and jot down your thoughts.

1. What did you learn from the way you played this game?

2. Were you successful? Did you achieve your goal?

3. What did you notice about your own behavior?

4. How did you feel during the game?

5. Did you feel powerful? Not powerful? Why?

6. Were you a leader or a follower?

7. Did you consider breaking the rules?

8. Did you break any rules? If yes, how do you feel about that?

9. Did you change rules? If yes, how do you feel about that?

10. Were you aware of others in the room?

11. What did you notice about other participants' behavior?

12. Did you have concern for your safety?

13. Did you have concern for the safety of others?

14. How energetic did you feel at the end of the game?

15. On a scale of 1 to 10, 10 being the most, to what extent did you encompass the whole picture?

16. What would you do differently next time?

PURPOSEFUL SPOT GAME DEVELOPMENT PLAN

Definition

"Encompassment is the practice of going with emergent energy instead of denying or resisting. The word *compass*, representing the whole circle, lies within *encompassment*. In coaching, encompassment means drawing a circle around you and the client so you both reside in the same circle. When you encompass a client, rapport and respect strengthen. Encompassment can happen through verbal language, physical gestures, or the sounds of silence."*

Instructions: Reflect on ways you might apply what you learned to your own life (home, work, and community).

1. What might I do differently?

2. How might I feel?

3. How will I know that I am more effective?

---

*Belf, T. *Coaching with Spirit: Allowing Success to Emerge.* San Francisco, CA: Jossey-Bass/Pfeiffer, 2002.

4. What might others say, notice, or feel?

5. What risks do I dare take?

6. What are possible payoffs and benefits?

7. How might I practice encompassment in my life?

Purposeful Spot Game Identity and the Infinite I Handout**

What if I soared to a bird's-eye view of my life to make choices? What if I made choices and commitments in accord with my *highest* values and purpose? What if I interacted positively and flexibly with my environment? Then I would transcend to a macro-perspective and *access* flow. Expanded thinking, high perspectives, broad vistas, and encompassing viewpoints are giving up to the infinite I.

Giving up is a paradox. It may seem like losing, but giving up can mean letting go of one level of control to participate at a higher level. Acting at your highest levels can bring peace and power.

Paradox: To feel alone, simply close your eyes; to feel connected with the universe, simply close your eyes. We separate; we join. There is no aloneness; there is no togetherness. Both-And, Alone-Together.

**T. Belf & C. Ward. *Simply Live It UP: Brief Solutions.* Bethesda, MD; Purposeful Press, 1997. Chapter 13. Identity and the Infinite I, pp. 199–205.

724. OTHER PERSPECTIVES: FOSTERING THE CREATIVE SPIRIT

Goals

- To demonstrate that there is always more than one way of looking at anything.

- To demonstrate that it is important to identify and assess the factors that limit our creativity.

- To help participants eliminate their own barriers to thinking creatively and to seeing other perspectives.

Group Size

Any size group.

Time Required

Two to three hours, depending on how long is spent viewing the films.

Materials

- An Other Perspectives Possible Solutions Sheet for the facilitator.
- An Other Perspectives Barriers to Creativity Handout for each participant.
- An Other Perspectives Lecturette for the facilitator.
- A monitor and a video player.
- Two different films rented on video:
  - *Patch Adams*, directed by Tom Shadyac in 1998 and distributed by Universal Studios. 115 minutes. (*Synopsis:* Patch Adams [Robin Williams] is studying to become a doctor, but he does not look, act, or think like a traditional doctor. For Patch, humor is the best medicine. He is always willing to do unusual things to make his patients laugh. A revealing film based on a story that goes beyond a traditional comedy.)

- *Baraka*, directed by Ron Fricke in 1992 and distributed by Magidson Productions. 96 minutes. (*Synopsis:* This film shows us an impressive mosaic of images not only of human groups but also of animals, statues, buildings, and natural elements. The main theme of the film is not presented in a conventional way. The images jump from a Buddhist ritual in Nepal to the Masai dances in Kenya or the Nô Japanese theatre. To sum up, it is an incredible and breathtaking journey through six continents and twenty-four countries.)

- A flip chart.
- Felt-tipped markers.
- Blank paper and pens or pencils for participants.

Physical Setting

A room large and flexible enough to allow participants to experience different kinds of activities, from watching a movie to relaxing while lying on the floor.

Process

1. Explain that the purpose of this activity is to help them to enhance their creative processes and to see things from other perspectives.

2. Give participants blank paper and pens or pencils and tell them to write the Roman numeral nine (IX) on a sheet of paper. When everyone has finished, tell them to "add one line to make six." Do not tell them anything else. Allow a few minutes and ask the participants to share their answers. Write their possible solutions on the flip chart. (Five minutes.)

3. Share any solutions not already mentioned from the Other Perspectives Possible Solutions Sheet, describing them and posting them on the flip chart. (Five minutes.)

4. Engage the group in a discussion of the following points about creativity:

   - What does solving this puzzle show us about seeing things differently?
   - Why don't some people consider alternatives easily?
   - What skills or behaviors would be useful for us to develop our ability to see different points of view?

- What kinds of behaviors would you like to start doing or stop doing that inhibit your own ability to see things from another perspective?

(Fifteen minutes.)

5. After wrapping up the discussion, ask the participants to select partners. Tell them that one member of each pair should show four fingers of one hand and hide his or her thumb. The partner should decide how many fingers are shown. (Probably everybody will say four, although they may be motivated because of the last activity to look for different solutions.) Tell everyone to get comfortable for watching a film.

6. Set up for showing *Patch Adams.* You will only show two different scenes from the film.

Show scene number 1 (Min. 9'23 to 11'50). This scene takes place in the psychiatric hospital, where Patch Adams has admitted himself voluntarily after a failed suicide attempt. In the hospital he meets Arthur, a patient obsessed with showing people four fingers of his hand and asking them: "How many fingers can you see?" Everybody says four. The scene shows Patch visiting Arthur to find out the solution. Arthur's answer is: "If you only focus on the problem, you will never see the solution. Look further. You have to see what other people do not see." (Five minutes.)

7. Engage the group in a discussion of the following questions and issues:

- What is the relationship between the creativity exercise we did earlier and the film clip you just saw?

- What factors restrict our ability to look beyond what we see?

- What does seeing what others do not see mean? How can we achieve that goal?

(Ten minutes.)

8. *Show scene number 2* (Min. 20' to 21'40). In this scene, Patch has left the psychiatric hospital and is now studying medicine. The scene begins when Patch and his new friend Truman, another student, are having breakfast. Truman is reflecting on the human mind and on the changing of behavioral patterns (the adoption of programmed answers) when a person grows older. Patch proposes to carry out the Hello Experiment. The objective of the experiment is "to change the programmed answer by changing the usual parameters." (Five minutes.)

9. Engage the group in a discussion of the following questions:

- What is your understanding of a programmed answer?

- What is the link between our programmed answers and our ability to exhibit creativity?

- How can we "de-program" ourselves?

(Ten minutes.)

10. To summarize the learnings of the session at this point, introduce the audience to some barriers to creativity. Distribute the Other Perspectives Barriers to Creativity Handout to each participant and use it as a basis for further discussion. (Ten minutes.)

11. Introduce the next section by stating that people have difficulty seeing problems and situations in more than one way. That is because we have lost our creative spirit. Once we are aware of this fact, it is much easier for us to use some special techniques that help us to unleash our creativity.

12. Show the film, *Baraka.*

> *Trainer's Note:* The purpose of this film is to show diversity using a film which is itself creative (it does not explain anything, it does not contain a word, and music plays a fundamental role) to show tensions and oppositions (nature versus culture, individual versus group, human versus animal life, urban versus rural life, modernity versus primitivism), to show how different we are and, at the same time, how alike we are. Due to the strength of the images shown and to the suitable sound track, the film can be used to accompany a relaxation exercise that allows new feelings to appear and helps participants acquire a positive attitude that nourishes their creative spirit.
>
> It is highly recommended that participants watch the whole movie, which lasts about ninety-six minutes. If this is not possible, any segment can be selected for viewing, as there is no context or plot.

(Up to ninety-six minutes.)

13. Engage the group in a discussion using the following questions, posting responses on the flip chart:

- What did you feel while watching this film? Why did you feel that way?

- What do you think *baraka* means? Why do you think the movie has this name?

- What do the set of images shown have in common? Explain.

- What have you learned about your own barriers to creative thinking?

(Ten minutes.)

14. Summarize the main learning induced by this session with the Other Perspectives Lecturette. (Five minutes.)

Submitted by Mila Gascó Hernández and Teresa Torres Coronas.

Mila Gascó Hernández, Ph.D., *has bachelor's and master's degrees in management and a Ph.D. in public management. She is a senior analyst in the International Institute on Governance in charge of the decentralization and local government team and the Information Society project. She is a professor in the Universitat Oberta de Catalunya and one of the Spanish associates of the Center for Research in Applied Creativity (in Canada). She is also co-author of the book* Retrieve Your Creativity *(Septemediciones, Spain).*

Teresa Torres Coronas, Ph.D., *has a bachelor's degree in economics and a Ph.D. in management. She won first prize in the 2000 edition of EADA related to management research. She is the author of the book* Valuing Brands *(Ediciones Gestión 2000, Spain), co-author of the book* Retrieve Your Creativity, *and author of many articles about intangible assets. She is a professor in the Universitat Rovira i Virgili and she is one of the Spanish associates of the Center for Research in Applied Creativity (in Canada).*

OTHER PERSPECTIVES POSSIBLE SOLUTIONS SHEET

Here are some possible solutions:

1. If we bisect the IX with a straight transverse line, we can get six in two different ways: (a) by counting six straight lines (three over the line and three underneath it) or (b) by turning the sheet of paper upside down so that the number six appears in Roman numerals above the line.

2. If you draw a curved line (circle) around the first character, you will create a clock whose hands point to 6:00.

3. If you add a curved line (taking the shape of the letter S) in front of the IX, you will get the number six in English.

Other Perspectives Barriers to Creativity Handout

Learning Barriers

We learn correct responses, routines, and patterns of behavior. We learn "the way things have always been done" and "the way things are supposed to be done." Over the years it becomes difficult for us to see and create new possibilities. The most obvious learning barriers to creativity are *prior learning* and *force of habit*.

Perceptual Barriers

From a lifetime of learning we are used to perceiving things in a particular way, often making it difficult for us to see new meanings, relationships, and ideas. Psychologists refer to our predisposition to perceive things in certain ways as a perceptual set, a mental set, or as functional fixedness. Perceptual barriers create the reverse of flexible, innovative thinking. Perceptual sets are tied to our tendency to make quick decisions and to jump to conclusions, rather than flexibly seeing alternatives. Perceptual blocks also prevent us from obtaining a complete and accurate picture of the real problem.

Being *flexible* is an important part of the effective cognitive process. Flexibility represents a capacity for change—whether a change in the meaning, interpretation, or use of information; a change in understanding of the task; a change of strategy for doing the task; or a change in direction of thinking. Flexibility allows an individual to see all the aspects of a problem and not just one of the facets. Being flexible allows us to see the parameters and boundaries of problems. Flexible people are capable of redefining problems and coming up with innovative solutions. One recommendation for being more creative, "Make the familiar strange," encourages people to see common objects and situations in new ways, to overcome too-familiar perceptions, and to look for new and different ideas. Creativity involves a transformational mental process, the perception of new meanings, combinations, and relationships.

Cultural Barriers

Cultural barriers to creativity are related to social influence, expectations, and pressures for conformity, which are based on social and institutional norms. Cultural blocks include habits and previous learning, "rules," cultural and family traditions, and more. Cultural barriers make us want to conform to the way we think others expect us to behave and to fear being different.

OTHER PERSPECTIVES LECTURETTE

What Creativity Is

Paul Torrance, who can be considered one of the fathers of creativity, once said that creativity is to want to know, to look twice, to listen to the smells, to build sand castles, to sing while taking a shower, to have a ball, to dig deep, to make holes to see through them.

For us, creativity is, then, to look for that which does not exist, to see what we usually see in a different way, to imagine, to solve problems, to fail, to experience, and, above all, to grow personally and professionally to become a unique person.

To have an open mind is a necessary condition to becoming a more creative person. Having an open mind requires an insatiable curiosity (related to the need to learn continuously), a commitment to verify knowledge through experience and to learn from mistakes, the willingness to accept ambiguity and fuzziness, the ability to develop a balance between art and science and logic and imagination, and the realization that everything is interrelated so diversity can help our understanding of the world rather than erode it.

Watching *Baraka* allowed us think about all of these issues.

725. Choices: Learning Effective Conflict-Management Strategies

Goals

- To acquaint participants with effective strategies for conflict management.

- To provide participants with a format for analyzing contingencies in conflict situations.

- To offer participants an opportunity to practice conflict management skills and receive performance feedback.

Group Size

Six to thirty participants in teams of three.

Time Required

One and one-half to two hours.

Materials

- One Choices Strategies for Managing Conflict handout for each participant.

- One Choices Strategies and Contingencies handout for each participant.

- One Choices Situations Worksheet for each participant.

- One Choices Popular Selections handout for each participant.

- Flip chart and felt-tipped markers.

- Pens or pencils for participants.

- Masking tape.

Physical Setting

A room large enough for the subgroups to work privately or breakout rooms.

Process

1. Introduce the topic of conflict management, describe the goals of the activity, and invite participants to contribute their preferred strategies for handling conflict situations. Write these on the flip chart. (Ten minutes.)

2. Distribute the Choices Strategies for Managing Conflict and the Choices Strategies and Contingencies handouts to participants. Provide a quick summary of the content, incorporating the contributions offered initially by the participants. (Ten minutes.)

3. Group participants into units of three and distribute the Choices Situations Worksheet and pens or pencils. Instruct subgroups to complete the worksheet as a team. Give them twenty minutes to finish in their groups. (Twenty minutes.)

4. Bring the large group together again and ask participants to reflect on their own behavior when they were faced with a conflict within their subgroup about a particular choice. Which conflict-management strategies were used? (Five minutes.)

5. Lead a discussion of their answers to the worksheet, posting their answers on the flip chart. Use the following questions:

   ■ Were different people's suggested answers within the subgroups similar or different?

   ■ What was the rationale for your response if it was different?

   ■ What did you learn about your personal strategies for managing conflict?

   ■ What might you do differently the next time you are in a conflict situation as a result of what you have learned during this activity?

   ■ How can you be certain to use what you have learned?

   (Twenty minutes.)

6. Provide a copy of the Choices Popular Selections handout for each participant and explain that these are not necessarily the "correct" answers, but the ones chosen most often by those who have filled out the worksheet previously. Discuss briefly why this would be and what the up side of each

answer is. Conclude by listing ways that participants can deal with conflict in new ways back on the job. (Twenty to thirty minutes.)

Variations

- With groups larger than thirty, additional facilitators can be used to provide summary dialogue and feedback at the conclusion of the activity.

- Individuals can complete the worksheet prior to working with others.

- All ten of the worksheet situations need not be used if time is short. Specific situations can be selected to match the needs of the training group.

- Teams can be larger than three; however, an odd number is desirable to eliminate stalemates.

- The first two handouts and additional readings on conflict may be assigned prior to the activity.

Submitted by Chuck Kormanski, Sr., and Chuck Kormanski, Jr.

Chuck Kormanski, Sr., Ed.D., is involved in organizational consulting and training, college teaching, and research in group and team development. Dr. Kormanski has published over twenty-five journal articles and book chapters in his field. He spent twenty-seven years at Penn State Altoona and is currently an assistant adjunct professor at St. Francis University and the University of Pittsburgh at Johnstown. He maintains a business and educational consulting practice in Hollidaysburg, Pennsylvania, and facilitates servant leadership programs for the Blair and Bedford County Chambers of Commerce. Dr. Kormanski is the author of The Team: Explorations in Group Process *(Love Publishing, 1999).*

Chuck Kormanski, Jr., M.S., is the assistant general manager for Mattress World, a bedding retail chain in central Pennsylvania. He teaches human resource management and international business at Penn State Altoona and management and marketing at Mt. Aloysius College.

Choices Strategies for Managing Conflict

Conflict is a naturally occurring phenomenon in group growth and development (Tuckman, 1965). Resistance and hostility eventually follow the initial stage (*forming*) of orientation (task focus) and dependency (relationship focus). This *storming* stage usually requires conflict management interventions by leadership in order to move the group forward toward the stages of *norming* (communication and cohesion) and *performing* (problem solving and interdependence).

When viewed from this perspective, conflict becomes an essential predecessor to continued growth and development. A leadership goal, then, may be managing the conflict in a productive way. An optimum level of conflict is seen as healthy and as providing alternatives, new insights, and different perspectives. Extremes are dangerous, however, as too much conflict creates chaos, and the absence of conflict is typically apathy.

Conflict and Leadership

Conflict and leadership are inseparable (Burns, 1978). As conflict increases, the need for effective leadership increases. Effective leadership requires knowledge of contingencies for conflict situations and skill in conflict management. There are five generic techniques for managing conflict. The leader could (1) withdraw from the conflict, (2) suppress or diffuse the conflict, (3) integrate the conflicting positions to form a consensus, (4) seek a compromise, or (5) use some type of authority and power (legitimate position, expertise, democratic voting, or other means) to resolve the conflict.

Conflict-Management Techniques

Knowledge of conflict management begins with understanding the situation in which the conflict is occurring. Each of the five techniques noted above has advantages and disadvantages; therefore, the initial intervention technique selected, as well as a back-up plan, is situational (Kormanski, 1982; Kormanski, 1999).

The advantages and disadvantages of each technique are presented in the Choices Strategies and Contingencies handout, arranged in a hierarchical order. Thus, for example, if integration is ineffective, either of the remaining two techniques (compromise or authority) can serve as a secondary intervention. The preceding two techniques (withdrawal or suppression) cannot be used, however, as once you have intervened it suggests that the conflict is important and needs active involvement by leadership. Per the hierarchy, authority is always the choice of last resort. Once it is used, there are no legitimate back-up interventions.

Conclusion

Being knowledgeable regarding conflict and effective conflict management techniques is only the first step of the process. One must develop the appropriate intervention skills to select and apply the techniques. The rapid, complex nature of change in our current world mandates that leaders possess skills to manage conflict. Lest we fear the process, Roger Lewin (1993) has suggested that the point at which a leader has the most potential for growth as a person is when the organization is right at the edge of chaos.

References

Burns, J. (1978). *Leadership*. New York: Harper & Row.

Kormanski, C. (1982). Leadership strategies for managing conflict. *Journal for Specialists in Group Work*, 7(2), 112–118.

Kormanski, C. (1999). *The team: Explorations in group process*. Denver, CO: Love.

Lewin, R. (1993). *Complexity: Life at the edge of chaos*. London: Orion.

Tuckman, B. (1965). Developmental sequence in small groups. *Psychological Bulletin*, 63, 384–399.

Choices Strategies and Contingencies

Withdrawal as a Strategy

Use When (Advantages)

- Choosing sides is to be avoided
- Critical information is missing
- The issue is outside the group
- Others are competent and delegation is appropriate
- You are powerless

Be Aware (Disadvantages)

- Legitimate action ceases
- Direct information stops
- Failure can be perceived
- Cannot be used in a crisis

Suppression (and Diffusion) as a Strategy

Use When (Advantages)

- A cooling down period is needed
- The issue is unimportant
- A relationship is important

Be Aware (Disadvantages)

- The issue may intensify
- You may appear weak and ineffective

Integration as a Strategy

Use When (Advantages)

- Group problem solving is needed
- New alternatives are helpful

- Group commitment is required
- Promoting openness and trust

Be Aware (Disadvantages)

- Group goals must be put first
- More time is required for dialogue
- It doesn't work with rigid, dull people

Compromise as a Strategy

Use When (Advantages)

- Power is equal
- Resources are limited
- A win-win settlement is desired

Be Aware (Disadvantages)

- Action (a third choice) can be weakened
- Inflation is encouraged
- A third party may be needed for negotiation

Authority as a Strategy

Use When (Advantages)

- A deadlock persists
- Others are incompetent
- Time is limited (crisis)
- An unpopular decision must be made
- Survival of the organization is critical

Be Aware (Disadvantages)

- Emotions intensify quickly
- Dependency is promoted
- Winners and losers are created

CHOICES SITUATIONS WORKSHEET

Instructions: Assume you are a group of top managers who are responsible for an organization of seven departments. Working as a team, choose an appropriate strategy to intervene in the situations below when the conflict must be managed in some way. Your choices are *withdrawal, suppression, integration, compromise,* and *authority.* Refer to the Choices Strategies for Managing Conflict sheet for some characteristics of each. Write your team's choice following each situation number.

Situation #1

Two employees of the support staff have requested the same two-week vacation period. They are the only two trained to carry out an essential task using a complex computer software program that cannot be mastered quickly. You have encouraged others to learn this process so there is more backup for the position, but heavy workloads have prevented this from occurring.

Situation #2

A sales manager has requested a raise because there are now two salespeople on commission earning higher salaries. The work performance of this individual currently does not merit a raise of the amount requested, mostly due to the person turning in critical reports late and missing a number of days of work. The person's sales group is one of the highest rated in the organization, but this may be the result of having superior individuals assigned to the team, rather than to the effectiveness of the manager.

Situation #3

It has become obvious that the copy machine located in a customer service area is being used for a variety of personal reasons, including reproducing obscene jokes. A few copies have sometimes been found lying on or near the machine at the close of the business day. You have mentioned the matter briefly in the organization's employee newsletter, but recently you have noticed an increase in the activity. Most of the office staff seems to be involved.

Situation #4

Three complaints have filtered upward to you from long-term employees concerning a newly hired individual. This person has a pierced nose and a visible tattoo. The work performance of the individual is adequate and the person does not have to see customers; however, the employees who have complained allege that the professional appearance of the office area has been compromised.

Situation #5

The organization has a flex-time schedule format that requires all employees to work the core hours of 10 a.m. to 3 p.m., Monday through Friday. Two department managers have complained that another department does not always maintain that policy. The manager of the department in question has responded by citing recent layoffs and additional work responsibilities as reasons for making exceptions to policy.

Situation #6

As a result of a recent downsizing, an office in a coveted location is now available. Three individuals have made a request to the department manager for the office. The manager has recommended that the office be given to one of the three. This individual has the highest performance rating, but was aided in obtaining employment with the company by the department manager, who is a good friend of the person's family. Colleagues prefer not to work with this individual, as there is seldom any evidence of teamwork.

Situation #7

Two department managers have requested a budget increase in the areas of travel and computer equipment. Each asks that your group support this request. The CEO, not your group, will make the final decision. You are aware that increasing funds for one department will result in a decrease for others, as the total budget figures for all of these categories are set.

Situation #8

Few of the management staff attended the Fourth of July picnic held at a department manager's country home last year. This particular manager, who has been a loyal team player for the past twenty-one years, has indicated that he/she plans to host the event again this year. Many of you have personally found the event to be boring, with little to do but talk and eat. Already, a few of the other managers have suggested that the event be held at a different location with a new format or else be cancelled.

Situation #9

It has come to your attention that a manager and a subordinate in the same department are having a romantic affair openly in the building. Both are married to other people. They have been taking extended lunch periods, yet both remain beyond quitting time to complete their work. Colleagues have begun to complain that neither is readily available mid-day and that they do not return messages in a timely manner.

Situation #10

Two loyal department managers are concerned that a newly hired manager who is wheelchair-bound has been given too much in the way of accommodations beyond what is required by the Americans with Disabilities Act. They have requested similar changes to make their own work lives easier. Specifically, they cite office size and location on the building's main floor as points of contention.

CHOICES POPULAR SELECTIONS

NOTE: The situations described on the Choices Situations Worksheet were designed to provide you with practice in analyzing and discussing conflict situations and contingencies. In a real-world setting, you would have had more data than was presented in the vignettes; thus, the selections below are simply presented as popular (not "correct") choices for intervention strategies in each situation. A second choice is also given in parentheses for each situation; these can be used as back-up strategies.

Situation #1: Compromise (Integration)

The limited resources of time and expertise, plus the desire for a win-win outcome, encourage *compromise* and make it an efficient strategy. *Integration* could be used to generate additional alternatives if more time were available to implement them, and this could be useful to avoid the dilemma again next year.

Situation #2: Integration (Authority)

A dialogue (*integration*) is needed to assess commitment, as well as to promote openness and trust. This would also provide an opportunity to discuss performance standards and expectations with the individual. *Authority* would be the backup choice and could involve clarifying and resetting performance goals.

Situation #3: Authority (Integration)

The combined issues of sexual harassment and customer service require an immediate intervention by *authority*. This may be seen by the employees as an unpopular move or as blown out of proportion (it's just a little bit of office fun), however critical to the implementation of the values of the organization. *Integration* could be used to clarify the importance of the issues, but *authority* would be needed to ensure immediate compliance.

Situation #4: Suppression (Integration)

Because only a few complaints were received and the employee is new, *suppressing* the situation and allowing time for people to get to know the individual as a person seems appropriate. An *integration* intervention can be used if the issue intensifies over time.

Situation #5: Integration (Compromise)

Sitting down with the key managers involved to discuss the issue and examine implications for the company as a whole would be advisable (*integration*). Input from all involved is critical, and each person must understand the others' points of view. If a consensus solution cannot be reached, then a *compromise* would be the next best step.

Situation #6: Authority (Integration)

It is the department manager's responsibility to assign office space, and this manager has provided a logical rationale for his or her choice; thus, *authority* is appropriate. An *integrative* follow-up would also be advisable to tackle a secondary concern of poor departmental teamwork, which appears to be surfacing.

Situation #7: Withdrawal (Suppression)

Because you are not involved in making the decision and you want to maintain good working relationships with both departments, it is to your advantage to *withdraw* from supporting either group. *Suppressing* the conflict until the budget process is completed could work if both managers have strong egos or are loyal colleagues.

Situation #8: Suppression (Compromise)

Even though few attend and are bored with the lack of activities, organizational loyalty is to be rewarded. You can *suppress* the conflict and model supportive behavior by attending the event yourselves. Respect for this manager and his advocacy of teamwork is important. As a *compromise,* you might form a task force to create a new, expanded event (at a different time and place) in the future that would be more family oriented, and you could designate the manager in question as the honorary host.

Situation #9: Authority (Compromise)

The complaints concerning accessibility of the employees and unauthorized extension of the lunch period are legitimate reasons for an *authoritative* intervention. Organizational values and how the company appears to its customers may also be at stake. Parameters should be established with the employees in question, using current company policy that is being violated. In addition, some "old-fashioned" advice about the dangers of such relationships could be given. As a *compromise*, intervene only with regard to company issues, such as not being available, and allow the two parties to decide their personal behavior when not in the workplace.

Situation #10: Integration (Authority)

The need for group solidarity and for managers to model the company's values with regard to such issues is important. A consensus approach is most likely to be helpful. An *integrative* dialogue to put issues on the table and engage in innovative problem solving is a preferred choice. *Authority* is an alternative if a problem-solving approach doesn't assure compliance with federal laws.

726. Performance Expectations: Making a Sandwich

Goals

- To understand the value of creating and communicating clear performance standards.

- To create performance objectives that are measurable.

- To demonstrate that creating behavioral objectives helps motivate learners and helps focus their attention on learning, making the learning outcome measurable.

Group Size

Any size group that the room can accommodate.

Time Required

Sixty to ninety minutes for activity and debriefing.

Materials

- One jar of peanut butter.
- One jar of jelly or jam.
- One loaf of white bread.
- One pair of thin plastic gloves.
- A plastic knife.
- One plate.
- Index cards, one per participant, no larger than 3 inches by 5 inches.
- Pens or pencils for participants.

- Flip chart and markers.
- Masking tape.
- Copies of the Performance Expectations Handout for all participants.

Physical Setting

A room large enough for the group's comfort. The group should be seated. The facilitator needs a table in the front of the room that is visible to everyone. A piece of flip-chart paper will serve as a tablecloth.

Process

1. Place the peanut butter and jelly jars, the bread, gloves, and the plate and knife on your "tablecloth."

2. Explain to the group that they are managers of a gourmet sandwich shop. A new employee is eager to begin the first day of work. The participants will be providing the new employee with a job aid: a process for making the simplest sandwich the store sells—a peanut butter and jelly sandwich.

3. Give everyone an index card and a pen or pencil. Explain that they will write instructions for making the sandwich for a new employee. Say that the new employee can read and write and that he or she is at least twenty-one years of age. Say, "Given this information about the employee, quickly write your instructions. Please do this quickly as this is a simple sandwich, one that everyone is familiar with. As soon as you are finished, wave your card in the air and I will collect it." (Five minutes.)

4. Walk around the room immediately in anticipation of collecting cards. Appear eager to collect them to apply pressure on participants to hurry.

5. Collect the cards and put them in order with the most vague instructions on the top and the most detailed at the bottom. Select five or six cards. Try to choose the least specific and those that make the most assumptions about the learner.

6. Ask for a volunteer to help read the first card you have selected. Say to the volunteer, "I'm your new employee. I have been very excited to start working here. I'd like to be the best sandwich maker in this deli. Although I've never eaten here before, I've heard it's a great place to eat. I brought my own gloves because I know hygiene is important." Put on the plastic gloves.

7. Ask the volunteer to read the instructions one step at a time. Follow the steps *literally*. For example, if it says to "put peanut butter on the bread," place the jar on the bread. If you are asked to take bread out of the plastic bags, tear the bag without untwisting the tie. (It is even better if the bread falls all over the table.) If a piece of bread falls on the floor, pick it up and be sure to use it later! If the recipe says to "spread the jelly" but does not say "with a knife," dip your fingers into the jelly and spread it on the bread. Be sure to tear the bread. Then say, "Oh, I ripped the bread. May I start over?" It is important that you assume the role of a learner who has *no prerequisite knowledge*. This new employee does not know how to use utensils (a knife), open a bag of bread, spread jelly or peanut butter evenly, align the edges of the bread, or close the sandwich. You must demonstrate lack of any prerequisite knowledge or skill in making a sandwich and lack of understanding of an attractive outcome. If possible, lick your fingers as you make the sandwich so that your lack of cleanliness and hygiene is apparent to the group. As you make an error in completing the sandwich, act apologetic. Act distressed as you realize you are not making a good impression on your new boss. Each time you make a serious error, ask the volunteer to pick another card, saying, "I don't think this is very good information. Let's try another set of instructions." You should learn from each mistake, so, for example, if the first card did not say to use a knife and you had to use your fingers, when you select a second card, say, "I guess I'm supposed to use this knife." Appear pleased that you have learned something.

8. Go through three or four cards until you complete one unappetizing sandwich, for example, too much peanut butter and not enough jelly; the bread not aligned nicely; or the bread soaked with jelly oozing out the sides. When you have finished making a sandwich, announce to your "manager," "I did it. Thank you for your help." Ask the volunteer to sit down. (Ten minutes.)

9. Ask the group: "Who's hungry? Would anyone like this sandwich?" No one will want it. Ask why not. (It is unhygienic and unappealing.) Debrief the experience and record key points on the flip chart. Ask:

   ■ I made a sandwich but no one will eat it. I did as I was told, so what makes my sandwich unappetizing? (The group will provide its own standards for an acceptable sandwich; the point is that no standards were provided to the "new employee.")

   ■ What assumptions were made of the employee? (Assumed prerequisite knowledge: skilled in using tools; knowledgeable of terms used in cooking and about ingredients; assumed employee had made—or eaten—this kind of sandwich before; assumed employee understood standards for sandwich making and hygiene; and so forth.)

- What should the manager have asked at the hiring point to learn what the new employee knew about making sandwiches? (Be sure to probe for both knowledge and skill requirements as well as the correct attitude about cleanliness.)

- Besides producing a finished product—a sandwich—what other expectations might the manager have had that were not communicated? (The proper amount of jelly and peanut butter, how to cut the bread, the need for cleanliness, and so on.)

(Fifteen minutes.)

10. Say: "Clarifying performance standards eliminates assumptions. A manager or trainer can help employees by making explicit what the product or result of the employee's effort will look like. To do that, we identify performance standards that follow the ABCDs of performance objectives. A is your *audience*, B is the *behavior* you expect, C is the *conditions* of the workplace where the performer performs, and D is your *degree* or criterion/standards. (Two minutes.)

11. Record on a flip chart the letter A and the word "audience." Say: "In our example, who is the audience? . . . Our new employee. Describing the audience helps you tailor the learning to their particular needs. Consider demographics such as gender and age, as well as learning style, culture, previous experience, and so on."

12. Record the letter B on the same flip chart with the word "behavior." Hang the paper on a wall. You will refer to it later. Say: "B is the behavior you want; that's the performance you expect. When you write a behavior, use an active verb. What behavior did we want from our new employee?" On another sheet of flip-chart paper, write the behavior: to make a peanut butter and jelly sandwich, or however the group describes the behavior. Say: "The words 'understand,' 'be aware of,' 'learn,' or 'be familiar with' are not good verbs to use; *you need a verb that is observable so that you can measure the performance*. For example, if you say, 'Explain the story,' the ability to explain can be observed by watching the person write the story or recite it to you verbally."

13. Say: "Obviously, just making a sandwich wasn't enough. Our new employee made a sandwich but it wasn't acceptable to the manager or to you." Write "Conditions" on the first flip chart now hanging on the wall.

Say: "Before we talk about our specific standards, let's look at *conditions*. Conditions are what the employee will be able to use or not be able to use when performing a task. For example, a pilot will use a checklist before takeoff. A checklist is a condition. In the workplace, employees are sometimes able to use reference materials, calculators, job aids, price lists, flowcharts, checklists, and other aids. Sometimes they are not allowed to use anything. For example, if you are expected to do something from memory, you will not be allowed to use a reference guide or a job aid. If you are denied the use of equipment or resources, most likely the condition will be 'from memory.' If our new employee will be making sandwiches during a busy lunch hour, what conditions should be included in the behavioral objective? A new employee may be allowed a job aid, but eventually this new employee will have to make every sandwich from memory. So 'from memory' becomes our condition." Write "from memory" on the second sheet of flip-chart paper that has the desired behavior written on it. It now reads "make a peanut butter and jelly sandwich from memory." (Five minutes.)

14. Say: "So far, our new employee will be able to make a peanut butter and jelly sandwich from memory. But that's not everything that's involved. It's clear what the behavior is—make a sandwich—and we know our conditions—the new employee is expected to make this sandwich from memory. But what are the standards? In our memory aid—ABCD—we said D is degree." Add D to the original flip-chart sheet and the word "degree." Say: "You didn't want to eat my sandwich because you thought it was unappetizing and wasn't made with good hygiene habits. What do we need to add to our behavioral objective that conveys our expectations about the appearance of the sandwich and how it is made?" Record all their comments, such as "without oozing jelly," "without soaking the bread," "spread evenly on the bread," "cut in half on a diagonal," "made by placing bread on a clean surface," "using clean hands," and so on. Then say: "These are your criteria for performance; in the memory aid ABCD, this is the D—degree. Degree is about accuracy, speed, or quality." Point to the statements they suggested that have to do with quality. If there are none about accuracy or speed, ask the group to identify these standards. Ask how long it should take to make a sandwich or how much jelly should be in the sandwich. For example, the store requirements could be that the sandwich must be made "in fewer than three minutes," or jelly must be "one-fourth inch thick," or that requirements are indicated in the company's sandwich handbook. (Five minutes.)

15. Add all of their suggested Ds to the flip-chart sheet on the wall with the behavior and the conditions. If there are now many Ds, ask the group if they are realistic and who determines the D. Explain that a manager should be able to determine the degree and the quantity needed for performance based on their own experience supervising the job, doing the task themselves, knowing the job description requirements, legal requirements, and others. In cases where there is a written standard, such as OSHA or ISO standards, these may be indicated in shorthand form, as for example, "per the ISO standards," "per OSHA standards," or "per company standards." However, tell the group to be careful that the standards are clear and are available to the employee to be used as a guide in learning. In some cases, the degree may not be important and may not be needed. For example, when citing performance expectations for listening to employee complaints to a new manager, it might be assumed that the listening behavior of a manager with a direct report includes the degree "always," as in "the manager will listen to concerns of direct reports (always)." Say that if the degree is obvious to everyone, they might choose not to include it. For example, for the behavior for a pilot to "land a plane" you might add "safely." You might also include "all the time" or it might be assumed that the pilot will always have a safe landing. Say: "It is wise, however, not to assume any standards and to avoid miscommunication and misinterpretation, so include the D whenever possible." (Five minutes.)

16. Your flip chart should now include the B, C, and D for the standard, such as "Make a peanut butter and jelly sandwich from memory according to The Gourmet Deli Procedures Manual." Ask the following questions to debrief:

   - How is having a B in the behavioral objective helpful? Who can benefit from indicating the B?

   - What purpose does it serve to indicate the conditions under which the performer will behave?

   - What resources exist for the manager or trainer to identify the degree?

   - What problems may have been avoided if the performance objectives had been given prior to the instruction to the "new employee" in our demonstration?

   - Using the new performance objective written on our flip-chart sheets, how would we measure the new employee's sandwich success? What would it look like? (Depending on what the group said, success might be that the sandwich is cut in half, there is no oozing of jelly, no soggy bread, or whatever.)

- Our objective is now written in a measurable fashion; what purposes are served by this correctly written objective?

- What assumptions might a manager need to check out with a direct report before starting a learning session?

(Twenty minutes.)

17. Provide everyone in the group with a copy of the Performance Expectations Handout to use as a reminder back on the job.

Submitted by Lynne Andia.

Lynne Andia is an OD consultant and teaches in the master's programs at West Chester University, West Chester, Pennsylvania, and at the Philadelphia College of Osteopathic Medicine. She has an M.Ed. from The Pennsylvania State University and an M.S. in organization development from American University.

Performance Expectations Handout

The ABCDs of Performance Objectives

A = audience

To whom is this instruction directed? This is usually indicated by function, such as "the manager," "the salesperson," or "the customer service rep."

B = behavior

The performance expected. Use active verbs such as toss (a ball), edit (a report), or operate (a forklift).

C = condition

The conditions under which a person will perform. What will the performer be allowed to use or not be allowed to use? For example:

- Using a checklist
- With a calculator
- With the aid of a flow chart
- From memory

D = degree

The standards or criteria, usually expressed in terms of quality, accuracy, or speed. These may be such things as:

- Without errors
- In fewer than ten minutes
- According to legal regulations
- For fifty yards or more

727. Persuasion? No Problem!
Evaluating Effective Presentation Skills

Goals*

- To explore various techniques used by presenters to persuade an audience.
- To encourage in-depth problem solving.

Group Size

Any number of participants divided into teams of five or six participants.

Time Required

Sixty to eighty minutes.

Materials

- Copies of the Persuasion? No Problem! "Do You See What I See?" worksheet for all participants.
- Pens or pencils for all participants.
- A flip chart and felt-tipped markers.

Physical Setting

Any room that will accommodate those involved in this activity, ideally in table groupings of five or six people.

---

*Note: While the ostensible purpose of this activity is to stimulate discussion of effective persuasion techniques, the underlying purpose is to encourage inquiry that goes beyond the surface. Such inquiry is necessary for problem solving that requires critical thinking.

Process

1. Divide the participants into groups of five or six, seated at tables. Give everyone a pen or pencil.

2. Explain the purpose of the activity: to develop their general problem-solving skills by sharpening their ability to discern similarities, differences, and emerging patterns in written materials.

3. Introduce the activity with an overview such as this:

   "Despite the time pressures we all face, it's important to take the time to define problems carefully and then to explore the multiple aspects of the problem before proceeding to find a solution. During this activity you will be asked to decide whether you agree with five different statements about persuasion. In each case, however, whether or not you agree with the statement is less important than what you can discern about the statement itself."

   (Five minutes.)

4. Give everyone a copy of the Persuasion? No Problem! "Do You See What I See?" worksheet and tell them to complete the worksheet individually. Explain that you will give them ten minutes to do so and to please work silently. (Ten minutes.)

5. Call time and ask participants to work in their subgroups to decide which, if any, of the assertions under each statement are true. (Twenty minutes.)

6. Allow approximately twenty minutes for the subgroups to discuss their answers. Encourage an in-depth analysis of each of the comments about the topic of persuasion, based on the notes they took earlier.

7. Call everyone together for a discussion of the persuasion statements themselves, using the following discussion starters:

   - What effective persuasion techniques have you seen recently on television?

   - Have you read any books lately in which a character or biographical figure used effective persuasion?

   - What role does listening play in persuading others?

   - Is it possible to be "ethically manipulative" in your persuasion efforts?

   - Which do you feel is more effective in persuading others: stories or statistics? Why?

- Think of the last time you were persuaded by someone to do something. What technique or tool did the persuader use?

- How important are singularity and simplicity of vision when it comes to persuasion?

- Could there be "too much of a good thing" as far as persuasion efforts are concerned? Give an example.

- How do effective leaders achieve a balance between dreams and reality?

- Discuss the possible meaning behind this statement by leadership guru Warren Bennis: "If I were to give off-the-cuff advice to anyone seeking to institute change, the first question I would ask is, 'How clear is your metaphor?'"

(Ten minutes.)

8. Share the answers to the questions, as follows: 1= a/b; 2 = c; 3 = b/c; 4 = a; 5 = d

9. Summarize by leading a large-group discussion of the following questions:

- What persuasive techniques worked in your group as you decided what was true?

- Which worked the most often? Why?

- Were persuasive techniques personality or skill driven?

- What role did inquiry play in the use of persuasion techniques?

- How important is inquiry to critical thinking and problem solving?

- What might you do differently to encourage better problem solving in the future? To persuade others of your views?

(Twenty minutes.)

Variations

- After debriefing and discussion of the answers, elicit historical examples of situations that were not analyzed deeply enough. For example, when junior engineer Roger Boisjoly advised his superiors on the Challenger mission that there was a problem with the O-ring, his warning fell on deaf ears.

- In a workshop that deals with creativity, lead a discussion of the popular definition of a creative person: one who looks at what everyone else is looking at but who sees what no one else sees. Discuss as well the criteria of both speed and accuracy in definitions of intelligence. Relate the discussion to the five items in the activity.

- In a workshop that focuses on problem solving, discuss the need for analysis that goes beyond the surface. Note H.L. Mencken's observation that "For every complex problem, there is one solution that is simple, neat, elegant . . . and wrong."

Submitted by Marlene Caroselli.

Marlene Caroselli, Ed.D., presents corporate training on a variety of subjects. She also presents motivational keynote addresses on a variety of subjects. She has written forty-nine books and curriculum guides to date. View them at her website— http://hometown.aol.com/mccpd—or at Amazon.com.

Persuasion? No Problem! "Do You See What I See?"

Instructions: Individually, and without speaking to others, determine which lettered statements following each numbered item are true. Note that it's possible that an item may have more than one statement that pertains to it. Also decide whether you agree with the statement itself and take notes for a later discussion on the topic of persuasion.

1. Effective persuaders don't hesitate to use books and television or movies to help them ascertain values, but they probably wouldn't turn to the radio for help.
   a. The first half alludes to visual tools; the second does not.
   b. The first half cites double-lettered references; the second half does not.
   c. The first half has tools written in an alliterative manner; the second half does not.
   d. All of the above.
   e. None of the above.

2. To improve your persuasion skills, listen, report, and declare, but don't compromise your values.
   a. The first half uses strong verbs; the second half does not.
   b. The first half is passive; the second half is not.
   c. The first half contains duo-syllabic exhortations; the second half does not.
   d. All of the above.
   e. None of the above.

3. If you have a persuasion project in mind, you should commit all your resources, communicate the pros and cons of the project, and convince others, using both anecdote and statistics, but you shouldn't deviate too far from your original intention.
   a. The first half is a parallel construction; the second half is not.
   b. The first half has a series of recommendations; the second half does not.
   c. The first half is alliterative in its recommendation; the second half is not.

d. All of the above.

e. None of the above.

4. To persuade well, you need to cite the alignment of resources and goals, the benefits that will accrue, and the constructs within which people will have to operate; but you don't need to generate an excessive number of possibilities.

a. The first half is alpha-sequential; the second half is not.

b. The first half contains infinitives; the second half does not.

c. The first half contains a turnaround phrase; the second half does not.

d. All of the above.

e. None of the above.

5. Among other things, successful persuaders know how to wow their followers and to bob with buoyancy when the waves of unethical opposition threaten to overwhelm them, but they don't know how to abandon their dreams very easily.

a. The first half is longer than the second half.

b. The first half contains a metaphor; the second half does not.

c. The first half contains palindromic words; the second half does not.

d. All of the above.

e. None of the above.

728. RULERS: DETERMINING OBJECTIVE MEASURES

Goals

- To demonstrate the issues that exist when members of a group must make subjective measurements.

- To demonstrate the challenges of objective measurement.

- To show how people create subjective measures when they do not have access to objective measures.

Group Size

Any group from five to several hundred in subgroups of six to eight.

Time Required

Approximately forty-five to fifty-five minutes, depending on the size of the total group and the amount of discussion.

Materials

- One envelope with a set of six or eight paper rulers per subgroup, prepared in advance by the facilitator.

- Copies of the Rulers Instruction Sheet for each participant.

- Paper and pencils for participants.

Physical Setting

Tables for the subgroups. If tables are not available, subgroups can sit on the floor or work within their rows in auditorium seating, but note that the instructions for what to measure would have to be modified.

Preparation

Prior to the workshop, prepare sets of rulers by making photocopies of actual twelve-inch rulers (in a variety of styles) on colored index stock. Use any photocopy machine that has an enlargement and reduction setting. Envelopes must contain identical sets of six to eight paper rulers. Ideally, each person in each subgroup should have a ruler, with an extra thrown in, so if there will be eight in a group, make nine rulers. No two rulers within an envelope should be the same length. One of the rulers should be blank; the longest ruler should be about fourteen inches long (120 percent enlargement); the shortest ruler should be about six inches long (52 percent reduction); no ruler should be within 3/4 inch of twelve inches.

Process

1. Explain that the purpose of the activity is to learn about objective measurement. Form participants into subgroups of six to eight and give everyone a sheet of blank paper and a pencil.

2. Distribute one envelope to each subgroup and one copy of the Rulers Instruction Sheet to each person.

3. Explain that each participant is to use one of the rulers in the envelope to answer the questions on the handout in silence. (*Note:* The instructions tell participants to measure "length" and "diameter," so they can be used no matter what type of tables are in the room.) (Five minutes.)

4. After about five minutes, ask everyone to make a final determination of the measurements and write their answers on the Instruction Sheets. When everyone has finished, say that each subgroup must now reach a consensus on their answers. Say that they will have fifteen minutes to do so. (Fifteen minutes.)

5. Circulate among the groups watching the process. (*Note:* Occasionally, a group becomes deadlocked trying to come up with some fancy formula to integrate everyone's answers. Also, occasionally one person decides that he or she knows the right answer and does not want to be part of the group answer.)

6. Before calling time, create columns heads similar to the following on an overhead transparency or flip chart:

Table	Length/Diameter	Height	Weight	How Determined

7. Draw everyone back into a large group discussion and post all subgroup results on the chart. The following points should be addressed:

- How did you compensate when you discovered that none of the rulers was correct? (Used 8½ by 11-inch notebook paper or the length of a forearm or whatever.)

- Which participants had blank rulers? What kinds of problems did they pose? (They are probably the most accurate since they do not mislead the user into believing that they have an accurate instrument.)

- How did you approach the assignment if your ruler was blank? Did you try to find a different ruler or decide to use your own "units" or simply go along for the ride? How is what you did typical of your behavior back on the job? (*Note:* If no one has kept a blank ruler, simply pull one out of an envelope and note that it is the only accurate ruler, that is, one unit.)

- What analogies can you draw between this activity and your place of work? (For example, if a supervisor is always holding the "longest ruler," while an employee has the "shortest" ruler, the situation is ripe for conflict and grievance.)

- How are situations like this analogous to communication with others? (We may think that we are talking about the same thing, but all too often we are not.)

- How was what you did here similar to performance measurement? (We have very different expectations because we lack agreement on the measurement we will use to evaluate progress, success, or failure of a project.)

- What do we do in the absence of mutually agreed metrics? (We guess! Exactly as everyone did when estimating the weight of the tables.)

(Fifteen minutes.)

8. Conclude by saying that the importance of using common metrics cannot be overemphasized. For example, the United States recently lost a satellite because some of the measurements were metric and others in U.S. measures. As another example, in the academic arena, we are usually interested in learning, but we have no efficient or reliable way to measure what has been learned so we rely on a lot of other measures that may not be accurate and that are highly subjective.

9. Gather everyone's thoughts on subjective versus objective measures and capture them on the flip chart, especially as it pertains to people's work back on the job. (Ten minutes.)

Variation

- Instead of distributing one envelope to each table, ask for one leader/volunteer from each table. Some leaders will distribute the rulers, others will circulate the envelope. Then during the debriefing, ask the participants how they felt about the process used to distribute the rulers. Ask participants how they felt if their leader decided which ruler each person should use. Participants often express strong dislike for this leadership style in a group setting. Good discussions usually follow.

Submitted by Bob Shaver.

Bob Shaver, MBA, is a faculty associate and director of the Basic Management Certificate Program at the University of Wisconsin-Madison School of Business. He has twenty years of industry and military experience, including ten years in managerial positions as a first-line supervisor, middle manager, and senior manager. For more than ten years, Mr. Shaver has designed and facilitated seminars on the future, instructional skills, leadership, management of change, motivation, problem solving, and survey design.

RULERS INSTRUCTION SHEET

Instructions: Using the ruler that you chose or that was provided for you, answer the following questions to the best of your ability without discussing your answers with others. Wait until the facilitator tells you to discuss the assignment as a group.

What is the length/diameter of the table at which you are seated?

Your best estimate:

Group consensus:

What is the height of the table?

Your best estimate:

Group consensus:

What is the weight of the table?

Your best estimate:

Group consensus:

How did *you* measure the table?

How confident are you of *your* answers on a scale of 1 to 10?

What process did *you* use to weigh the table?

How did the *group* reach consensus on each of the measurements?

How confident are you of the *group's* answers on a scale of 1 to 10?

729. TEAR IT UP:
LEARNING THREE TYPES OF INTERACTION

Goals

- To compare and contrast the concepts of individualism, competition, and cooperation.

- To explore feelings and reactions during the three types of social interaction.

- To identify appropriate uses for the three types of interactions.

Group Size

Ten to thirty participants.

Time Required

One hour to one hour and fifteen minutes.

Materials

- A prepared overhead transparency or flip-chart sheet of Tear It Up: Three Types of Interaction as well as a prepared transparency or flip-chart sheet for *each one* of the following headings:

  Individualistic Interaction

  Competitive Interaction

  Cooperative Interaction

- Transparency and flip-chart markers for recording data.

- Three blank sheets of paper and a pencil for each participant.

- One sheet of construction paper (any color) and a glue stick for each subgroup.

- An overhead projector.
- A flip chart and masking tape.

Physical Setting

Any room in which everyone can see the flip chart or projector screen and where subgroups can work comfortably.

Process

1. Prior to the session, prepare the overhead transparencies or flip-chart sheets. Introduce the activity by telling participants that they will be exploring three basic types of social interaction: Individualistic, Competitive, and Cooperative.

2. Display the overhead transparency or flip-chart sheet that describes the Three Types of Interaction and read aloud the terms and definitions.

3. For each of the three words, elicit game or sports examples from the participants. Some examples might be:

   - *Individualistic:* solitaire card game, mountain climbing, swimming, gymnastics

   - *Competitive:* chess, tug of war, basketball, drag racing

   - *Cooperative:* leap frog, see-saw, football team, relay team

   (Five minutes.)

4. Explain to the participants that they will be experiencing three quick, but graphic examples of these interactions. State that, as the interactions take place, they are to focus on their *feelings* and *reactions.*

5. Distribute three sheets of paper and a pencil to each participant. Instruct participants to take one sheet of paper, then introduce the *individualistic task* to the group by saying, "Each person is to tear his or her sheet to form a shape that meets all of the following criteria: two straight sides, two curved sides, and a hole. Any and all shapes that meet these criteria are acceptable." Repeat the criteria if necessary and/or write them on the flip chart.

6. Allow several minutes for individuals to complete the task. Do not provide any additional information for the task if participants ask questions. (Five minutes.)

The 2003 Annual: Volume 1, Training/© 2003 John Wiley & Sons, Inc.

7. Once the participants complete the task, instruct them to hold up their shapes and to view what others have made. The shapes for this task might include figures that look like this:

8. Ask the participants to describe their feelings and reactions during the task. Using the prepared transparency or flip-chart sheet for "Individualistic Interaction," record the descriptive words that are generated from the discussion (for example, successful, non-threatened, satisfied, confused, alone). (Five minutes.)

9. Divide the large group into subgroups of three to five members each. When everyone is settled, instruct participants to use a different sheet of paper for the next task. Introduce the *competitive task* to the group by saying, "Each person is to tear his or her sheet to form a circle. The goal is to tear the *roundest* circle in your group. The winning circle will be judged by others for its *roundness*."

10. Allow several minutes for individuals to complete the task, then instruct each group to select its *roundest* circle and to place an identifying mark on it. (Ten minutes.)

11. Collect the circles of the chosen finalists and place them on the overhead projector. Explain that the group as a whole will now select the best circle from among these. Using an "applause meter," judge the best circle and announce the winner. (For large groups, three circles may be chosen as first-, second-, and third-place winners.) (Five minutes.)

12. Ask the participants to describe their feelings and reactions during the task. Using the prepared transparency or flip-chart sheet for "Competitive Interaction," record the descriptive words that are generated from the discussion (for example, anxious, angry, threatened, motivated, energized). (Five minutes.)

13. Instruct participants to use the last sheet of paper. Introduce the *cooperative task* to the group by saying, "The goal is for each group to decide on one shape that every person in the group will use to tear his or her

sheet. The group will then form a collage symbolizing cooperation. The team members are to construct their collage by gluing them to the construction paper that will be provided."

14. Distribute one sheet of colored construction paper and a glue stick to each group. Allow several minutes for groups to complete their collages. Instruct each group to display its final product. Some examples of the collage designs might include figures that look like this:

 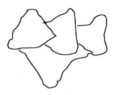 

(Ten minutes.)

15. Ask the participants to describe their feelings and reactions during the task. Using the prepared transparency or flip-chart sheet for "Cooperative Interaction," record the descriptive words that are generated from the discussion (for example, supported, teamwork, pride, trust). (Five minutes.)

16. Lead a whole-group discussion using these questions:

- Overall, what were your feelings and reactions to these three types of interaction?

- What were some reactions that you observed other participants exhibiting?

- How can we relate these feelings and reactions to how we interact with others in the workplace?

- We recognize that each of these three social interactions has advantages and disadvantages. In what workplace circumstances would an individualistic approach be beneficial? A competitive approach? A cooperative approach?

- How can we use this information to improve workplace performance?

(Fifteen minutes.)

Variation

■ If time allows, participants within each team can close the activity by compiling a list of responses to the following lead-in: "Cooperation is like [fill in] because [fill in]." Each team then shares its responses with the large group.

Submitted by Lorraine Ukens.

Lorraine Ukens, *owner of Team-ing With Success, is a performance improvement consultant who specializes in team building and experiential learning. She has spoken at many conferences and is the author of several training activity books, games, simulations, and other text contributions, as well as the editor of the book* What Smart Trainers Know *(Jossey-Bass/Pfeiffer, 2001). She also teaches a graduate course in training and development at Towson University in Maryland and is a past president of the Maryland chapter of ASTD.*

Tear It Up: Three Types of Interaction

Individualistic: when one person works alone to reach a goal

Competitive: when one or more persons work against others toward a single goal

Cooperative: when two or more persons work together toward a single goal

730. DECODE: WORKING WITH DIFFERENT INSTRUCTIONS

Goals

- To explore factors that facilitate or inhibit a person from assuming a take-charge leadership style when it is appropriate. (*Note:* Do not share this particular goal with participants until after the debriefing.)
- To learn how to work effectively in teams.

Group Size

Any number divided into subgroups of four to seven. Best dynamics are with fifteen to thirty participants.

Time Required

Approximately thirty minutes.

Materials

- One copy of the Decode Instruction Sheet for each participant.
- One copy of the Decode Secret Instructions Sheet.
- One copy of the Decode Cryptogram for each participant.
- A copy of the Decode Answer Key for the facilitator.
- A transparency of the Decode Cryptogram (optional).
- A transparency of the Decode Answer Key (optional).
- Index cards (or blank sheets of paper) and pencils for participants.
- Flip chart and felt-tipped markers.
- An overhead projector (optional).
- Timer.
- Whistle.

Physical Setting

Any room that will accommodate the participants, preferably with tables for working.

Process

1. Explain that the goal of the activity is to learn to work together more effectively in teams. Divide participants into groups of four to seven members each. Seat each group at a table.

2. Brief participants by asking how many of them have solved cryptogram puzzles before. Have people briefly share their knowledge with others. Explain what a cryptogram is using the information from the Decode Instruction Sheet. Explain that all groups will be asked to solve the same cryptogram. (Five minutes.)

3. Explain that if a team correctly and completely solves the cryptogram within two minutes, it will earn two hundred points. If it takes more than two minutes but fewer than three minutes, the team will earn fifty points.

4. Explain that before receiving the cryptogram, each participant will receive an Instruction Sheet with hints on how to solve cryptograms. Participants will be allowed to study this sheet for two minutes only. They may not mark up the Instruction Sheet, but they may take notes on an index card (or a blank piece of paper) that you will give them. The Instruction Sheets will be taken back after two minutes.

5. Explain that, at any time after receiving the cryptogram, a group can send one of its members to ask for help from the facilitator. The facilitator will decode any *one* of the words in the cryptogram selected by the group member. Be sure that they understand this point.

6. Insert the Decode Secret Instructions Sheet in the middle of a pile of regular Instruction Sheets. Place the appropriate number of Instruction Sheets, face down, at each table. Make sure that the Secret Instructions Sheet is included in one of the piles. Give everyone an index card or blank paper and a pencil for note taking.

7. Set the timer for two minutes. Ask participants to pick up *one* of the Instruction Sheets and study it independently and silently, taking notes if they wish. After two minutes, blow the whistle, announce the end of the self-instruction period, and ask participants to place their Instruction Sheets in the middle of the table face down.

8. Now distribute Decode Cryptograms by placing the appropriate number of cryptograms, face down, at each table.

9. Begin by setting the timer for two minutes and asking teams to begin decoding the cryptogram. Remind participants that you will decode any *one* of the words for the benefit of each group.

10. Monitor the session. Observe the behavior of the "leader" (the person who received the Secret Instructions Sheet). When participants come to you to decode a word, consult the Decode Answer Key and give the correct word. (Two minutes.)

11. If any group has completely and correctly decoded the message before two minutes are over, tell them they have earned two hundred points. At the end of two minutes, announce the time and set the timer for another minute. At the end of three minutes, announce the end of the session. If the groups have not yet solved the cryptogram, read the correct solution or write it on the flip chart. (Three minutes.)

12. Explain that one of the participants received a Secret Instructions Sheet that gave the best strategy for winning the game. Say that this simulated specialized competency on the part of that participant and gave that person a leadership role.

13. Explain the rationale by setting up hypothetical situations: "If you know that hijackers are going to crash the plane, how do you organize the passengers to break down the cockpit door? If you have to locate a terrorist before he slips the net, how do you organize a search party?" Discuss the appropriate use of the *command-and-control* style of leadership, which has received bad press in these participatory days. Through discussion, bring the group to the point of agreeing that if there is an emergency and you are the most competent person around, there's a lot to be said for taking charge. (Five minutes.)

14. To gain maximum insight from the activity and to relate it to the instructional objective, conduct a debriefing session. Use selected questions from the following list and post learning points on the flip chart:

   ▪ The special instructions given to a randomly selected participant gave that person additional knowledge. Did this guarantee that he or she was automatically accepted as a leader? What additional skills and characteristics are required for being an effective leader?

   ▪ Why was the assumption made that the teams were in competition? Are there times in our lives when we mistakenly refuse to cooperate with others?

- How did the selected person communicate the strategy to teammates and to the entire group? If you were the leader, how would you have done this differently?
- How did the selected person persuade others to follow the cooperative strategy? If you were the leader, how would you have done this differently?
- How did the selected person interact with other participants? If you were the leader, how would you have interacted with others?
- Most other groups that have played this game have failed to implement the recommended strategy. What do you think were some of the reasons for the inability of the leaders of the previous groups to implement the preferred strategy?
- How do the previous relationships and shared experiences among participants make the leader's task easier or more difficult? Is it more likely that someone with knowledge of others in the group would succeed?
- Did anyone else come up with the same strategy? What did this participant do?
- What if there were another participant who received the same secret instructions? How would this have changed the leader's task?
- How did the time limit hinder the leader? How did the time limit help the leader? How would you have acted as a leader if you had ample time?
- Have you ever been in a situation where you had an effective strategy for meeting a challenge but held back sharing it with others? Why did this happen?
- What can we learn about our behavior back on the job from this activity?

(Fifteen minutes.)

Submitted by Sivasailam "Thiagi" Thiagarajan.

Sivasailam "Thiagi" Thiagarajan. For the past three decades, Thiagi has been making a living by having fun and helping others have fun. Thiagi has lived in three countries and has consulted in twenty-five others. He is currently the Resident Mad Genius at QB International, a training design organization that blends e-learning and facilitated learning. Thiagi publishes a monthly online newsletter, "Play for Performance," that is archived at www.thiagi.com.

DECODE INSTRUCTION SHEET

You are probably familiar with codes and cryptograms from your childhood days. In a cryptogram, each letter in the message is replaced by another letter of the alphabet. For example, LET THE GAMES BEGIN! May become this cryptogram:

YZF FOZ JUKZH CZJVQ!

In the cryptogram Y replaces L, Z replaces E, F replaces T, and so on. Notice that the same letter substitutions are used throughout this cryptogram: Every E in the sentence is replaced by a Z, and every T is replaced by an F.

Here's some information to help you solve cryptograms:

Letter Frequency

The most commonly used letters of the English language are *e, t, a, i, o, n, s, h,* and *r.*

The letters that are most commonly found at the beginning of words are *t, a, o, d,* and *w.*

The letters that are most commonly found at the end of words are *e, s, d,* and *t.*

Word Frequency

One-letter words are either *a* or *I.*

The most common two-letter words are *to, of, in, it, is, as, at, be, we, he, so, on, an, or, do, if, up, by,* and *my.*

The most common three-letter words are *the, and, are, for, not, but, had, has, was, all, any, one, man, out, you, his, her,* and *can.*

The most common four-letter words are *that, with, have, this, will, your, from, they, want, been, good, much, some,* and *very.*

Decode Secret Instructions Sheet

The other participants are learning how to solve cryptograms, but you have been selected to receive some *secret* instructions.

Forget the mechanics of solving a cryptogram! Here's the best strategy for winning the game:

- Teams should cooperate with each other.
- Each team should ask the facilitator to decode a different word.
- Teams should share their decoded words with each other.
- They should help each other to decode the entire message.
- *All* teams can win as long as they decode the message within the time limit.
- When the game begins, share this strategy with everyone.
- Convince them to use this strategy.

DECODE CRYPTOGRAM

ISV'B JZZXYH BPJB BPH SVQE

___'_ _____ ____ ___ ____

UJE BS UCV CZ BS FSYTHBH.

___ __ ___ __ __ _____ .

ZSYHBCYHZ BPH AHZB UJE BS

_____ ___ ____ ___ __

UCV CZ BS FSSTHWJBH UCBP

___ __ __ _____ ____

SBPHWZ—Z. BPCJMJWJOJV

_____—_. _____

DECODE ANSWER KEY

ISV'B JZZXYH BPJB BPH SVQE

DON'T ASSUME THAT THE ONLY

UJE BS UCV CZ BS FSYTHBH.

WAY TO WIN IS TO COMPETE.

ZSYHBCYHZ BPH AHZB UJE BS

SOMETIMES THE BEST WAY TO

UCV CZ BS FSSTHWJBH UCBP

WIN IS TO COOPERATE WITH

SBPHWZ—Z. BPCJMJWJOJV

OTHERS—S. THIAGARAJAN

731. Aardvark and Antelope: Examining Team Leadership

Goal

- To demonstrate in a creative way the idea that one cannot rely on the team leader/expert to make all the decisions.

Group Size

Eight to twenty people, whether from intact teams or not.

Time Required

Twenty to thirty minutes, depending on group size.

Materials

- Name tags for participants.
- Two different colored marking pens.
- One aardvark and one antelope stuffed animal (optional).

Physical Setting

A space large enough for the group to sit or stand in a U-shape.

Process

1. Explain that the activity you are about to do concerns various aspects of teamwork.

2. Have everyone write out and affix a name tag to the front of his or her outfit and then stand or be seated in a U-shape on the floor or by drawing up their chairs.

3. Introduce the person at the end of the "U" as the "fount of all knowledge about aardvarks." Hand that person one of the markers and say: "Whenever anyone needs to know anything about aardvarks, he or she has to come to [Jane], who is the fount of all knowledge about aardvarks."

4. Introduce the person at the other end of the "U" as the "fount of all knowledge about antelopes." Hand that person a different colored marker. State: "Whenever anyone needs to know anything about antelopes, he or she has to come to [Bob], the fount of all knowledge about antelopes."

5. Explain to the group the rules of the activity:

> "This is how it works: [Jane], you tell the person next to you [Sally] 'This marker is an aardvark.' [Sally], because she is NOT the fount of all knowledge, must ask you, [Jane], 'A what?' before accepting the aardvark. [Jane], you must reply, 'An aardvark.' Now that [Sally] understands, [he or she] is allowed to take the marker from [Jane].
>
> "Now [Sally] in turn must explain the aardvark to the next person in line, [Kelly]. But because [Sally] is NOT the fount of all knowledge, she has to go back to the fount of all knowledge [Jane] and ask 'A what?' To this [Jane] will reply 'an aardvark.' [Sally] will then tell [Kelly] 'It's an aardvark.' And so the process continues. The only person who can verify that the object is indeed an aardvark is [Jane]. The same thing holds true for [Bob] and the antelopes."

6. Make sure both "sides" understand the rules before you continue. Clarify that their goal is to ensure that [Bob] understands about aardvarks and that [Jane] understands about antelopes, but remembering that, as they pass the marker down the line, the founts of all knowledge must verify the information each time the marker passes from one team member to the next.

7. Then stand back and watch the confusion, especially when the two pens intersect at the midway point. Note what happens for the debriefing. (About ten minutes.)

8. Pull the group back together to debrief the activity with the following questions:

- What do you think about members of a group being designated as the founts of all knowledge?

- Does this happen in real groups?

- Why was it necessary to keep going back to these people? What sorts of problems did it cause?

The 2003 Annual: Volume 1, Training/© 2003 John Wiley & Sons, Inc.

- Do you see this dynamic at work on any current team of which you are a member? How does it play out in real life?

- How can we prevent this dynamic from occurring back on the job?

(Ten minutes.)

Submitted by Kristin J. Arnold.

Kristin J. Arnold, MBA, CPCM, specializes in coaching executives and their leadership, management, and employee teams, particularly in the areas of strategic and business planning, process improvement, decision making, and collaborative problem solving. An accomplished author and editor of several professional articles and books, as well as a featured columnist in The Daily Press, *a Tribune Publishing Group newspaper, Ms. Arnold is regarded as an expert in team development and process improvement techniques. With building extraordinary teams as her signature service, Ms. Arnold has provided process facilitation, training, and coaching support to both public and private sector initiatives.*

732. Let's Get Personal: Using Slogans to Introduce Oneself

Goals

- To establish a warm, personal tone at the beginning of a training event.

- To allow participants an opportunity to use personal slogans as a safe way to introduce themselves as part of the getting-acquainted process.

- To provide trainers with a creative way to establish a desired atmosphere for learning.

Group Size

Any size group of participants who do not know one another well, in subgroups of three to five.

Time Required

Twenty-five to forty-five minutes, depending on the number of participants.

Materials

- A handout containing one of the Let's Get Personal slogans that illustrates the facilitator's personal philosophy, prepared in advance.

- One copy of the Let's Get Personal Slogans Sheet for each participant.

- Paper and pens or pencils for participants.

- A flip chart and felt-tipped markers.

- One large sheet of flip-chart paper and a marker per participant.

- Masking tape.

Physical Setting

Any area large enough for participants to be seated comfortably and that has plenty of wall space for posting slogans.

Process

1. Distribute the handout you prepared in advance with a slogan that represents your personal philosophy about the topic being discussed. Give each participant a pen or pencil and a piece of paper also.

2. Explain that you have selected the slogan(s) on the handout as your way to introduce yourself and your personal philosophy about the topic (or about life, if that is appropriate in this setting) and as a way to set the mood for the training that is to follow. Do not discuss the slogan at this point. (Two minutes.)

3. Ask participants to assemble in subgroups of three to five to discuss their reactions to your selection and what it implies about you personally in your role as their trainer. Tell them to jot down their ideas. (Five minutes.)

4. Have everyone come together and lead a discussion of the expectations they may have formed of you and of the upcoming session based on the slogan you chose. Post pertinent points on the flip chart. (Ten minutes.)

5. Distribute Let's Get Personal Slogans Sheets to participants. Ask participants to review the slogans individually and select *one* that they believe best indicates how they will work with others during the workshop (or what kind of people they are, if this suits the purpose of the workshop), and to write a few notes that explain the basis of their selection. (Five minutes.)

6. Reconvene the large group and have everyone write the slogan he or she chose, along with one or two brief reasons for that choice, on a piece of flip-chart paper and post it on the wall. Have them sign their sheets. (Five minutes.)

7. Have everyone mill about reading what is there, asking for clarification from the appropriate participant if necessary. Discuss all the posted sheets briefly in turn. (Five to ten minutes.)

8. Debrief the activity by asking what expectations they formed about others based on the slogans that others chose. Discuss similarities among participants based on the slogans selected and why they were selected.

Sum up the discussion on the flip chart with what the results mean for the upcoming workshop. (Ten minutes.)

Variations

- The slogans selected by the trainer can be included as the front page in the participant manual instead of being distributed as a separate handout.

- Participants can be asked to develop their own personal slogans instead of selecting one from the handout.

- Slogans selected by the participants can be posted in the training room and used to reestablish the desired mood throughout the training session.

- Participants can be asked to free associate in writing about the slogan of their choice. This entails writing whatever comes to mind without thinking or censoring beforehand and can yield some good insights.

- This activity can provide a jumping-off point for discussion of values or stereotyping. Participants can be asked to introduce one another by making assumptions about the other person based on the slogan chosen, but with no discussion with that person.

Submitted by Phyliss Cooke and Tara L. Kuther.

Phyliss Cooke, Ph.D., is a licensed psychologist and consultant in private practice with twenty-five years' experience in the field of consulting and the application of behavioral science to business policy and practices. From 1977 through 1988 she was a senior consultant and dean of the Intern Program and the master's degree program at University Associates, Inc. Since 1988 Dr. Cooke has consulted extensively with Native American clients, First Nations clients in Canada, and clients in Pacific Rim countries on issues of cultural awareness, communication, and management practices. She has made numerous contributions to the Annuals.

Tara L. Kuther, Ph.D., is an assistant professor of developmental psychology at Western Connecticut State University. Dr. Kuther has taught undergraduate and graduate courses at a variety of institutions, including Fordham University, Lehman College (CUNY), and Teachers College, Columbia University. Dr. Kuther's psychological research on adolescents and young adults, as well as on ethical issues in research and teaching, have appeared in over twenty scholarly journals and books.

LET'S GET PERSONAL SLOGANS SHEET

"One way to control the future is to invent it."—*author unknown*

"Success in leading a planned change is as much a question of 'will' as it is of 'skill.'"—*author unknown*

"Participation is something that top management decides that middle management should do with their subordinates."—*author unknown*

"Leaders write the cookbook rather than read it."—*author unknown*

"Once you have established a vision, you will have to develop strategies to guide your planning and take actions to achieve your goals."
—*author unknown*

"It isn't the mountain ahead that wears you down—it's the pebble in your shoe."—*author unknown*

"Problems cannot be solved at the same level of awareness that created them."—*Albert Einstein*

"When called by a panther—don't answer."—*Ogden Nash*

"You cannot control the length of your life, but you can control its width and depth."—*author unknown*

"Why worry about what you cannot control when you can control the things that matter?"—*author unknown*

"Difficulties in life can make us bitter or better—the choice is ours!"
—*author unknown*

"Be sure that the words you speak are sweet—you may have to eat them!"
—*author unknown*

"If you aren't going all the way, why go at all?"—*Joe Namath*

The 2003 Annual: Volume 1, Training/© 2003 John Wiley & Sons, Inc.

733. Yo-Yos: Using Kinesthetic Methods for Learning

Goals

- To give participants an opportunity to train and lead a small group.
- To help groups and teams bond through developing and accomplishing a common goal.
- To provide an unusual and enjoyable kinesthetic learning experience.

Group Size

Ten to forty participants.

Time Required

Forty-five to sixty minutes.

Materials

- One yo-yo per participant from a wide assortment of colors and designs. (Note that if you wish to use color or design as a way to form subgroups, you will need to have the appropriate numbers of colors/designs.)
- One box or bag to hold the yo-yos.
- Flip chart and felt-tipped markers.
- Blank paper and pens or pencils for participants.
- Prizes or awards for winning teams (optional).

Physical Setting

A room with enough space for groups of four or five to spread out comfortably while standing and using the yo-yos.

Facilitator Note

Even the most taciturn manager today will probably enjoy using a yo-yo. It seems to remind them of their younger, more carefree days. Although not everyone was a yo-yo "expert," most people have had at least some experience with a yo-yo. For many, yo-yo activities can provide a much-needed kinesthetic or "hands-on" component to a training or team-building session.

Process

1. Briefly describe the goals of the activity, then tell participants to each choose a yo-yo from a box or bag of mixed design yo-yos. Tell them to form groups of four to six. (If desired, do this by having all those holding the same design or color of yo-yo form a group.)

2. Explain to the participants that their first task is to play with their individual yo-yos to determine what their skill levels are. Give them five minutes to practice within their small groups. (Five minutes.)

3. Call an end to the practice session and tell subgroups to determine by consensus the most accomplished "yo-yoer" in their subgroup. (Two minutes.)

4. When all subgroups have chosen, explain to participants that the most accomplished person in each subgroup is to teach the rest of the members a stunt, a trick, or a move that everyone in the group can do together. (This may just involve sending the yo-yos up and down in unison or some kind of repetitive pattern. However, group presentations can be extraordinarily complex.) Each subgroup must also come up with a group name (for example, the "Spin Doctors" or "Blue Moons"). Give them time to decide a name and a movement. (Ten minutes.)

5. Reconvene the large group and ask subgroups one at a time to share their group names and then demonstrate their stunts or tricks for the large group. (Ten minutes.)

6. Have the participants return to their small groups, give them blank paper and pencils, and allow them from five to ten minutes to process their answers to questions such as the following, which you may write on the flip chart:

   ■ How did you choose your group leader/expert?

   ■ How did you decide what to "perform" and at what level?

- What techniques did the leader/expert use to teach and motivate your group members?

- How satisfied were you with your group's performance?

Tell them to wrap up with any key learnings. (Ten minutes.)

7. Reconvene the large group to discuss participants' responses and learning experiences as time allows. If desired, note these on the flip chart also. (*Note:* Participants will be especially delighted if allowed to keep their yo-yos!) (Ten minutes.)

Variations

- Give participants from individual work units or teams the same basic yo-yo and ask them to complete two tasks: first, to develop, as a work unit or team, a humorous skit using the yo-yos to demonstrate something dysfunctional about their team or department. Examples could be communication breakdowns, power clashes, impassable hierarchies, lack of trust, or whatever is true for them. (For example, one group in the past showed people trying to wrest the yo-yos away from each other. Another demonstrated individuals who, in their haste to pass the yo-yos, were facing away from each other and kept dropping them.) Then, one at a time, ask the small groups to perform the skits demonstrating their own dysfunction for the large group. Once everyone has had some good laughs from the first round, ask individual groups to develop a demonstration of a collective goal or vision for their team. (For example, one group showed the seamless passing of the yo-yo from one team member to another through bumpy or challenging times; another showed individuals being willing to take risks and try difficult maneuvers with their yo-yos without fear of punishment or reprisal.) Again, one group at a time, demonstrate and then discuss the team's goal or vision for the large group. Ask participants to return to their small groups and, in ten to fifteen minutes, discuss the following questions:

  - Which task was the more difficult, the "dysfunction" or the "vision," and why?

  - What would need to change or be done differently in order to resolve the challenges or dysfunctions presented in the first round?

  - What needs to be done, stopped, or changed in order for the vision to become a reality?

  - Other insights or learnings from this activity?

Reconvene the large group and discuss responses and learnings, as time allows. Note and compare these on flip charts as time allows. Encourage teams to identify and articulate both their "dysfunctions" and goals/visions in a supportive environment.

- If you like, you can present small prizes for categories such as "most creative," "most graceful," "most skillful," and so on.

Submitted by Donna L. Goldstein.

Donna L. Goldstein, Ed.D., *is managing director of Development Associates International, a management consulting and training firm in Hollywood, Florida. Dr. Goldstein and her colleagues have helped over 275 organizations worldwide to create happier staffs, healthier teams, and more productive and profitable workforces. She holds a doctorate in human resource development from Florida International University. She has contributed to fourteen books on HR and OD, including McGraw Hill's 1997–2002* Training and Performance Sourcebooks.

734. Inner Child: Applying New Knowledge in a Creative Way*

Goals

- To identify ways to implement or apply skills learned in workshops.

- To demonstrate how quickly the creativeness of a group can be generated and tapped in any workshop.

- To develop participants' awareness of behaviors that can release and generate creative thinking on demand.

- To bring closure to a workshop topic.

Group Size

Ten to twenty-five people who have been working on personal creativity or who are looking for ways to increase workplace morale, in subgroups of four to six. More can be accommodated if the room is large and the seating is movable.

Time Required

Up to sixty minutes.

Materials

- Copies of the Inner Child Creative Ideas Listing for each participant.

- Paper and pencils or pens for each participant.

---

*Based on an activity in the *Have Balloons, Will Travel* workbook, written by Robert Alan Black, Ph.D., and published by Cre8ng Places Press in 1997 and re-released as *Have Balloons, Crayons and Hoola Hoops; Let's Meet* in 2000.

- A flip chart and felt-tipped markers for each subgroup.
- A flip chart and felt-tipped markers for the facilitator.
- Small prizes (optional).

Physical Setting

A room, preferably with tables that will seat four to six. If the room has auditorium seating, participants can form clusters of four to six in their areas of the auditorium or room.

Process

1. Explain to the group that one of the primary goals of any training program is to help participants gather new information and experience and learn how to apply it, understand the processes used, and be able to creatively apply all of what they have learned to their own workplaces.

2. Say to the group, "One of our primary goals in this program is to have each of you be able to take the content and the tools taught and apply them *creatively* in your own workplaces. It has been discovered that, the more creative the working environment is, the more creativity occurs. This activity is one way to help you tap your own creativity on demand and to raise your present creative level whenever you need to."

3. Then say, "It is known that children until the age of six or seven are normally more naturally creative than at any other time in their lives. After they enter school, their natural creativity tends to be lessened, dulled, or even squelched. Would you accept that being childlike would help you to be more creative?"

   If you receive unanimous agreement, move to the next step. If you receive varied or almost no agreement, ask them to assume that being childlike may be a quick way to help themselves to be more creative and to go with that assumption for the moment.

4. Give everyone blank paper and a pencil and ask them to spend a few minutes thinking of creative, more childlike ways that they could approach their work days. Have them jot down their ideas. (Five minutes.)

5. Ask everyone to form small groups of four to six. Give each group a flip chart and markers and tell them to come up with a list of specific behaviors or actions that they think of as childlike or fun that they could do

every day on the job to make a difference. Have each group choose a recorder to write their lists on the flip chart. (Ten minutes.)

6. Now tell the groups to combine creativity skills they learned during the workshop with several of the "childlike" behaviors they have come up with. Challenge each group to identify three combinations of childlike behavior and creative, fun things to do back on the job. Give them another ten minutes to do this. (Ten minutes.)

7. Bring the large group back together and ask each subgroup to share their *most creative* new idea. Record their ideas on a flip chart in front of the room and discuss them briefly, asking for clarification, if necessary. (Fifteen minutes.)

8. (Optional) Award a prize, certificate, or token gift that might represent creativity to the group members and help them to remember the lessons they have learned.

9. Then ask the groups to discuss what would happen if they actually did some of the activities that have been listed in their workplaces and how they might feel afterward. Use the following questions to promote discussion:

   ■ What would be the benefit of using a new behavior?

   ■ If the original idea is too outlandish for your organization or department, how could you adapt it to your workplace?

   (Ten minutes.)

10. Provide copies of the Inner Child Creative Ideas Listing and challenge everyone to "be more 'childlike' from now on" as they return to their jobs.

Variation

■ Follow up by using some of the activities that are feasible for the rest of your workshop. Choose a few and use them as energizers throughout the program.

Submitted by Robert Alan Black, Ph.D.

Robert Alan Black, Ph.D., *founder of Cre8ng People, Places & Possibilities, is a creative thinking consultant and professional speaker who specializes in the S.P.R.E.A.D.ng™ of Creative Thinking throughout workplaces world-wide. During more than thirty-five years of creative work, he has been a licensed architect, graphics and signage designer, interior designer, TV news writer and editor, freelance cartoonist, freelance writer, college art professor, and creative thinking and leadership consultant. He has had over two hundred articles published and has written nine books on creative thinking, leading, communicating, and teaming. He also serves as an adjunct professor at Columbus State University in Columbus, Georgia, and has been involved with the annual Creative Problem Solving Institute since 1978. He is a member of the National Speakers Association, Georgia Speakers Association, American Creativity Association, Creative Education Foundation, National Storytelling Association, and the Southern Order of Storytellers.*

Inner Child Creative Ideas Listing

What would happen if you did all of the following today? Take the creative challenge and add more fun to your life!

1. Give yourself a special sticker for everything you do today.

2. Dot all your i's with heart shapes.

3. Sing into a make-believe microphone.

4. Grow a colored soft drink mustache.

5. Smile at everyone in the room or everyone you meet.

6. Read a book of your favorite cartoonist's work.

7. Dunk your muffin or donut in milk or coffee.

8. Create a game where you make up the rules as you go along.

9. Order and eat only "fun" food for a day.

10. Buy and share a dozen donuts with new or old friends.

11. Deliberately, in a different, funny way, step on sidewalk cracks wherever you walk today.

12. Create and wear funny hats to a meeting or while you work at your desk.

735. Golf Game: Keeping Accurate Score*

Goals

- To emphasize the critically important aspects of performance measurement in a lighthearted way.

- To raise awareness about one's own use of performance feedback and measurement.

- To use an analogy (keeping score in golf) to help the learner better relate to the principles and concepts being presented.

Group Size

Any number.

Time Required

Approximately forty-five minutes.

Materials

- One copy of the Golf Game Lecturette for the facilitator.

- One copy of the Golf Game Assessment for each participant (and extra blank copies for them to take home, if desired).

- One copy of the Golf Game Scoring Sheet for each participant.

- Pens or pencils for participants.

- A flip chart and felt-tipped markers.

Physical Setting

Any room with writing surfaces for participants.

---

*This activity is adapted from Peter R. Garber's book and training program entitled *Management Lessons from Golf.*

Process

1. Explain that you will be doing a quick self-assessment of participants' use of performance feedback on the job using a golf analogy. Say that they don't have to have any technical knowledge about golf other than the fact that each golf hole has an established number of strokes that a skilled golfer should not exceed to make "par" and that each time a golf ball is hit it counts one point or stroke.

2. Use the Golf Game Lecturette as the basis for your own explanation of the concepts or simply read the lecturette to participants. (Five minutes.)

3. Lead a discussion of the points that were made and post them on the flip chart. (Ten minutes.)

4. Give participants copies of the Golf Game Assessment and pens or pencils. Tell them they will have five minutes to fill it out. (Five minutes.)

5. When everyone has finished, give them copies of the Golf Game Scoring Sheet and ask them to complete it, thinking only about their own behavior on the job. (Five minutes.)

6. Ask for sample scores and lead a discussion of what these may indicate about the people in the group and their use of performance feedback. Use the following questions for discussion, posting answers on the flip chart:

   - What does a score of 7 or 8 indicate about your own use of performance feedback?

   - Was there a difference in how well you kept track of others' performance and how you kept track of your own?

   - What techniques do you typically use to measure your own performance on the job?

   - What techniques do you use to measure the performance of others?

   - If you are not currently keeping some kind of "score" for employees at your workplace, what kind of performance measurement systems can you put into place in the future?

   - If you do give people feedback on their performance, how timely is this feedback?

   - How can you use your performance measurement systems to help people improve their performance rather than just hear how they are doing currently?

- With increased awareness of the importance of performance feedback, what will you do differently when you return to the job site?

- How can you commit to making this change?

(Fifteen minutes.)

7. Wrap up the discussion, suggesting that participants write down some ideas for improvement and check themselves at some date in the next few weeks and then again in about six months. Give out extra copies of the assessment if desired.

Submitted by Peter R. Garber.

Peter R. Garber *is manager of affirmative action for PPG Industries, Inc., in Pittsburgh, Pennsylvania. He is the author of five management books, including his most recent work,* Turbulent Change: Every Working Person's Survival Guide, *and is a regular contributor of activities and learning instruments in the* Annuals.

Golf Game Lecturette

The game of golf has enjoyed renewed interest over the past several years. Golfing superstars like Tiger Woods have raised the sport to new levels of excellence. The game of golf provides many analogies and lessons that we can easily apply to the business world.

For example, golf requires that one play by the rules, learn and master the fundamentals of the game, and continue to strive to improve one's performance—which is very similar to business. It is especially important in golf that you keep accurate score. In golf every stroke counts the same, one. A drive that goes three hundred yards or more counts the same as a six-inch putt. And both can be just as difficult to make and as important to the final outcome of the game or contest.

Measurement of work performance is critical to improving your organization's bottom-line results. The difference between being highly successful and not reaching your goals can often be measured in the smallest of increments. Thus, accurate measurement is critically important in business as well as in golf.

Unfortunately, many golfers have trouble keeping accurate score of their performance or are unhappy with their performance. They can be very creative in solving this problem! For instance, golfers who do not want to have to take an extra shot (because the lower the score the better) have been known to illegally move a ball to a better position when they think no one is looking. Then there are those supposed "practice" swings that are not counted, even when they were actually sincere attempts to hit the ball. And believe it or not, some golfers intentionally miscount the number of strokes they have taken on a hole! This last point deserves additional comment. One of the great curiosities of golf is that even the most talented business and financial people have difficulty counting over one hundred when playing just eighteen holes of golf! There is probably even more cheating done on the golf course than on tax returns!

As I said earlier, keeping accurate score is just as important in business. Keeping score allows you to measure your performance from one day to the next, week to week, year to year. If you do not have an accurate score, you may be misled concerning your level of performance and not address critical problems that might exist, which can ultimately cause you to lose customers. Keeping score in business can be accomplished in any number of ways and can go beyond just reporting your profits and/or losses. Keeping score in business might involve measuring customer satisfaction by the number of complaints or compliments received. It might be measured by the morale and attitude of the organization's employees. Sales trends and projections can be other important measures. How people are performing on their jobs is also an extremely important measure to both the employee and his or her supervisor. Everyone has the need to know how well he or she is performing.

Golfers return to the golf course to see whether they can improve their scores. The same also needs to be true for employees on the job—they should return every day eager to improve their results. However, without feedback, an employee may not know whether his or her performance is improving, staying the same, or even getting worse. Without feedback, reaching higher performance levels can be extremely difficult, if not impossible.

To illustrate, what would it be like if we took measurement away from a golfer? Imagine that immediately after each shot you blindfolded a golfer and led him or her to the next shot without any idea how well or poorly the ball was hit and gave no feedback about performance or score. How much do you think the golfer would enjoy the game under these circumstances?

In the business world, we often create such a scenario with employees. Typically, employees receive very little feedback about how well they are performing their jobs other than summary information given a long time afterward. This would be like being told what your golf score was last weekend a year later. Obviously, it would be of much less meaning and interest to you at that point. The usefulness of the information is also greatly diminished. To support performance improvement, feedback must be immediate. The more immediate and accurate the measurement or score, the more useful it becomes. Employees as well as stakeholders can greatly benefit from receiving timely and accurate information concerning their performance and the performance of the organization. Managers or supervisors must continually look for ways to improve the way they measure performance to make it as accurate and timely as possible.

GOLF GAME ASSESSMENT

Hole #1: Par 4

Instructions: Circle "Yes" or "No" for each question as it relates to the way you measure and give feedback about your own or others' performance on the job.

1. Do you keep accurate score when measuring your own performance at work?

    Yes   No

2. Do you give others immediate feedback on their performance at work?

    Yes   No

3. Do you use measurements to improve your performance?

    Yes   No

4. Do you use measurements to help others improve their performance?

    Yes   No

GOLF GAME SCORING SHEET

Hole #1: Par 4

Instructions: Taking another lesson from golf, use the following "scorecard" to help you think of more accurate and timely ways to keep score on critical measures in your business. Transfer your answers from the Assessment to this sheet. Give yourself two points for every "no" answer and one point for every "yes." For any answer for which you answered no, think about ways that you can improve your performance and jot them down for later group discussion.

Item	Answer	Score (Strokes)
1. Do you keep accurate score when measuring your own performance at work?		
2. Do you give others immediate feedback on their performance at work?		
3. Do you use measurements to improve your performance?		
4. Do you use measurements to help others improve their performance?		
Total Strokes		

736. Intrinsic/Extrinsic Motivators: Encouraging Creativity

Group Size

Members of existing work groups, teams, cross-functional groups, randomly assigned groups, or "stranger" groups in subgroups of five to eight participants.

Time Required

One hour and thirty minutes to one hour and forty-five minutes.

Materials

- A copy of the Intrinsic/Extrinsic Motivators Questionnaire for each participant.

- A copy of the Intrinsic/Extrinsic Motivators' Role in Creativity Handout for each participant.

- A pencil for each participant.

- A flip chart and a felt-tipped marker for each subgroup.

- Masking tape for posting.

Physical Setting

A room in which subgroups can work undisturbed. A table and chairs for each subgroup.

Process

1. Introduce the goals by saying that this interactive, experience-based activity is designed to increase participants' awareness of creativity and creative processes. Say that participants will examine their own jobs, discuss ways intrinsic and extrinsic motivators affect their creativity on the job, and develop some ways to enhance and support creativity in the workplace. Say that the role tacit knowledge plays in the creative process will also be discussed.

2. Distribute the Internal/External Motivators Questionnaire and a pencil to each participant. Ask participants to write their own answers to Questions 1 and 2. (Five minutes.)

3. After about five minutes, assign participants to subgroups of approximately equal size, from five to eight in each. Give each subgroup a flip chart and felt-tipped markers. Ask subgroups to choose one member in each who will record their answers on the flip chart and report group results orally. Tell the subgroups to use consensus or majority vote to decide which responses will be written on the flip chart. Tell the recorders that they are to write *at least two responses from each participant* for Question 1 on the flip chart. (Ten minutes.)

4. Ask subgroups to discuss and compare the ranking of major work activities they have listed for Question 2 for (a) level of difficulty, (b) potential to motivate, and (c) opportunity to add value. Have the recorders write on the flip chart at least two responses each participant has given for Question 2. (Twenty minutes.)

5. Distribute a copy of the Intrinsic/Extrinsic Motivators' Role in Creativity Handout to each participant. Ask participants to read this handout silently and then individually record their answers to Questions 3 and 4 on the Questionnaire. (Fifteen minutes.)

6. Now ask subgroup members to take turns reading aloud their answers to Question 3. Have the recorder write each person's responses on the flip chart. (Ten minutes.)

7. Ask subgroup members to take turns reading aloud their responses to Question 4 and then to agree on a total of six answers to be recorded. Tell recorders to list these responses on the flip chart. (Ten minutes.)

8. Ask participants to silently compare their own responses to Questions 1 and 2 with their own responses to Questions 3 and 4 and then answer Question 5. Ask subgroup members to report their answers to Question 5 to the recorder, who is to record these answers on the flip chart. (Ten minutes.)

9. Bring the group together and summarize in a large group discussion, using the following questions:

   ■ What was the most important part of this activity for you?

   ■ What have you learned about motivation?

   ■ What impact will having done this activity have for you back in the workplace?

   ■ How will what you have learned change your leadership style or future participation in a group?

   ■ What will you do differently based on what you have learned?

   (Ten minutes.)

10. Summarize and write on a flip chart the overall accomplishments the participants have brought out, as well as their goals for the future, emphasizing the importance of intrinsic motivation in the workplace as well as extrinsic rewards. Encourage participants to foster and appropriately reward one another's creative accomplishments at work. (If any participants work together, they can create agreements to this effect.) (Five minutes.)

Submitted by Elizabeth A. Smith.

Elizabeth A. Smith, Ph.D., is chief knowledge officer, CRG Medical, L.P., and adjunct professor, Business and Public Administration, University of Houston Clear Lake. Her professional interests include creativity, productivity, motivation, quality, and explicit and tacit knowledge. She has authored two books, Creating Productive Organizations *(manual and facilitator's guide) and* The Productivity Manual *(2nd ed.), as well as numerous articles and experiential learning activities. Dr. Smith is a member of the American Society for Quality, American Society for Training & Development, and Sigma Xi.*

Intrinsic/Extrinsic Motivators Questionnaire

Instructions: Answer questions 1 and 2 below and then wait for further instructions. You will have ten minutes to complete the first two questions.

1. How could you do your job in a more creative manner? List some ways in the space below:

2. List four or five major work activities or jobs you perform on a regular basis in the left-hand boxes on the chart below. Use a seven-point scale that ranges from 1 (low) to 7 (high) to rate each work activity on three separate dimensions: (a) level of difficulty, (b) potential to motivate, and (c) opportunity to add value.

Major Work Activity	Level of Difficulty	Potential to Motivate	Opportunity to Add Value
1.			
2.			
3.			
4.			
5.			

3. List five motivators or types of rewards that would encourage you to do your job in a more creative manner.

4. List three motivators or types of rewards from Question 3 above that you believe would *definitely increase your creativity*. Indicate whether these motivators are realistic or unrealistic in terms of your job or work setting. Indicate whether each is intrinsic or extrinsic.

Motivators	Realistic/ Unrealistic	Intrinsic	Extrinsic
1.			
2.			
3.			

5. List three types of work activities you like to perform and the motivators or rewards that would stimulate and reinforce your creativity.

Work Activity	Rewards That Reinforce Creativity
1.	
2.	
3.	

INTERNAL/EXTERNAL MOTIVATORS' ROLE IN CREATIVITY HANDOUT

Creativity, innovation, and an *entrepreneurial culture* are key elements in an organization's success. Organizations that downsize, reorganize, or face unexpected turbulence in the marketplace desperately need creative people who literally can do more with less. For their part, creative people want to work in organizations that openly encourage and recognize their creative talents. However, few organizations do a good job of recognizing and adequately rewarding the creative efforts of their people.

Extrinsic and Intrinsic Motivators and Rewards

Extrinsic rewards are tangible and easy to describe and measure, such as pay raises, bonuses, expense accounts, and other types of financial compensation. Monetary rewards encourage people to take the surest or quickest, not necessarily the most creative, route to gain the reward. Many upper-level managers and administrators who have little daily contact with employees believe that everyone wants money or its equivalent. Managers who strongly believe that monetary rewards are the best motivators seldom consider how individual differences and personal preferences affect productivity.

Intrinsic rewards are self-administered and provide immediate satisfaction, for instance, having a peer tell you that you did a great job on your report. The opportunity to do a difficult job in a competent manner and be recognized for it is another example of a self-administered reward. Most intrinsic motivators are based on feelings of accomplishment, feeling that one has done something worthwhile, or having an opportunity for self-development. Creative people are especially likely to be motivated intrinsically—by the need to self-actualize (Maslow, 1970), the need to achieve and maintain competence (White, 1959), and by their innate desire to be creative (Herzberg, 1968). Recognition from peers and work associates is one of the best rewards of all for these people.

Several studies have shown the relationship between creativity and intrinsic motivation. Personal data collected by Crutchfield (1961) indicate that high levels of intrinsic motivation accompany the work of notably creative people. Intrinsic rewards play prime roles in nurturing and enhancing creative performance (Amabile, 1983). "Task-involved" intrinsic motivation will lead to higher levels of creativity than will "ego-involved" extrinsic motivation (Crutchfield, 1962). Intrinsically motivated people feel freer to take risks because those risks carry virtually no liability, except those risks that are self-imposed (Lepper & Green, 1978). Overall, intrinsic rewards have been shown to have a greater positive impact on creativity than have extrinsic motivators (Amabile, 1996; Robinson & Stern, 1997; Thomas, 2000).

Some Fortune 500 companies have inserted the word "creativity" in statements of their corporate values and quality policies and incorporated creativity into their organizations' recognition and reward systems. More progressive organizations recognize that people are motivated by *intrinsic* or nonmonetary rewards, and their use to reward employees' creative thoughts, acts, and accomplishments is gradually increasing.

Creativity is defined as a mental process leading to ideas, theories, solutions, products, and artistic forms that are unique. Creative people have the ability or disposition to produce uncommon, remotely associated, or clever responses (Guilford, 1968). Novel ideas and creative endeavors in music and art, for example, can be variations on a given theme. Creative people often have quite different personalities, as well as thinking and problem-solving styles, and they display their creativity in unique ways.

Corporate Creativity

A company is considered creative when its employees do something new and potentially useful without being directly shown or taught how to do so. Corporate creativity is expressed through entirely new activities or innovations and also by improving or changing what has already been done (Robinson & Stern, 1997). Leaders of competitive, successful organizations have begun to recognize the prime roles that creativity and innovation play in the marketplace. These leaders know that corporate creativity is essential to achieve their business goals and vital to the long-term survival and success of their organizations. For instance, leaders at Glaxo Wellcome, a pharmaceutical company, are gradually building a distributed entrepreneurial and innovative culture to encourage transfer of learning, creation of new knowledge, and sharing of experience. They encourage the self-renewal efforts of their employees by giving them the opportunity and some funds to pursue avenues that might lead to breakthrough discoveries.

Companies that lack open communication channels and dynamic, supportive organizational cultures that nurture creativity and innovation have a hard time competing in the marketplace today. Unfortunately, many workers stop trying to be creative when they work in unsupportive work environments.

Individual Creativity

Everyone is creative in one way or another. However, there are wide individual differences among creative processes and among ways in which creativity is expressed. Most creative work is done by ordinary people who bring a fresh perspective to their work (Amabile, 1996). Taylor (1988) said that creative people integrate facts, knowledge, impressions, and feelings into a new form. Sternberg (1988) proposed that creative people incorporate new ideas into existing knowledge by breaking through longstanding boundaries and limitations in their respective fields. According to Robinson and Stern (1997), creative people engage in unexpected, unplanned creative acts that often result from self-initiated activities.

Expressions of Creativity

People express and demonstrate their creativity in problem solving, thinking and reasoning, and through other creative actions.

Problem Solving

Creative people are sensitive to problems and recognize "good" or intriguing problems in their fields. They solve these problems by searching for gaps in knowledge, recognizing patterns or similarities among problems, and taking intellectual risks. They set their own rules for problem solving rather than following rules used by others. Although they risk failure, they also take advantage of chance.

Thinking and Reasoning

Creative people have flexible, divergent thought processes. They take intellectual risks, avoid the traps of conventional thinking, and challenge longstanding assumptions. Creative people ask a lot of questions and look for reasons why things happen the way they do. Because they often have a nontraditional view of the world, they examine problems from a different perspective. Many creative ideas that initially seem illogical and undoable to others become logical in their view, which others appreciate only in hindsight. Creative people use lateral thinking to see beyond blind spots in the organization. They find new patterns and develop ways to solve problems and improve how they do their jobs.

Actions

Creative people balance instability within themselves with the motivation to reach a high level of organization and stability (Sternberg, 1988). Most creative people have a strong, restless inner drive to perform at a high level or to self-actualize in order to satisfy their "self" needs (Maslow, 1970). They keep on working toward a goal despite the odds against them. To illustrate, 3M Corporation's former CEO, William McKnight, once ordered Richard Drew, a young employee, to stop working on a project because he thought it would never work. "Drew disregarded the order and went on to invent masking tape, which paved the way for the creation of Scotch tape, 3M's defining product" (Sutton, 2001). Highly motivated people like Drew use their creative energy to reduce the gap between their own visions and current reality (Senge, 1990). They openly demonstrate their motivation through eagerness, energy, and enthusiasm. When creative people have challenging work they enjoy doing, they may modify their own jobs so they can be even more creative.

Individual Differences

People differ in the amount of creativity they have and in how they express that creativity. They also differ in their beliefs, attitudes, and behaviors. No two people are motivated by the exact same thing. Individual differences in perceptions, work experience, and willingness to do certain kinds of work affect the types of motivators and rewards people want. The stage where people are in their careers also affects the type of motivators they select (Smith, 1998). A newly hired twenty-year-old, for instance, might want a pay raise, while a person who has been with the company for fifteen years might want to spend time Friday afternoons working on a pet project that management has killed.

The job itself often has the potential to motivate an employee, such as when it provides an exciting opportunity to do something new. People are motivated intrinsically when they are given the freedom to pursue their own interests or design their own jobs and do things their own way. Many people relish the chance to add their unique brand of value to their jobs. This "something extra" often goes beyond the basic expectations of supervisors, team leaders, and customers. When people are genuinely motivated by their work and also receive the kind of intrinsic reward they really want, their job satisfaction and productivity are high (Smith, 1995; Smith 1998).

Encouraging and Supporting Creativity in the Workplace

Given that creative people tend to be intrinsically motivated, the following guidelines may be helpful for managers who wish to recognize, encourage, and reward creativity.

1. Provide a strong, supportive, open, flexible work environment that recognizes, fosters, and rewards creativity, innovation, and risk taking. For instance, recognize and support early stages of creative thoughts and actions by reducing personal, social, and organizational restraining forces that block or reduce creativity (Smith, 1998). Use traditional brainstorming techniques, storyboarding, and breakout group discussions, for example, to develop creative ideas and solutions (Hiam, 1998).

2. Ask people what motivates them. They will be surprised, but delighted to give you an honest answer. Recognize and reward creative processes and creative acts in ways that closely match a person's unique needs. Most intrinsic motivators come from the job itself, so it is vital to match people with jobs that are intrinsically motivating to them.

3. Encourage people to engage in self-initiated activities that let them choose problems to work on that interest them and that they believe they can solve. Give participants some free time and a small budget to pursue long-standing interests that may be unrelated to their jobs. They will be thrilled. You may be surprised at how much they can do on a small budget. These self-initiated activities often produce novel solutions to longstanding problems, or result in a new product.

4. Have special functions or award ceremonies to recognize and reward each person's unique creative talents and to showcase the importance of creativity and innovation. Whenever possible, involve the person's peers and work associates. Keep telling people that their creative achievements and unique efforts and contributions truly make a difference and affect the overall success of the organization.

5. Provide people with diverse stimuli, such as intriguing problems they have not previously encountered. Encourage them to view something they have already brought to a certain level from a totally different perspective. Many new ideas come from people in completely different fields of study, or by "cross-fertilization." People from diverse disciplines see the same things from new, fresh perspectives that rarely have boundaries. Putting people who have a wide range of thinking styles together often produces "creative abrasion," a necessary first step in the discovery process.

6. Encourage communication that does not follow existing formal lines of communication in the company. This latitude helps people to exchange information that can lead to breakthroughs. Company email and electronic discussion or idea rooms can be used to test out and exchange ideas. Encourage cross-disciplinary and cross-functional communication through knowledge networking, knowledge fairs, and mentoring programs. Frustrated or temporarily discouraged workers can never learn to become intrapreneurs and create their own positive work environments in an organization that doesn't recognize or reward creative endeavors.

7. Encourage the use of tacit knowledge or "know how," rather than explicit knowledge or "know what." Explicit knowledge, like academic information and technical data, is easy to communicate, codify, store in databases, and access. Tacit knowledge, action-oriented knowledge based on common sense, often comes from insights and by learning from others. Tacit knowledge is revealed by telling stories, chatting about problems, discussing projects, and exchanging ideas about what works and what does not. Knowledge fairs are also excellent sources of tacit knowledge. Tacit knowledge plays a prime role in creativity because creative processes are brought out through one-on-one learning experiences and face-to-face communication that allow people to directly test out and exchange ideas (Smith, 2002). Opportunities to acquire, share, and use tacit knowledge not only facilitate communication of creative ideas, but help build a culture in which creativity becomes contagious.

References

Amabile, T.M. (1983). *The social psychology of creativity.* New York: Springer-Verlag.

Amabile, T.M. (1996). *Creativity in context.* Boulder, CO: Westview Publishers.

Crutchfield, R. (1961). The creative process. In *Proceedings of the Conference on "the Creative Person"* (pp. VI.1–VI.16). Lake Tahoe, CA: University of California Alumni Center.

Crutchfield, R. (1962). Conformity and creative thinking. In H. Gruber, G. Terrell, & M. Wertheimer (Eds.). *Contemporary approaches in creative thinking* (pp. 120–140). New York: Atherton.

Guildford, J.P. (1968). *Intelligence, creativity, and their educational implications.* San Diego, CA: Robert R. Knapp.

Herzberg, F. (1968, January/February). One more time: How do you motivate employees? *Harvard Business Review,* pp. 53–62.

Hiam, A. (1998). *The manager's pocket guide to creativity.* Amherst, MA: HRD Press.

Lepper, M., & Green, D. (1978). *The hidden costs of rewards.* Hillsdale, NJ: Lawrence Erlbaum.

Maslow, A.H. (1970). *Motivation and personality* (2nd ed.). New York: Harper & Row.

Robinson, A.G., & Stern, S. (1997). *Corporate creativity.* San Francisco, CA: Berrett-Koehler.

Senge, P.M. (1990). *The fifth discipline.* New York: Doubleday/Currency.

Smith, E.A. (1995). *Creating productive organizations.* Boca Raton, FL: St. Lucie/CRC Press.

Smith, E.A. (1998). The role of creativity in motivation and productivity. In D.J. Sumanth, W.B. Werther, & J.A. Edosomwan (Eds.), *Proceedings of the Seventh International Conference on Productivity and Quality Research* (pp. 395–408). Norcross, GA: Engineering & Management Press.

Smith, E.A. (2002). The role of tacit and explicit knowledge in the workplace. *The Journal of Workplace Learning, 6*(2).

Sutton, R.I. (2001, September). The weird rules of creativity. *Harvard Business Review,* pp. 94–103.

Sternberg, R.J. (1988). A three-facet model of creativity. In R.J. Sternberg (Ed.), *The nature of creativity.* Cambridge, MA: Cambridge University Press.

Taylor, C.W. (1988). Various approaches to and definitions of creativity. In R.J. Sternberg (Ed.), *The nature of creativity.* Cambridge, MA: Cambridge University Press.

Thomas, K.W. (2000). *Intrinsic motivation at work.* San Francisco, CA: Berrett-Koehler.

White, R.W. (1959). Motivation reconsidered: The concept of competence. *Psychological Review, 66,* 297–334.

737. WHEN I MANAGE, WHEN I LEAD: SEPARATING THE FUNCTIONS

Goals

- To demonstrate ways in which leadership differs from management.
- To allow participants to learn the distinguishing characteristics of leadership from their own experience.
- To allow participants to learn about leadership from one another.

Group Size

Any size group in subgroups of five to seven.

Time Required

Approximately sixty minutes.

Materials

- One set of activity cards, prepared in advance, for each subgroup.
- One copy of the When I Manage, When I Lead Notes for the facilitator.
- One copy of the When I Manage, When I Lead Summary for each participant.
- A flip chart and felt-tipped markers.
- Masking tape.

Physical Setting

Tables and chairs arranged so that each subgroup can work without disturbing others.

Process

1. Create the activity cards in advance by copying the When I Manage, When I Lead Activity Cards onto index stock and cutting the cards and shuffling them. (Note that the activity cards describe the differing qualities of management and leadership in a nonjudgmental way, providing a structured way for participants to discuss these differences and learn from one another's opinions and experiences.)

2. Open the session with a brief lecturette on leadership and management, taken from material on the When I Manage, When I Lead Notes. Explain that leadership is a complex set of communication, motivational, psychological, and relationship skills that is different from management. Say that management skills center around the organization and execution of tasks, whereas leadership is about generating and directing energy and commitment among a group of people. While both are necessary to achieve results, management involves skills that are more concrete, while leadership is less tangible. (This introduction can be very brief because most of the learning will come from the interaction among the participants.) (Three to five minutes.)

3. Invite the participants to divide into small groups of five to seven people. When everyone is seated comfortably at tables or in circles, give each group one set of activity cards.

4. Place the two title cards ("When I manage . . ." and "When I lead . . .") next to each other face up on each of the tables. Then shuffle the remaining twenty playing cards and place them face down in the center of the table.

5. Instruct the groups to turn over one playing card at a time and to discuss among themselves whether the word or phrase on the card pertains more to *leadership* or to *management*. When the group has reached consensus, they are to place the card under the appropriate title card. Tell them to continue turning over playing cards one at a time and deciding where each goes. At the end of the activity, there will be two piles of cards, one describing leadership and one describing management. (Fifteen minutes.)

6. Call the group together and draw a vertical line down the flip chart and write "Management" at the top of one column and "Leadership" at the top of the other. Ask the group what characteristics describe leadership and what characteristics describe management. Record their responses. Use as many sheets of newsprint paper as necessary, taping extra sheets to the wall. Stop to discuss areas of disagreement as they occur. If needed,

use the When I Manage, When I Lead Summary to decide which list an item belongs on. (Twenty minutes.)

7. After everyone is satisfied with the listing on the flip chart, give participants copies of the Summary to keep. Wrap up by asking the following questions:

- What do the characteristics we have listed for management have in common?

- What do the characteristics we have listed for leadership have in common?

- In which domain do each of you feel more comfortable? What are some reasons for that?

- Is there any tension between the characteristics of management and the characteristics of leadership? Is this a real or perceived tension? Can we both manage and lead at the same time? Give an example.

(Fifteen minutes.)

8. End the activity by noting that leaders are often faced with dilemmas that create the impression they must choose between management and leadership, between short-term results and long-term goals, whereas the art of leadership is finding a way to do both. A careful examination of the common characteristics of management and leadership should demonstrate that they are not mutually exclusive. Take comments and close the session. (Five minutes.)

Variations

- Distribute the When I Manage, When I Lead Summary at the beginning of the activity and use it as a discussion tool, having groups come up with scenarios for each of the pairings.

- Hand-letter the activity cards on 3" x 5" cards, using a larger size for the headings.

Submitted by Steve Sphar.

Steve Sphar, J.D., is an internal organization development consultant for the California State Teachers' Retirement System. He has counseled managers and employees in both the private and public sectors for over fifteen years. He is a frequent contributor to professional publications, including the Annual and the McGraw-Hill Training and Performance Sourcebook.

WHEN I MANAGE, WHEN I LEAD ACTIVITY CARDS

When I Manage, I . . .	When I Lead, I . . .
Provide Structure	Provide Support
Am a Builder	Am an Architect
Maintain	Develop
Ask, "How and When?"	Ask, "Why?"
Do Things Right	Do the Right Thing

When I Manage, I . . .	When I Lead, I . . .
Administrate	Instigate
Keep an Eye on the Bottom Line	Keep an Eye on the Horizon
Give Answers	Ask Questions
Talk Tactics	Talk Strategy
Use Common Sense	Use Imagination

The 2003 Annual: Volume 1, Training/© 2003 John Wiley & Sons, Inc.

WHEN I MANAGE, WHEN I LEAD NOTES

When we act as *managers,* we build the project, we maintain structures that guide the work, we pay attention to details, we solve problems with practical answers, we get the job done on time and under budget. These are positive qualities.

When we act as *leaders,* we use a different set of skills that utilize our ability to motive and inspire others to commit their energy to a common purpose. So when we act as leaders, we develop and support people's growth, we see the big picture, we guide and articulate the vision, we provide direction without micromanaging, we dare to dream, and sometimes we stir things up. These are also positive qualities.

WHEN I MANAGE, WHEN I LEAD SUMMARY

All of the descriptions on the activity cards are intended to have positive connotations. The words pertaining to management describe the logistical, practical aspects of what management is all about: the orderly planning, organizing, and execution of tasks and activities. Those pertaining to leadership refer to seeing the big picture and to helping others see it too.

When I Manage, I . . .	When I Lead, I . . .
Provide Structure	Provide Support
Am a Builder	Am an Architect
Maintain	Develop
Ask, "How and When?"	Ask, "Why?"
Do Things Right	Do the Right Thing
Administrate	Instigate
Keep an Eye on the Bottom Line	Keep an Eye on the Horizon
Give Answers	Ask Questions
Talk Tactics	Talk Strategy
Use Common Sense	Use Imagination

738. Meet My Leader: Using Analogy to Describe Traits

Goals

- To identify the differences between ineffective and effective leaders.

- To use more of the human senses to accelerate learning.

Group Size

Any number of subgroups of four to five participants.

Time Required

Approximately sixty minutes.

Materials

- A collection of common objects such as pieces of fruit (orange, banana, apple, pear—one type of fruit per subgroup) or office supplies (pencil, marker, scissors, tape—one type of office supply per subgroup).

- One felt-tipped marker (different colors) for each subgroup.

- Blank paper and pencils for participants.

- A flip chart and felt-tipped markers.

- Masking tape.

Physical Setting

A room large enough for people to move from place to place and for the participants to discuss the objects without disturbing one another.

Process

1. Before participants arrive, based on the number of groups you will have, create enough stations at different places along the walls to accommodate four or five people each. At each station, tape a blank sheet of newsprint to the wall and set out a colored marker (a different color for each station) and one piece of fruit, an office supply, or other object of your choice.

2. After everyone arrives, explain to the participants that the concept of leadership is complex and that the activity they are about to do will help them to unravel some of the mystery through analogy.

3. Form subgroups of four or five participants each and direct each group to stand along the wall at a separate sheet of flip-chart paper. Ask each group to choose a recorder. (Two minutes.)

4. Write the following phrases on the flip chart while everyone is moving around:
   - How the object *feels* like my leader
   - How the object *sees* like my leader
   - How the object *moves* like my leader
   - How the object *hears* like my leader

5. Ask participants to think about leaders they work for currently as they handle their station's object and answer the questions you have written, first silently, and then sharing with the others in their subgroups as the recorder writes their answers on the piece of flip-chart paper. (Ten minutes.)

6. Have all subgroups move to a new station and repeat the process, taking their own colored marker along for later identification purposes. (Five minutes.)

7. Switch stations again and repeat the process until everyone has visited every station. (Five minutes per station.)

8. Pull the large group together for discussion. Use the notes that have been recorded on the newsprint sheets and the following questions for discussion:
   - What were the distinguishing features of each object you handled and the analogous leadership characteristics?
   - How were the various descriptions of leaders the same or different from one another at each station?
   - In what ways were the various objects like leaders you admire?

Record the answers on a flip chart with the heading "Effective Leaders Are . . ."

- In what ways was each object like leaders you find ineffective?

Record their answers on the flip chart with the heading "Ineffective Leaders Are . . ." (Ten minutes.)

9. Now say, "Let's compare the lists of characteristics we created for effective and for ineffective leaders. What can you conclude from these observations?" Write their answers on the flip chart. (Five minutes.)

10. Give the following potential definition of effective and ineffective leaders:

   "An *ineffective* leader will get the task done, but an *effective* leader will get the task done and assure that those working on the task still have a good relationship with one another and would be willing to work together again."

11. Provide time for participants to reflect and apply what they have learned. Tell them to take a few minutes to reflect on their own characteristics, attitudes, and skills as a leader and to check them against the lists of characteristics of both effective and ineffective leaders.

12. Have participants identify one to two areas they intend to focus on developing and to form pairs to discuss with one another how they might achieve this goal back on the job. Give them blank paper and pencils to write down their thoughts and ways they can encourage each other to remember the lessons learned. (Ten minutes.)

Variation

- Substitute other words for the word leader, such as "colleague," "direct report," "customer," "vendor," "accountant," or "human resources director."

Submitted by Lois B. Hart.

Lois B. Hart, Ed.D., *is director of the Women's Leadership Institute and president of Leadership Dynamics. Dr. Hart has thirty years' experience as a trainer, facilitator, and consultant presenting programs on leadership, teams, conflict, and facilitation. She is co-author with Ken Blanchard and Mario Tamayo of* Celebrate! *(2002). She has written twenty-one other books, including* 50 Activities for Developing Leaders, Learning from Conflict, Training Methods That Work, *and* Faultless Facilitation.

739. Lasso Your Vision, Mission, and Values: Building Team Support and Commitment

Goals

- To create ownership and understanding of an organization's or team's vision, mission, and values statements.

- To evaluate current actions that contribute to the vision, mission, and values becoming a reality.

- To identify actions to strengthen the vision, mission, and values, making them a part of the everyday culture of the team or organization.

Group Size

Five to thirty participants from the same organization or intact team or work group.

Time Required

Sixty to ninety minutes, depending on the amount of discussion generated.

Materials

- Copies of the organization's Vision, Mission and Values statements printed on pieces of flip-chart paper or reproduced on overhead transparencies.

- At least twenty sheets of flip-chart paper with lassos drawn at the top of the sheets posted at the front of the room.

- A sheet of flip-chart paper with the Code Key (see Step 11) on it.

- A flip chart and felt-tipped markers or an overhead projector and transparency markers.

- Extra flip-chart paper.

- A different color felt-tipped marker for each subgroup.

- Masking tape.
- A timing device.

Physical Setting

A room large enough to post flip-chart paper around the room, allowing small groups to meet at the different charts and discuss them without interference from other groups.

Process

1. Place the company's or team's vision, mission, and values statements (previously printed on flip-chart paper) on the wall at the front of the room (or show them on an overhead projector). (If this is a first time the group has seen these statements, begin by sharing definitions of vision, mission, and values, and/or by giving a brief overview of how these specific ones were developed.)

2. Begin by telling the group:

   "All too often the vision, mission, and values statements of a company [team] simply become laminated artwork hanging on the wall or words on paper hidden in strategic plans. Our goal is to make these statements living, breathing realities that define how we make decisions and act with our customers and with one another. The first step in this process is to be sure that everyone really understands what our vision, mission, and values statements are saying about how we want to operate as a company [team]. To accomplish this, we are going to take a few minutes to look at each of them, using a technique from the rodeo to help us make the statements come to life for us."

3. Share the technique by asking the question:

   "How many have ever watched a rodeo? Remember the part where the cowboy tries to lasso the calf? It's a tough job, but most of the time the cowboy is able to do it. Sometimes the calf wins! Well, we are going to see the words in our vision, mission, and values statements as calves—and we are the cowboys. We are going to lasso the most important words in those statements. Our lasso is a magic marker. Let's start with the vision statement."

4. Read the vision statement to the group. Then ask: "As you hear this statement, what words jump out at you as most important and meaningful?"

Emphasize that key words are words that give the statement its meat. Tell them to focus as much as possible on action words that are descriptive.

5. As individuals call out a word, write it inside one of the lassos that you had previously drawn on individual pieces of flip-chart paper. *Each word goes in a separate lasso, on a separate piece of flip-chart paper posted at a different place in the room.* Have volunteers post each piece of chart paper on the wall as you continue capturing words from the group. (Five minutes.)

6. When all key words in the vision statement have been lassoed, move on to the mission statement and repeat the process. Then move on to the values statement, repeating the process. At the conclusion of this phase, the walls will be filled with chart paper, each sheet holding a lasso with a key word contained in it. (Ten minutes.)

7. Tell the group:

> "Now that we've captured the key words from our vision, mission, and values statements, it's time to 'wrap' some meaning around them. We are going to spend the next thirty minutes doing this. To keep our rodeo analogy, you'll notice that all lassoed words have chutes coming out from them (represented by the blank chart paper). Our next job is to change these words into actions. As you look at each of the words inside a lasso, ask yourself: 'What does it look like when whatever that word represents is really happening?' We are going to capture some of your ideas by breaking into smaller groups."

8. Divide the participants into smaller groups. One way to do it is to say:

> "To get started, let's break into some smaller groups. In the next sixty seconds, line up in order by the amount of time you have worked here at this organization: Go!"

At the end of sixty seconds count off by the number of teams you want (for example, if you want to break the group into five teams, have them count 1, 2, 3, 4, 5, 1, 2, 3, 4, 5, and so on). (*Note:* The value of this method is that you create teams composed of a mix of longtime employees, newer hires, and those in between.)

9. Give each subgroup a different colored marker and give the following directions:

> "During the next thirty minutes, your team is to visit each chute (chart) and talk together quietly about the lassoed word. Discuss what it means to you and what specific *actions* would illustrate that the idea it represents is in effect in your organization. Your job is to record *actual examples* of what that word is like in action. Be a little

creative—you can write the words, draw a picture, draw a symbol, or anything you want. The goal is for each chute to have information recorded by each team. We'll be able to tell who wrote what because your group's marker color will be on each page. If your group talks about one of these words and either does not understand it or just cannot think of anything to put on the chart, put a question mark on the chart with your marker. But try really hard to think of one or more actual examples to illustrate what this concept means to you— how it looks in action—right now."

Give the group an opportunity to ask questions to clarify the task. Then set the timer for thirty minutes.

10. During this phase, wander around and give guidance and help as necessary to be sure participants understand what they are supposed to be doing. Give the participants a five-minute warning and a two-minute warning and remind them that they need to visit every chart. (Thirty minutes.)

11. Give everyone an opportunity to relax for a few minutes. While people are taking this stretch break, double-check the charts to be sure each group visited each one and post the Code Key where everyone can see it as follows.

    * (star) = We're doing great!
    ? (question) = We're really not sure.
    – (minus) = We need some work!

12. Call everyone together and announce that it is time for a quick check to evaluate how the organization (or team) is doing in terms of actually living its vision, mission, and values. Tell the group:

    "Imagine that you had to very quickly evaluate how well this company (or team) is doing right this minute in terms of each of these key words. In your breakout teams, take ten minutes to go to each chart, read the lassoed word, quickly review the information that all the other teams and your team have written, and then choose one of the code symbols on the Code Key I have posted to evaluate how well we are doing overall in exemplifying what *that particular word or concept* means. Write the code your group decides on the chart with the same color marker you used before and move on to another chart. Keep going until you have revisited all the lassoed words." (Ten minutes.)

13. Give the group a five-minute and a two-minute warning, reminding them that the goal is to write a code on each chart.

14. After ten minutes, call time. Thank everyone for their hard work and bring closure using the following questions:

- What have you learned about our organization's vision, mission, and values statements through this activity?
- What common themes are present?
- What parts of the vision need some work? The mission? The values?
- What are some changes you would like to make in how you personally carry out the organization's vision, mission, and values? What would you change about the way you deal with your customers and/or teammates as a result of this activity?
- Do you think it is important for all of us to have the same picture of what the vision, mission, and value statements mean? Why or why not?
- How have you felt today about sharing your ideas with other members of this group?
- When a word received a number of minus signs, what does that indicate? Which seem to need special work?
- What do we have to celebrate about how our organization is living its vision, mission, and values?
- What will you do differently as a result of this activity when you return to the job?

(Ten minutes.)

15. Document any follow-up actions that participants plan to take—either to reinforce the positives or to reposition the negatives—as a result of this activity on a flip chart. (Five minutes.)

Variations

- Use this process, but only focus on one of the items, such as mission, rather than all three.
- Use this process to discuss a project mission, a problem being solved, or a customer complaint.
- With very large groups (such as an entire organization), conduct a number of focus groups, using members of the management team as facilitators. Once everyone has participated in a focus group, prepare a summary report that identifies all the key words lassoed and the evaluation codes

given. Let supervisors share the feedback with their work groups and have them lead discussions about what their work groups can do to model the vision, mission, and values.

Submitted by Cher Holton.

Cher Holton, Ph.D., *president of the Holton Consulting Group, Inc., is an impact consultant focusing on rekindling the human spirit. She is Certified Speaking Professional and Certified Management Consultant and is author of* The Manager's Short Course to a Long Career; Living at the Speed of Life: Staying in Control in a World Gone Bonkers!; Suppose: Questions to Turbo-Charge Your Business and Your Life; *and* From Ballroom to Bottom Line: In Business and In Life.

Introduction
to the Inventories, Questionnaires, and Surveys Section

Inventories, questionnaires, and surveys are valuable tools for the HRD professional. These feedback tools help respondents take an objective look at themselves and at their organizations. These tools also help to explain how a particular theory applies to them or to their situations.

Inventories, questionnaires, and surveys are useful in a number of training and consulting situations: privately for self-diagnosis; one-on-one to plan individual development; in a small group to open discussion; in a work team to help the team to focus on its highest priorities; or in an organization to gather data to achieve progress.

You will find that the use of inventories, questionnaires, and surveys enriches, personalizes, and deepens training, development, and intervention designs. Many can be combined with other experiential learning activities or articles in this or other *Annuals* to design an exciting, involving, practical, and well-rounded intervention.

Each instrument includes the background necessary for understanding, presenting, and using it. Interpretive information, scales, and scoring sheets are also provided. In addition, we include the reliability and validity data contributed by the authors. If you wish additional information on any of these instruments, contact the authors directly. You will find their addresses and telephone numbers in the "Contributors" listing near the end of this volume.

Other assessment tools that address a wider variety of topics can be found in our comprehensive *Reference Guide to Handbooks and Annuals*. This guide indexes all the instruments that we have published to date in the *Annuals*. You will find this complete, up-to-date, and easy-to-use resource valuable for locating other instruments, as well as for locating experiential learning activities and articles. A print version of the *Reference Guide* is available for volumes through 1999. An online supplement covering the years through 2003 can be found at www.pfeiffer.com/go/supplement.

The 2003 Annual: Volume 1, Training includes four assessment tools in the following categories:

Individual Development

Readiness for Online Learning Self-Assessment, by Ryan Watkins

Communication

Online Social Presence Self-Assessment (OSPSA), by Chih-Hsiung Tu

Consulting and Facilitating

Evaluating Training: Before, During, and After, by Susan Boyd

Organizations

The Knowledge Management Assessment Tool (KMAT), by David J. Maier and James L. Moseley

READINESS FOR ONLINE LEARNING SELF-ASSESSMENT

Ryan Watkins

Abstract: Today, online learning opportunities are commonly available as a means for satisfying our educational desires and/or training requirements, but there is often a question of whether or not learners are likely to succeed. Deciding whether or not online learning is "right" for someone is rarely a straightforward process. This self-assessment provides trainers and supervisors with a quick, yet comprehensive, way to help respondents analyze their readiness for success in an online environment. It can be used to appraise not only respondents' technical preparedness for the online learning environment, but also to examine their online communication skills and study habits. It also provides a guide for examining which, if any, online learning environments offer respondents the best opportunities for success.

In response to consumer demands and technological advances, many organizations (including educational institutions, corporations, and government agencies) have moved toward offering employees, students, and others the opportunity to learn at a distance. Offering valid and useful learning opportunities at a time and place more convenient for the learner has become a priority for many organizations and is offering learners unprecedented access to learning experiences.

However, anticipating someone's success as a learner at a distance is not always easy. The online learning environment can be much different from those learning environments most of us have experienced previously. The potential online learner, however, should not be intimidated, as most online learning environments are designed so that learners with a variety of learning styles and preferences can find success.

The likelihood of success does, nonetheless, depend on a variety of factors. Several are necessarily related to technical proficiencies, while others are indicators of preferences as a learner. The Readiness for Online Learning Self-Assessment provides a quick, yet comprehensive, analysis of respondents' preparedness for success in an online learning environment.

SUGGESTED IMPLEMENTATION

The assessment is designed to assist trainers or supervisors in asking the "right" questions, both about respondents' preparedness for an online learning experience and about which types of online learning experiences they are best prepared for. The assessment is based on the fundamental characteristics for success that the author has identified through experience both as an online learner and as an instructor.

The self-assessment is divided into two sections. The first is designed to assist the respondent in determining whether he or she is ready for an online learning experience. The second is to assist him or her in choosing the desirable characteristics of an online learning experience, given his or her personal characteristics. This will enable instructors or supervisors to choose learning experiences that will best suit the individual.

ADMINISTRATION

Give respondents copies of the Readiness for Online Learning Self-Assessment and pencils and ask them to complete both sections as honestly as possible, based on their own experiences online as well as in the conventional classroom. Tell them to use only their own learning experiences as a basis for their answers, rather than what they have read or heard from others. Tell them it will take between ten and fifteen minutes to complete the assessment.

When everyone has finished, give them all copies of the Scoring Sheet and ask them to total their scores for each part of the assessment. When everyone has written his or her scores in the proper places, hand out copies of the Interpretation Sheet. Let everyone check his or her own results and lead a discussion of the implications for respondents for how they should approach upcoming online classes. Ask for the range of scores, as you may want to provide extra help for those who scored especially low and/or provide additional technical resources so that they will be successful.

Use the results to plan events best suited to the respondents' needs and abilities. The assessment can be taken again at a later date after respondents have had more experience online.

RELIABILITY AND VALIDITY

This instrument has some face validity in that the author and others he has known concur that the items are important for success with online learning. The assessment has not been statistically validated nor scientifically tested, but the author's experience is that taking these questions into account when considering online learning for any individual or group can be extremely useful.

References and Related Readings

Kaufman, R., Watkins, R., & Guerra, I. (2001). The future of distance education: Defining and sustaining useful results. *Educational Technology, 41*(3), 19–26.

Kaufman, R., Watkins, R., & Leigh, D. (2001). *Useful educational results: Defining, prioritizing and achieving.* Lancaster, PA: Proactive Publishing.

Watkins, R. (2000). How distance education is changing workforce development. *Quarterly Review of Distance Education, 1*(3), 241–246.

Watkins, R. (in press). Determining if distance education is the right choice: Applied strategic thinking in education. *Computers in the Schools, 20*(2).

Watkins, R., & Corry, M. (in press). Virtual universities: Challenging the conventions of education. In W. Haddad & A. Draxler (Eds.), *Technologies for education: Potentials, parameters and prospects.* Paris: UNESCO.

Watkins, R., & Kaufman, R. (2002). Strategic audit for distance education. In M. Silberman (Ed.), *The 2002 team and organization development sourcebook.* New York: McGraw-Hill.

Watkins, R., & Kaufman, R. (in press). Strategic planning for distance education. In M. Moore (Ed.), *Handbook of American distance education.* University Park, PA: Penn State University Press.

Watkins, R., & Schlosser, C. (2000). Capabilities based educational equivalency units: Beginning a professional dialogue on useful models for educational equivalency. *American Journal of Distance Education, 14*(3), 34–47.

Ryan Watkins is an assistant professor of educational technology leadership at George Washington University. He has published more than thirty articles on the topics of distance education, instructional design, needs assessment, and strategic planning. He is also co-author of Useful Educational Results *with Roger Kaufman and Doug Leigh.*

READINESS FOR ONLINE LEARNING SELF-ASSESSMENT*

Ryan Watkins

Part One

Instructions: As you read the questions below, ask yourself: "Am I ready for on-line learning?" Answer by circling the appropriate number from 1 (low agreement) to 6 (high agreement).

	Low Agreement			High Agreement		
	1	2	3	4	5	6

Technology

1. Do you have adequate bandwidth (speed of access to Internet resources) to access the files required for the learning experience? 1 2 3 4 5 6

2. If needed, will you have access to technical assistance (either through the learning experience or elsewhere)? 1 2 3 4 5 6

3. Do you have the basic computer skills for navigating the Internet and the learning experience itself (e.g., search engines, downloading files, installing software)? 1 2 3 4 5 6

4. Do you own the software necessary for completing the learning experience (Adobe Acrobat, MS Office, QuickTime, Flash, and so forth)? 1 2 3 4 5 6

5. Does your computer have the required components for the learning experience (enough RAM, speakers, desktop video conferencing)? 1 2 3 4 5 6

*I would like to thank Richard Lemmer, Cynthia Fish, Janice Levie, Diane Atkinson, and Dr. Mike Corry of George Washington University; Dr. Lya Visser of Nova Southeastern University; Dr. Roger Kaufman of Florida State University; Ingrid Guerra of the University of Michigan–Dearborn; and Monte Watkins of Accenture Consulting, as well as the other online learners and instructors who have provided me with constructive feedback in the development of this self-assessment.

Low Agreement			High Agreement		
1	2	3	4	5	6

6. Do you have anti-virus software that can protect your computer from a variety of viruses?   1   2   3   4   5   6

7. Can you download files from the Internet to the hard drive of your computer?   1   2   3   4   5   6

Self-Directed Learning

8. Will the learning experience you are considering provide you with enough useful skills and knowledge so that you can stay motivated throughout?   1   2   3   4   5   6

9. Are you able to invest the time to complete the daily/weekly required activities of the learning experience?   1   2   3   4   5   6

10. Would your friends/colleagues say that you successfully finish challenges that you take on?   1   2   3   4   5   6

11. Are you committed to learning and applying what you learn?   1   2   3   4   5   6

12. Do you have a personal support structure in place to assist you in keeping motivated throughout the learning experience?   1   2   3   4   5   6

Online Relationships

13. Do you feel comfortable knowing that other learners will most likely only know you through online discussions?   1   2   3   4   5   6

14. Are you able to express your mood, emotions, and humor accurately through your writing?   1   2   3   4   5   6

15. Would you be able to remain motivated knowing that the instructor was not online at all times and was therefore unable to provide immediate responses to questions and concerns?   1   2   3   4   5   6

The 2003 Annual: Volume 1, Training/© 2003 John Wiley & Sons, Inc.

Part Two

Instructions: As you read the questions below, ask yourself: "Which types of on-line learning experiences am I ready for?" Use the same scale as before, with 1 as low agreement and 6 as high agreement.

	Low Agreement			High Agreement		
	1	2	3	4	5	6

Online Video

1. Do you feel comfortable taking notes while watching a video on the computer?   1   2   3   4   5   6

2. Will you be comfortable relating the content of short video clips (one to three minutes, typically) to the extensive information you have read online or in required texts?   1   2   3   4   5   6

Chat Rooms

3. Would you feel comfortable reading online while typing?   1   2   3   4   5   6

4. Can you follow along with more than one online conversation at a time?   1   2   3   4   5   6

5. Are you comfortable knowing that you may not be able to participate in all of the conversations occurring online at the same time?   1   2   3   4   5   6

Discussion Groups

6. Can you accurately express your ideas, comments, and questions through writing?   1   2   3   4   5   6

7. Can you keep focused on the topic of a discussion, even when there are time delays between comments?   1   2   3   4   5   6

8. Do you perform better when you are given additional time to compose a response to a question?   1   2   3   4   5   6

Low Agreement			High Agreement		
1	2	3	4	5	6

Online Readings

9. Are you comfortable reading documents longer than one page on a computer screen?

     1   2   3   4   5   6

10. Do you have access to a printer for those documents that are too long for you to read online?

     1   2   3   4   5   6

11. Do you take notes on challenging material while reading it on the computer?

     1   2   3   4   5   6

Peer Evaluations

12. Would you be comfortable providing a fellow learner with constructive feedback on his or her work?

     1   2   3   4   5   6

13. Would you be comfortable receiving constructive, but potentially less favorable, feedback on your work from fellow learners whom you do not know personally?

     1   2   3   4   5   6

Group Projects

14. Do you know how to use the attachment features of your email (view email attachments and attach files to an email message)?

     1   2   3   4   5   6

15. Would you be comfortable knowing that part of your grade would be based on the contribution/input of another learner with whom you only interact online?

     1   2   3   4   5   6

16. Will you be comfortable working with other learners in different time zones?

     1   2   3   4   5   6

17. Is your schedule such that you can provide prompt and timely feedback to and ask questions of project team members?

     1   2   3   4   5   6

	Low Agreement			**High Agreement**		
	1	2	3	4	5	6

Learner Support

18. Will you feel comfortable if the online
learning experience offers you little
contact with the instructor (or tutor)? 1 2 3 4 5 6

19. Are you confident that you will not
require much technical and adminis-
trative support for a successful online
learning experience? 1 2 3 4 5 6

20. Has the prospective learning experience
been designed to keep you actively involved throughout the learning process? 1 2 3 4 5 6

READINESS FOR ONLINE LEARNING
SELF-ASSESSMENT SCORING SHEET

Part One

Instructions: Enter the response value you chose for each item in Part One of the Readiness for Online Learning Self-Assessment in the table below:

Question Number	Response Value
Question 1	
Question 2	
Question 3	
Question 4	
Question 5	
Question 6	
Question 7	
Question 8	
Question 9	
Question 10	
Question 11	
Question 12	
Question 13	
Question 14	
Question 15	
Total	

Part Two

Instructions: Enter the response value you chose for each item in Part Two of the Readiness for Online Learning Self-Assessment in the table below:

Question Number	Response Value
Question 1	
Question 2	
Question 3	
Question 4	
Question 5	
Question 6	
Question 7	
Question 8	
Question 9	
Question 10	
Question 11	
Question 12	
Question 13	
Question 14	
Question 15	
Question 16	
Question 17	
Question 18	
Question 19	
Question 20	
Total	

Readiness for Online Learning
Self-Assessment Interpretation Sheet

Part One

Scores from 81 to 90

A variety of online learning environments will likely be supportive of your interests and comfortable for you as a learner. Still, you should attempt to choose your online learning experiences based on your strengths in the second section of the self-assessment. Matching your strengths with the offerings of the online learning experience will still be essential for choosing an environment in which you are likely to succeed. Viable online learning experiences should provide you with a list of both the technologies required and the types of learning events offered.

Scores from 71 to 80

Entering an online learning experience is likely a good opportunity for you to expand your skills and knowledge, although you may have to spend additional time gaining the skills required for the online environment. If your score was low due to a lack of available technology, then finding additional technology resources (perhaps at public libraries) may be an alternative. If you responded that multiple dimensions of self-directed learning might be challenging, then study habits and time management may be a good place to start. The additional time required should be factored into your decision to take an online course.

Scores from 15 to 70

There are likely several areas in which you may want to gain additional experience before entering an online learning environment. Review the factors for which your response was 4 or below, and look for opportunities to expand on your experiences in those areas.

Part Two

Scores from 108 to 120

You are likely to benefit from a variety of online learning experiences. You already have many of the skills required for successful participation in an online course, so you can focus on the learning experience itself. You should still try to match the components of the online learning experience with the strengths you have identified. Viable online learning experiences should provide you with a list of both the technologies required and the types of learning events offered during the experience.

Scores from 96 to 107

Some aspects of an online learning experience may be a challenge, but overall you should have the skills for successful participation in the majority of course activities. You will likely want to spend some additional time during the learning experience to gain the skills in those areas that you identified as being 4 or below, so factor this into your choice of online learning experience.

Scores from 20 to 95

There are likely several areas in which you may want to gain additional experience before entering an online learning environment. Review the factors for which your response was 4 or below, and look for opportunities to expand on your experiences in those areas.

EVALUATING TRAINING: BEFORE, DURING, AND AFTER

Susan Boyd

Abstract: Evaluation can be a great support to the learning process and an aid to both the instructor and the learners. Many instructors think of evaluation as simply a form at the end of the class, the traditional smile sheets that have the learners rate the instructor, content, and environment. But evaluation really begins at the time the learner registers for class, continues during class so that the instructor can gauge and adjust to the learners' needs, and, most importantly, continues after class to ensure training has made a difference back on the job. The author provides seven sample evaluation forms to be used throughout the training process.

Evaluating the learners prior to, during, and after training can provide invaluable feedback about the training results of a program. Information gathered through evaluation sheets can be used at different times:

- To determine whether the learner has met the prerequisites for the class;
- To adjust the instruction to the learners' needs during the program;
- To make changes to the course material and curriculum for future training classes;
- To solve equipment, materials, logistics, and other problems before the next class;
- To identify future training needs and courses for individuals and departments; and
- To gather evidence that training has made a difference back on the job.

Samples of forms used for a variety of purposes are presented here. These are actual forms that have been used to evaluate training programs in the past. Modify and use them to meet your own training program needs. Forms can be sent to participants through email or over the Internet. You can collect the information online, summarize it, and keep an evaluation database to better analyze results over a number of programs.

Use of the Evaluation Forms

The use of each of the evaluation forms that follow is described below. They all can be adapted to specific training needs.

Prior to Class

Pre-Screening Questionnaire. Learners are asked to fill out and submit forms two or three weeks prior to a class. The information is used to better tailor the instruction, grouping/seating, and materials to the learners' needs.

During Class

Comfort Level Rating Form.   Learners complete this form during a class. The instructor/trainer uses the information to determine the level of confidence that participants have in using the skills they are learning and to identify areas of mastery and topics to review. This type of form would typically be completed periodically throughout a two-to-four-day class and before the lunch break in a one-day class. The trainer can use the information to pair up individuals for review sessions and to adjust course content for the future.

At the End of Class

Learner Commitment Statement.   Learners complete this form at the end of a workshop, identifying how they will use the skills they have learned when they are back on the job. The instructor can send reminders to participants about two weeks later so that they can put the training points into action.

Class Evaluation Form.   Learners complete this form at the end of a workshop, rating their satisfaction with course content, the instructor, the materials, and the classroom environment. Respondents are asked to identify the most relevant parts of the program for them and to provide suggestions for improvement.

Instructor Feedback Form.   Instructors complete this type of form immediately after a class, rating individual learners on whether they have mastered the planned objectives and listing problems/changes they would like to make with the material, room, equipment, and so forth, prior to any future session.

Follow-Up Evaluation After Class

Learner Follow-Up Form.   Learners complete this form from three to six weeks after a session to check their mastery of the material and demonstrate how they are using the skills that were taught. They may also identify additional training needs at this point.

Supervisor Follow-Up Form.   Supervisors complete this form from three to six weeks after having their staff trained to evaluate the changes in on-the-job behavior or skill levels that can be attributed to the training session. They may also identify future training needs at this point.

Susan Boyd is *president of Susan Boyd Associates, which specializes in job-specific computer training programs. She is the author of* Accelerate Computer Learning with Analogies *and a contributor to the 1999, 2001, and 2002* Training & Performance Sourcebook. *Ms. Boyd has over twenty years' experience in the training and computer education field and is a member of the International Who's Who in Information Technology. Ms. Boyd is a national conference speaker and published author of over twenty training articles.*

SAMPLE PRE-SCREENING QUESTIONNAIRE

Susan Boyd

Name: _____

Phone: _____

Title: _____ Email: _____

Instructions: Your feedback is important so that we can better tailor the upcoming workshop to your needs. Please review the course description and then complete the checklist below about yourself. We look forward to meeting you at the workshop.

1. Years of experience in this field
   - ☐ Less than 1 year
   - ☐ 1 to 3 years
   - ☐ 4 to 5 years
   - ☐ 6 to 7 years
   - ☐ 8 to 10 years
   - ☐ 11+ years

2. Typical training problems (check all that apply)
   - ☐ Training slow versus fast learners
   - ☐ Using various review techniques
   - ☐ Learners do not meet the prerequisites
   - ☐ Dealing with the afternoon blahs
   - ☐ Ending a training session
   - ☐ Keeping learners actively involved
   - ☐ Keeping myself motivated throughout the day
   - ☐ Using questioning techniques
   - ☐ Learners feel course is irrelevant to their needs
   - ☐ Learners do not have management's support to apply skills
   - ☐ Evaluating learners' progress

☐ Beginning a training session

☐ Keeping the class interested in the materials

☐ Dealing with the "know it all" learner

☐ Giving one-on-one attention without losing the rest of the class

3. My biggest training challenge is. . . .

4. I like to improve my training by. . . .

5. I hope this course will. . . .

6. I hope this course will not. . . .

Sample Comfort Level Rating Form

Susan Boyd

Name: _____

Date: _____

1. I am most comfortable with the following topics covered so far. (List three.)

2. I need review and more practice time on the following topics. (List three.)

3. To enhance my learning, I wish the trainer would. . . .

4. To enhance my learning, I need to. . . .

5. On a scale of 1 to 5 (1 = feeling confused/overwhelmed, 3 = feeling okay, 5 = feeling I've mastered all the skills so far), I would rate my comfort level with the system so far as. . . .

Sample Learner Commitment Statement

Susan Boyd

Name: _____

Course Date: _____

Instructions: Review your learning goal and notes you have made during the course so far, as well as the posted suggestions from the activities in which you have participated. Feel free to ask the presenter for suggestions.

1. My biggest challenge is. . . .

2. Through this workshop, I have learned the following techniques that I could use to address this challenge:

3. As a result of this session, I plan to accomplish the following action items in the next few months:

Place this form in an envelope and address it to yourself. I'll mail it back to you by the end of the month so that you can have a reminder to put your commitment into ACTION!

SAMPLE CLASS EVALUATION FORM

Susan Boyd

Name: _____

Date: _____

Instructor: _____

Instructions: Your feedback is important to us. Please evaluate the following areas of the course on the following rating scale:

5 = Strongly Agree   4 = Agree   3 = Uncertain   2 = Disagree   1 = Strongly Disagree

1. The course content and exercises met my learning goals.   5   4   3   2   1

2. The instructor was knowledgeable about the content and presented the information in a clear, concise manner.   5   4   3   2   1

3. The course activities were job-oriented and helped reinforce the learning.   5   4   3   2   1

4. The course pacing and schedule were appropriate to class needs.   5   4   3   2   1

5. The course materials and reference cards will be useful back on the job.   5   4   3   2   1

6. The facilitator was patient and helpful in providing assistance.   5   4   3   2   1

7. I would recommend this type of training program to others.   5   4   3   2   1

8. I feel that I have mastered the basics of the course and can begin using what I have learned on my job.   5   4   3   2   1

9. What I liked best about the training session was. . . .

10. I wish we had more time to. . . .

11. For future courses, I would suggest the following enhancements/improvements:

12. Overall, I feel the workshop was. . . .

The 2003 Annual: Volume 1, Training/© 2003 John Wiley & Sons, Inc.

SAMPLE INSTRUCTOR FEEDBACK FORM

Susan Boyd

Instructor: _____

Course Date: _____

Course Title: _____

Level: _____

Location: _____

Number of Learners: _____

Learner Assessment

Name	Met Pre-requisites?	Mastered Objectives?	Comments, Suggested Follow-Up

1. Overall, how would you describe this class and how well participants mastered the course objectives?

2. What learning challenges did you encounter, how did you handle them, and what do you suggest for future classes on this topic?

3. Did the equipment (hardware, software, A/V) function properly?
   ☐ Yes ☐ No (explain)

4. Were class materials satisfactory (that is, the right materials, right amount, good copy quality, and so forth)? ☐ Yes ☐ No (explain)

5. What worked well with this class?

6. What did not work well with this class?

7. What enhancements would you recommend for this course?

8. What overall follow-up is needed before the next class?

SAMPLE LEARNER FOLLOW-UP FORM

Susan Boyd

Name: _____

Date: _____

Supervisor: _____

Course Name: _____

Date: _____

Instructor: _____

The purpose of this follow-up evaluation process is to identify how you are using the skills you learned in the training session now that you are back in your job environment. Your feedback is important to us, as we use this information to identify enhancements needed for this course, as well as to develop future training sessions.

1. Are you using the software/skills you learned in the training course?
   ☐ Yes ☐ No (explain)

2. Listed on the next page are the topics that were covered in class. Use the codes to describe how often you use these topics and at what skill level.

Frequency of Use: 3 = Daily; 2 = Weekly; 1 = Occasionally; 0 = Have not used

Mastery Level: 3 = Mastered; 2 = Can do, but with help; 1 = Have problems; 0 = Never use

Topic	Frequency of Use	Mastery Level
Logging into Windows NT	_____	_____
Changing Windows NT and Novell passwords	_____	_____
Moving and sizing windows, arranging on same screen	_____	_____
Opening multiple applications and switching between them	_____	_____
Copying between applications	_____	_____
Changing screen colors	_____	_____
Changing screen colors/screen saver in Windows	_____	_____
Read, send mail, manage mail (delete and file in folders)	_____	_____

3. Now that you have completed the course and also used the software back on the job, what enhancements would you suggest to improve the training class?

4. How has the PC impacted your job? Discuss any advantages or improvements still needed for you to use it effectively.

5. Identify any future training needs. Use the reverse side of this sheet if necessary.

SAMPLE SUPERVISOR FOLLOW-UP FORM

Susan Boyd

Name: _____

Department: _____

Present date: _____

Date your group received training: _____

The purpose of this follow-up evaluation is to identify how your group is using the skills that were taught at the Introductory PC Training class now that they are back in the job environment. Your feedback is important to us, as we use this information to identify ways to enhance the present course, as well as to determine needs for future training sessions. Please use the reverse side of the sheet if needed for additional comments.

1. Your group was taught the following basic PC skills during the Introductory PC Training class: basic terminology, logging in and changing passwords, opening/closing/moving/sizing/arranging windows, using Advanta-specific applications on the PC, switching between applications, Excel basics (settlement/research only), and mail (credit and settlement/research groups only)

   Do you feel your group has mastered the skills taught in the training course? ☐ Yes ☐ No

   Please discuss their comfort and competency level.

2. Now that your group has completed the course and also used the software back on the job, what enhancements would you suggest to improve the Introductory PC Training class or the training program in general?

3. What concerns and suggestions do you have regarding the PC implementation and support process?

4. Identify any future training needs for yourself and specify the time frame.

5. Identify any future training needs for your group and specify the time frame.

6. What business benefits do you see from using the PC on your job?

7. How has the Introductory PC Training class contributed to realizing these benefits in your unit?

THE KNOWLEDGE MANAGEMENT ASSESSMENT TOOL (KMAT)

David J. Maier and James L. Moseley

Abstract: The Knowledge Management Assessment Tool (KMAT) is a diagnostic survey that helps an organization determine the effectiveness of its knowledge management (KM) practices. It is administered to employees to assess the presence of such practices in their work. Respondents rate their level of agreement with thirty statements on five KM dimensions: identification and creation, collection and capture, storage and organization, sharing and distribution, and application and use.

The concept of knowledge management is receiving considerable attention in the literature as a result of dramatic increases in competition and the resulting need for organizations to foster innovation, increase productivity and revenue, provide better customer service, and reduce costs and product development cycle times. Despite all the attention given to knowledge management by both scholars and practitioners, there is little consensus as to the exact nature and processes that are involved. Consequently, there is no commonly accepted method to measure its application in organizations.

Attempts to describe knowledge management have ranged from very broad conceptual statements to more specific descriptions of the processes and the goals involved. In developing a tool to assess the effectiveness of knowledge management practices in an organization in a systematic way, we have come up with the following definition that is both prescriptive and conceptual: *Knowledge management is a discipline that promotes an integrated approach to the creation, collection, storage, organization, dissemination, and application of all of an organization's information and intellectual assets—both explicit and tacit— leveraged to optimize performance and reduce costs.*

The KMAT was derived through a literature and Internet search of the five KM dimensions: identification and creation, collection and capture, storage and organization, sharing and distribution, and application and use. The authors looked for themes and common threads and framed statements to reflect them.

DESCRIPTION OF THE ASSESSMENT

The KMAT consists of thirty statements, six for each of the five dimensions of the knowledge management process. Individuals completing the assessment simply read each statement and reflect on how it pertains to their work. These reflections are quantified by one of six responses from 6 (strongly agree) to 1 (strongly disagree).

The respondents transfer their responses from the instrument to Section 1 of the Scoring Sheet, which is then collected and tabulated for analysis (Sections 2 and 3). Because the data are intended for viewing in the aggregate and have no real value to the individual, the administrator does the scoring. It is recommended that administration of the assessment be done online and scoring accomplished electronically if at all possible. In piloting the instrument, it was found that it took approximately thirty minutes to complete as a paper-and-pencil assessment.

THEORY BEHIND THE ASSESSMENT

The knowledge management construct has been examined and applied in a wide variety of disciplines, including business process reengineering, decision support systems, expert and executive information systems, total quality management, business intelligence, library and information science, information technology, e-learning, learning organizations, computer-supported collaborative work, and document management.

A growing body of literature indicates certain common dimensions of the knowledge management construct. Five that appear to be particularly important relate to knowledge identification and creation, collection and capture, storage and organization, sharing and dissemination, and application and use. These dimensions, described below, represent an integrated and procedural approach to the knowledge management discipline.

Knowledge Identification and Creation

The process begins with identifying and creating the *knowledge*, which can be defined as the transformation of *data* (isolated facts with no meaning) and *information* (interpreted data with meaning) into a value-added resource through experience and logical inferences. Knowledge thus becomes an actionable resource in an organization. It provides employees with the ability to perform a particular task or identify hidden trends and unusual patterns within data and information for operational and strategic decision making. Identification and creation of knowledge is often accomplished through interviews, observation, brainstorming sessions, focus groups, portfolio analysis, root-cause analysis, and other similar techniques that generate new ideas and knowledge. These are very often led by experts in the particular domain.

Knowledge Collection and Capture

Once knowledge has been identified and created, it can be collected and captured either on paper or in an electronic format. Organizational intranet portals, knowledge bases, and network servers are the most effective methods.

Job analyses, work documentation, organizational audits, and case studies are examples of collection instruments used by organizations.

Because an overwhelming amount of knowledge often exists in an organization, it should be prioritized; only that which is critical to the organization's competitive edge and knowledge management goals should be collected and captured. It is also essential that the means by which knowledge moves through an organization, or the "information flow," be collected and captured. This will aid in the improvement of ineffective processes that hinder the knowledge management initiative.

Knowledge Storage and Organization

How knowledge is stored and organized is vital to the success of a knowledge management initiative. The unorganized storage of knowledge causes significant losses in employee time, productivity, and customer service quality. It will ultimately "bottleneck" the process and render it useless.

Because people think about information differently, depending on their position and needs, it must be organized or categorized in multiple ways to allow quick and easy retrieval. Typical classification schemes for organizing include product line, industry, activity, and department or function.

Knowledge Sharing and Dissemination

The sharing and dissemination of knowledge within an organization is one of the two primary goals of a knowledge management initiative. Such sharing improves business processes, increases productivity, and fosters innovation, allowing an organization to maintain a competitive edge. The previous three knowledge management dimensions discussed feed into this one.

While knowledge can be shared and disseminated through many traditional, non-electronic means, such as meetings and memos, the advanced electronic technologies now available offer the best solution for large, often global organizations that contain enormous volumes of knowledge. Such technologies include email, threaded discussion, knowledge bases, groupware and collaboration tools, online whiteboards, search engines and agents, intranet portals, e-business portals, customer relationship management software, learning and document management software, and digital libraries.

Knowledge Application and Use

After successful implementation of the previous four dimensions, an organization is ready to apply and use its newfound knowledge or "corporate memory." Organizational knowledge can be applied and used in many ways. Technology such as online analytical processing (OLAP) provides an organization with the ability to analyze information and look for relationships, trends, patterns, exceptions, and other valuable, often "hidden" information. Data-mining tools present in OLAP and other business intelligence (BI) software allow an organization to make logical inferences and draw conclusions about specific business areas using statistical models and algorithms. Consumer trends, competitive product offerings and pricing, current marketing campaigns, research and development projects, and human and capital asset utilization are examples of these business areas.

Whether technological or non-technological techniques are used, the results are the same. Organizations that make use of their corporate memory tend to surpass their competition in exploiting collective experiences, meeting customer demands, managing increasing complexity and globalization, and improving the bottom line through strategic and operational decision making.

Each of the five dimensions can be further examined in terms of two perspectives: explicit knowledge and tacit knowledge.

Explicit Knowledge

Explicit knowledge represents *recorded* information, intelligence, and expertise. These include organizational databases and data warehouses, market reports, sales reports and presentations, product specifications and white papers, press releases, news stories, price sheets, training materials, job descriptions, documentation, annual reports, organizational charts, minutes of meetings, strategic plans, and the like.

Tacit Knowledge

Tacit knowledge represents *personal expertise* not formally recorded and therefore essentially unofficial. It includes facts that give rise to corporate memory and knowledge, processes, procedures, mechanisms, and strategies. It also includes the prejudices, values, intuitions, biases, and trust that cause employees to think and act. This information, sometimes referred to as "intellectual assets," is neither easily recorded within the organization nor easily shared among employees.

ADMINISTRATION

The survey is intended to be completed by all of the employees within an organization. Although administration within a work unit would certainly yield valuable data, sustainability is more an organization-wide concept. If large quantities of data are anticipated for aggregation, an online instrument with electronic scoring is recommended, thus providing an easy way to collect and score the data. For smaller data sets, administration can be conducted with paper and pencil, with scoring done manually, by following the instructions provided in Sections 1, 2, and 3 of the KMAT Scoring Sheet. All responses are best kept confidential and scores revealed as organizational or departmental averages only. The instrument takes approximately thirty minutes to complete.

THE SCORING PROCESS

The KMAT Scoring Sheet is in three sections. Section 1 is to be completed by the employee. Sections 2 and 3, containing aggregated data, are to be completed by an organizational administrator. The scoring process is as follows:

Section 1

1. Participants transfer their responses from the survey pages to the appropriate spaces in Section 1 of the KMAT Scoring Sheet.
2. Participants add their responses for each dimension and record these sums.

Section 2

1. An administrator (unless scoring is done electronically) places the aggregate totals for each dimension in the appropriate total box in Section 2 of the KMAT Scoring Sheet.
2. The number of respondents in each category is written in each N box.
3. The adjusted total (the average score) is calculated by dividing the total of each dimension by N.

Section 3

1. An administrator (unless scoring is done electronically) adds the total scores of all participants for each question and places this value in the appropriate subtotal box.

2. Then he or she adds the subtotals for both explicit and tacit knowledge and places this value in the proper total box and places the total number of participants in the N box.

3. Then the administrator divides the total for each dimension by N to find the adjusted totals (averages).

INTERPRETATION OF SCORES

Two different Scoring Sheets (Sections 2 and 3) are provided to make it easier to interpret the aggregated results. Section 2 presents scores according to the five knowledge management dimensions and should be evaluated using the following scale for each of the five dimensions:

31 to 36   The organization (or department) exhibits highly effective knowledge management practices in this area.

26 to 30   The organization (or department) exhibits very effective knowledge management practices on this dimension.

21 to 25   The organization (or department) exhibits moderately effective knowledge management practices on this dimension.

16 to 20   The organization (or department) exhibits moderately ineffective knowledge management practices in this area.

11 to 15   The organization (or department) exhibits very ineffective knowledge management practices on this dimension.

6 to 10   The organization (or department) exhibits extremely ineffective knowledge management practices on this dimension.

Section 3 of the Scoring Sheet arrays responses by the type of knowledge—explicit or tacit—and should be evaluated using the following scale for each of the two types of knowledge:

15 to 26	The organization (or department) exhibits highly effective knowledge management practices on this dimension.
27 to 39	The organization (or department) exhibits very effective knowledge management practices on this dimension.
40 to 52	The organization (or department) exhibits moderately effective knowledge management practices on this dimension.
53 to 65	The organization (or department) exhibits moderately ineffective knowledge management practices on this dimension.
66 to 78	The organization (or department) exhibits very ineffective knowledge management practices on this dimension.
79 to 90	The organization (or department) exhibits extremely ineffective knowledge management practices on this dimension.

POSTING THE DATA

The results can be posted and compared with previous assessments to show progress for the entire organization. The scores can be presented in a number of ways, including:

- Scores for the entire organization;

- Breakdowns of scores by business unit (human resources, engineering, marketing, accounting, and so forth);

- Breakdowns of scores by knowledge management dimension (identification and creation, collection and capture, storage and organization, sharing and dissemination, and application and use); or

- Breakdowns of scores by type of knowledge: explicit or tacit.

Care should be taken to ensure that there are at least five respondents from each business unit to assure anonymity.

OTHER SUGGESTED USES

Although the instrument is primarily intended to generate dialogue, inquiry, and action planning organization-wide, it also can be used to examine the effectiveness of knowledge management practices within or between departments and with external clients (customers, partners, vendors, and suppliers). This is an important factor in identifying "information flow" and knowledge-sharing bottlenecks.

RELIABILITY AND VALIDITY

The KMAT survey, an informal diagnostic tool, was piloted with corporate managers responsible for organization development, information management, and process improvement and revised based on their feedback. It has both content and face validity. (Content validity is the degree to which items on the survey represent the content that the survey is designed to measure. Face validity is the subjective appraisal of what the content of the survey measures.) The population that piloted the survey concurred on both kinds of validity. Reliability data for the KMAT survey is not available. The authors suggest being mindful of stability over time and increasing the number of survey items to test reliability.

David J. Maier is a project leader of information systems at the Barbara Ann Karmanos Cancer Institute, Detroit, Michigan. He has taught courses in business, information systems, knowledge management, and human resource development and currently teaches at Wayne State University in the College of Education's instructional technology program. He is the recipient of numerous awards, a contributor to two books on performance improvement, a member of ASTD, and a board member of ISPI, Michigan Chapter.

James L. Moseley, Ed.D., LPC, CHES, is associate professor of community medicine in the School of Medicine at Wayne State University. He also teaches in the College of Education's instructional technology program. He is a licensed professional counselor and a certified health education specialist. He is the recipient of numerous teaching and service awards, the co-author of two books, the author of a variety of articles and book chapters, and member of both ISPI and ASTD.

KNOWLEDGE MANAGEMENT ASSESSMENT TOOL (KMAT)

David J. Maier and James L. Moseley

Instructions: This survey is designed to allow you to register your opinions regarding your organization and its external relationships. Please review each of the following statements and circle the response that best represents your opinion about your organization, using the following scale.

6 = Strongly Agree   5 = Agree   4 = Mildly Agree
3 = Mildly Disagree   2 = Disagree   1 = Strongly Disagree

Item	Response					
1. The generation of new ideas and knowledge is highly valued.	1	2	3	4	5	6
2. Job analyses are frequently performed to determine job duties and requirements.	1	2	3	4	5	6
3. An electronic knowledge base exists to store new ideas, knowledge, solutions, and best practices.	1	2	3	4	5	6
4. Documents are proactively shared with employees.	1	2	3	4	5	6
5. The collective experience of employees is an integral part of decision making.	1	2	3	4	5	6
6. Suggestions and multiple viewpoints are often sought for decision making and organization development.	1	2	3	4	5	6
7. The development of job documentation is encouraged.	1	2	3	4	5	6
8. Information from many sources is stored in an integrated manner and cross-referenced, facilitating better communication and decision making.	1	2	3	4	5	6
9. No policies or technical security issues prevent the sharing of information and knowledge.	1	2	3	4	5	6

6 = Strongly Agree 5 = Agree 4 = Mildly Agree
3 = Mildly Disagree 2 = Disagree 1 = Strongly Disagree

Item	Response
10. Job responsibilities are carried out and decisions are made based on all the necessary information and knowledge.	1 2 3 4 5 6
11. Experience is highly valued.	1 2 3 4 5 6
12. Documents can be posted on an organizational intranet portal or saved on a network server.	1 2 3 4 5 6
13. The information and knowledge you receive is accurate and up-to-date.	1 2 3 4 5 6
14. An organizational intranet portal exists where information and knowledge relevant to job requirements may be retrieved.	1 2 3 4 5 6
15. New ideas and knowledge are frequently applied.	1 2 3 4 5 6
16. Brainstorming and other similar techniques are often used to generate and record new ideas and knowledge.	1 2 3 4 5 6
17. New ideas and knowledge are recorded for future use.	1 2 3 4 5 6
18. It is common practice to store work documents on an organizational server, rather than on personal computers.	1 2 3 4 5 6
19. Electronic and/or non-electronic collaboration, teamwork, and cooperation are a part of doing business.	1 2 3 4 5 6
20. Recorded knowledge and best practices are used for training, staff development, and organizational development.	1 2 3 4 5 6
21. Tips and tools, job aids, and case studies of best practices are available for performance objectives.	1 2 3 4 5 6

Item			**Response**			

22. On-the-job time is available to gather information and knowledge from others.   1   2   3   4   5   6

23. Information is stored and organized in a way that makes it intuitively easy and quick to locate.   1   2   3   4   5   6

24. Collaborative meetings to gather information and share knowledge are productive.   1   2   3   4   5   6

25. Advanced technologies, such as data warehousing, mining, and modeling, are used to leverage data and information for strategic and operational decision making.   1   2   3   4   5   6

26. There is a directory of experts for each major knowledge domain.   1   2   3   4   5   6

27. Concept mapping, sometimes called "mind mapping," is a common technique used to gather new information and knowledge.   1   2   3   4   5   6

28. Documents stored on an organizational server or intranet contain timely and useful knowledge for our job responsibilities.   1   2   3   4   5   6

29. Incentives are in place that motivate staff to share knowledge.   1   2   3   4   5   6

30. Expert systems and knowledge bases are used to aid in decision making.   1   2   3   4   5   6

KMAT Employee Scoring Sheet

Instructions

1. Enter the department or business unit for which you work in the space provided.

2. Transfer your score on each item from the Knowledge Management Assessment Tool to the corresponding numbered blank.

3. Add your responses for each dimension vertically and place the total in the appropriate blank at the bottom of each column.

Section 1

Your department or business unit:				
Knowledge Identification and Creation	Knowledge Collection and Capture	Knowledge Storage and Organization	Knowledge Sharing and Dissemination	Knowledge Application and Use
1.	2.	3.	4.	5.
6.	7.	8.	9.	10.
11.	12.	13.	14.	15.
16.	17.	18.	19.	20.
21.	22.	23.	24.	25.
26.	27.	28.	29.	30.
Total:	Total:	Total:	Total:	Total:

KMAT ADMINISTRATOR SCORING SHEET 1

Five-Dimensional Analysis

Instructions

1. Add the total scores of all participants within whatever subunit or organizational division you have chosen for each dimension and place this value in the total box.

2. Place the total number of respondents in the N box.

3. Divide the total number for each dimension by N to find the adjusted total (average score for that dimension).

Section 2

Dimension	Total	N	Adjusted Total (Total/N)
Knowledge Identification and Creation			
Knowledge Collection and Capture			
Knowledge Storage and Organization			
Knowledge Sharing and Dissemination			
Knowledge Application and Use			

KMAT ADMINISTRATOR SCORING SHEET 2

Explicit/Tacit Analysis

Instructions

1. Add the total scores of all respondents for *each question* and place this value in the respective subtotal box.

2. Add the subtotals in each column to obtain total scores for explicit knowledge and for tacit knowledge.

3. Place the total number of participants in the N box for each column.

4. Divide the total for each dimension by N to find the adjusted total (average for that dimension).

Section 3

**Explicit Knowledge
Management Practices**

**Tacit Knowledge
Management Practices**

Question	Subtotal
2	
4	
7	
9	
12	
14	
16	
18	
20	
21	
23	
24	
26	
28	
30	
Total	
N	
Adjusted Total (Total/N)	

Question	Subtotal
1	
3	
5	
6	
8	
10	
11	
13	
15	
17	
19	
22	
26	
27	
29	
Total	
N	
Adjusted Total (Total/N)	

Introduction

to the Presentation and Discussion Resources Section

The Presentation and Discussion Resources Section is a collection of articles of use to every facilitator. The theories, background information, models, and methods will challenge facilitators' thinking, enrich their professional development, and assist their internal and external clients with productive change. These articles may be used as a basis for lecturettes, as handouts in training sessions, or as background reading material.

This section will provide you with a variety of useful ideas, theoretical opinions, teachable models, practical strategies, and proven intervention methods. The articles will add richness and depth to your training and consulting knowledge and skills. They will challenge you to think differently, explore new concepts, and experiment with new interventions. The articles will continue to add a fresh perspective to your work.

The 2003 Annual: Volume 1, Training includes twelve articles, in the following categories:

Individual Development: Personal Growth

Finding Fulfillment by Living Your Passions, by Richard Chang

Individual Development: Stress and Burnout

Stress Management Training for Trainers, by Herbert S. Kindler

Communication: Coaching and Encouraging

Coaching the Superstars: Learning the Lessons of Hardship,
by Barbara Pate Glacel

Communication: Communication in Organizations

I Hear America Speaking: Lessons for Leaders, by Marlene Caroselli

Problem Solving: Models, Methods, and Techniques

Learner-Driven Teaching Methods: Developing Critical Thinking Skills, by Elizabeth A. Smith

Groups and Teams: Techniques to Use with Groups

Trainer Survival Skills, by Susan Boyd

Consulting: Consulting Strategies and Techniques

Getting the Most from a Good Story, by Lori L. Silverman and Mary B. Wacker

Consulting: Interface with Clients

Delivering Effective Presentations: A Review of Techniques for Enhancing Audience Involvement, by Ira J. Morrow

Facilitating: Theories and Models of Facilitating

Designing Curricula for Learning Environments: Using a Facilitative Teaching Approach to Empower Learners, by Sharon Drew Morgen

Facilitating: Techniques and Strategies

Why Learning Games Are Important and How to Create Your Own Games, by Carolyn Nilson

Facilitating: Evaluation

Delivering Effective Training Presentations, by Julie A. Furst-Bowe

Leadership: Theories and Models

Training for Leadership Development: Three Process Keys, by Marshall Sashkin

As with previous *Annuals,* this volume covers a wide variety of topics. The range of articles presented encourages thought-provoking discussion about the present and future of HRD. Other articles on specific subjects can be located by using our comprehensive *Reference Guide to Handbooks and Annuals.* The guide is updated regularly and indexes the contents of all the *Annuals* and the *Handbooks of Structured Experiences.* With each revision, the *Reference Guide* becomes a complete, up-to-date, and easy-to-use resource for selecting appropriate materials from the *Annuals* and *Handbooks.* A print version of the *Reference Guide* is available for volumes through 1999. An online supplement covering the years through 2003 can be found at www.pfeiffer.com/go/supplement.

Here, and in the *Reference Guide*, we have done our best to categorize the articles for easy reference; however, many of the articles encompass a range of topics, disciplines, and applications. If you do not find what you are looking for under one category, check a related category. In some cases we may place an article in the "Training" *Annual* that also has implications for "Consulting," and vice versa. As the field of HRD continues to grow and develop, there is more and more crossover between training and consulting. Explore all the contents of both volumes of the *Annual* in order to realize the full potential for learning and development that each offers.

FINDING FULFILLMENT BY LIVING YOUR PASSIONS

Richard Chang

Abstract: Finding your passion and integrating it into your life can lead to greater personal satisfaction, self-esteem, empowerment, energy, and success. This article discusses reasons that people do not follow their passions. It describes four ways to discover your passions: epiphany, change, intuition, and experience. It tells how to differentiate passions from interests and defines the two types of passion: content-based and context-based. Finally, it describes the process of integrating your passion into your life by identifying your purposes, building perspective, creating an action plan, implementing the plan, and staying the course.

Is Something Missing?

The happiest people may be the ones who have found ways to make their passions in life be their "work," whether it is work they are paid for or work they do voluntarily. These people don't work, as many of us do, to enable them to engage in their passions intermittently—when they can find the time. For such people, what they do is not work in the sense of toil; it is enjoyable and meaningful.

Unfortunately, the majority of people have not managed this level of satisfaction, even if they know what their passions are. Many people have given up their dreams of doing something they really care about. More unfortunate are those who have not discovered something to be passionate about. These people view their work simply as a necessity, as something they have to do in order to support themselves and their families and meet the expectations of society. They follow the path that opens before them without questioning its meaning or the satisfaction they derive from it. They may blame their lack of fulfillment or unhappiness on others, not realizing that energy and fulfillment come from within. They may regret the choices they have made or think that something is missing from their lives but not know what to do about it. Often, they do not realize that there is another way to lead their lives.

A positive source of passion gives meaning and excitement and purpose to life. With a little help, many people can begin to discover or rediscover what their passions are and change their lives to better reflect what is in their hearts.

When we think of "living our passions," we often think of people such as successful musicians, athletes, artists, dancers, and medical researchers. But there are many other examples of everyday people who have found ways to do what they care about and to feel good about how they earn their living or spend their free time. For instance, one man took early retirement from a corporate job and opened a motorcycle-repair shop; another person volunteers with an animal rescue organization; and a third is taking night courses to become a landscape designer. One attorney who wanted to "run away and join the circus" as a child now does volunteer work at a children's hospital—as "Chucky the Clown"! These people overcame the deterrents to fulfillment and found ways to live their passions. When we find the courage to pursue our passions, we often achieve things we might not previously have dreamed possible, as we open ourselves to the inspiration, energy, and commitment that come from within.

DETERRENTS TO DISCOVERING YOUR PASSION

What prevents us from discovering our passions and our potentials? People often cite constraining life circumstances, such as lack of education; lack of money; too many other commitments; or lack of opportunities for women, for people of their race, for people of their age, and so on. But what really holds most people back is the basic emotion of fear. Many people fear the unknown. Some fear the disapproval or scorn of others. Fear of change and fear of risk lead them to create scenarios of failure and self-limiting action. At the least, they are afraid of making fools of themselves by trying something new. Self-doubt and fear of failure lead to inertia. Inertia becomes a habit, and they become so inured to their routines that they become almost numb, moving through life or their jobs in a state of apathy.

FOUR WAYS TO DISCOVER YOUR PASSION

There are four basic ways in which people can discover their passions:

1. *Discovery by Epiphany:* An epiphany is a (usually unexpected) life-changing experience that creates a sudden and intense awareness. The effect is a powerful "wake-up call." Such a realization does not always result from a major life event; it can occur in a moment of solitude or in the midst of daily life.

2. *Discovery Through Change:* Major life changes, such as birth, marriage, divorce, illness, recovery, a change of job, and death, can cause you to look at how you live your life and what you value. As you travel the road of life, a stumble or the call of a bird may reveal to you a new road that you were not aware of.

3. *Discovery Through Intuition:* You must sense your passion in order to identify it. For some, this is easy; they have always sensed the course they wish to pursue, even if they have had to work hard to make it happen.

4. *Discovery Through Experience:* For others, discovering their passions requires experimentation. This may occur gradually and subtly, as we weed out our likes and dislikes and find that we gravitate continually to a particular type of action. Or it may occur when we are introduced to something new that we had not experienced before. A gradual realization that something calls to us reveals a passion that we had not known before. Discovery through experience may require some experimentation, taking some risks, and trying something new.

Sometimes, discovering a passion requires shutting out the distractions of everyday life and focusing on the messages of the heart. It is easier to examine our lives if we are distanced—however briefly—from them. This adds perspective to our reflection. Part of this examination may include reflection on the past, on what you loved to do and how you felt when engaged in various activities. Part of it includes an assessment of what you like and dislike in the present, what gives you energy or saps it, and what gives you a sense of fulfillment or joy. You can ask those close to you to help you identify what you seem to do well and most eagerly, what your strengths and talents are, and what your weaknesses are, based on their observations of you. You may be surprised at what others think you excel in.

Then you can look toward the future. What things do you hope to be doing? If you could start over, what would you hope to accomplish? What vision of your future most appeals to you? Narrow this down as best you can.

Take all the information you have gleaned and look for connections between the things you have identified. Then do some exploration to test your assumptions. If you think that something may be a passion, try different aspects of it (for example, reading about it, taking a class, talking to those who live with it, or doing it on a volunteer basis in your free time).

How to Recognize a Passion

It may not always be easy to distinguish between a passion and an interest. Both may be something that you look forward to doing. However, a primary indication that you are passionate about what you are doing is when you find that you lose all sense of time while you are engaged in it. This has been called "flow" and being in a "zone." It is a state in which you become completely absorbed in what you are doing. There are indications that an activity is more than an interest if:

- You lose track of time when you are engaged in it;
- You perform beyond your normal capabilities when you are engaged in it;
- Your energy level is higher when you are engaged in it;
- You feel rejuvenated and good after engaging in it;
- You become excited when you think about it;
- Your enthusiasm for it is consistent over time;
- You feel more confident or empowered when you are engaged in it;
- Others notice or comment on your involvement or performance in it; and/or
- You dream about it.

If you are not aware of your passions, you can open yourself to opportunities and experiences that can reveal them. Reading books, taking classes, going new places, talking with friends and relatives, and trying new activities all can help you to identify preferences. By reflecting on your past and current experiences and the feelings they evoke, you can begin to identify your passions.

TYPES OF PASSION

There are two types of passion: content-based and context-based.

- Content-based passion centers around a single subject or activity, such as painting, baseball, motorcycles, fishing, chess, or spelunking.
- Context-based passion centers around a theme, rather than a specific topic or activity. Examples include helping, learning, creating, competing, and organizing.

It may take some experimentation to discern whether one's primary passion is content-based or context-based. For example, a person who is devoted to a particular sport in school may discover upon entering the work world that what really motivates him is the rush he gets from trying to achieve his personal best or from the thrill of competition. A person who enjoys doing crafts may discover that she also enjoys photography. For these people, it is the *type* of doing that matters, rather than the specific medium in which it is done.

A friend of mine, an editor, enjoys interior decorating, quilting, and gift wrapping. She also enjoys reading mystery stories and introducing compatible people. After some reflection, she realized that her passion was "identifying patterns—finding and putting together things that match or complement one another." Such a context-based passion may be more difficult to identify at first, but it often allows a lot of leeway in its expression.

Of course, any individual may have more than one passion and may find more than one way in which to express his or her passions and integrate them into his or her life.

INTEGRATING YOUR PASSION INTO YOUR LIFE

To begin, you need to have a sense of where you are now, what you hope to accomplish, what you are willing to sacrifice, and what you hope to gain, in order to begin living your passion and benefiting from it.

Identify Your Purposes

First, you need to identify your purposes, the reasons for pursuing your passions. Passion without purpose is not likely to lead very far and may result in "going off the deep end," losing a perspective of reality, and/or abandoning the important things in life for the temporarily exciting. A passion is not a purpose in itself. A purpose may be to earn a living, to create something in a particular area of endeavor, to build self-satisfaction, or to help others. You may have more than one purpose, which is fine, as long as they are complementary. You also may have several options for action in regard to your passion, and it is a good idea to identify and explore as many as possible before making a decision. Try to anticipate the possible outcomes of each option. In the end, your purposes bring significance to the pursuit of your passion.

Build Perspective

Second, you need perspective. Perspective involves both the heart and the head. One danger in embracing your passion is ignoring your current circumstances. Part of perspective is an analysis of one's talent. Loving to play baseball does not mean that you have what it takes to become a professional athlete. But it may lead you to become a coach for a school or community league. A geologist friend who loves art (but who has limited artistic talent) chose to study the history of art as an avocation and now gives lectures at his city's art museum. A content-based passion often becomes an avocation or recreation. Another part of perspective is identifying what it will take to pursue your passion and what you are willing to give up to attain your goal. You do not want to give up more than you will gain or give up something you will regret losing in the long run. The secret is to find a way to pursue your passion within the bounds of current reality. A passion without perspective easily can become an obsession, which is not a healthy state.

Create an Action Plan

As with any new venture, you need to develop an action plan. What actions will you take? What structure will you have to build to support your plan? Will you need to obtain more knowledge? How will you do that? What networking can you do? What contacts can you make that will help? Consider the effects on those you care about. Consider timing and opportunities. Do some investigation. Assess what is realistic and what is not. Identify what will help you to achieve your goal and what will not. Incorporate what you learn into your plan.

Build in some flexibility and contingency plans. Few roads are completely smooth, and anticipation of challenges and setbacks (and your responses to these) can help to keep you from becoming discouraged and getting off track.

Before you begin to implement your plan, set the stage. Inform those close to you of what you are planning to do—at least to some degree. You do not have to solicit their approval, but you probably don't want to burn your bridges, either. As far as possible, create the physical conditions conducive to your progress. Identify those habits that might hinder your progress and refine your routines to support your action plan. Seek out people who understand your passion and will be supportive of your progress.

Implement Your Plan

Beginning to implement your action plan requires leaving your comfort zone and taking some risks. What these risks involve depends on your particular plan and situation. Continue to use both your head and your heart as you make choices and decisions. When you perform with passion, you view challenges as opportunities rather than as obstacles.

As you proceed, you will change. Others will notice your sense of purpose and empowerment and your energy. You can enlist others to help you achieve your goals, and you can serve as a role model for others who have not yet begun to identify and live their passions.

Stay the Course

As with any other endeavor, integrating your passion into your life requires sticking with it. Few things that are worth achieving come easily or quickly. For example, many of us have vowed to engage in healthy living or to change our dietary habits, only to tire of the effort and become engulfed in our old ways of doing things. The difference here is that when you are pursuing a passion, your heart is in it as well as your head. This helps to build willpower and commitment, even in the face of setbacks.

Remember that any good action plan is flexible. If you run up against a reality that you had not envisioned, amend the plan rather than giving up on your passion altogether. View changes to your plan as improvements rather than as failures. There are many roads to satisfaction, and you may discover rewards that you never knew existed.

Finally, be open to opportunity. It is amazing what comes our way when we are open to recognizing, appreciating, and utilizing it.

Richard Chang is CEO of Richard Chang Associates, Inc., a performance-improvement consulting, training, and publishing firm with headquarters in Irvine, California. His specialties include strategic planning, performance measurement, quality improvement, organization development, change management, product realization, customer service, and human resource development. He has consulted to a wide range of organizations and has served as chair of the board of ASTD and as a judge for the Malcolm Baldrige National Quality Award. He is the author or co-author of more than twenty books, including The Passion Plan: A Step-by-Step Guide to Discovering, Developing, and Living Your Passion, *published in 2000 by Jossey-Bass.*

Stress Management Training for Trainers

Herbert S. Kindler

Abstract: Trainers often pay more attention to the needs of their clients than they do to their own well-being. This article indicates three key variables trainers should self-monitor and suggests actions to take to avoid burnout and reduce the risk of stress-related illness.

You already know that effective stress management requires exercise, good nutrition, interpersonal coping skills, rest, and deep relaxation. So why do you still feel stressed more often than you want to admit?

Because real learning is knowledge *in action*. The challenge is to act on what we know. We know that the most serious aspect of excessive, prolonged stress is greater susceptibility to illness. We know that hormones released under stress influence our immune systems. So it stands to reason that if stress is an intense continuing or frequent occurrence, immune resistance is suppressed and may lead to disease. The risk of asthma, arthritis, migraine, peptic ulcers, diabetes, and cardiovascular disease sharply increases with high stress levels over time. The immune function can be compromised to the point at which it can speed the metastasis of cancer, exacerbate plaque formation in arteries, and increase the likelihood of viral infections.

Last week a trainer-friend told me that a dull pain in his groin sent him to his internist and then to a urologist. His prostate was enlarged and his PSA (prostate-specific antigens) indicated high risk for cancer and need for a definitive biopsy.

His priorities shifted as his illusion of invulnerability burst. He committed himself to lifestyle changes aimed at reducing his stress level—changes he previously put off because he was too busy. What will it take for *you* to act on what you know?

Training is a high-stress profession. Your nervous system is bombarded daily with phone calls, faxes, email, voice mail, flyers, meetings, and just plain noise. You tax your body with travel. You push yourself with deadlines. You are pressured to learn constantly changing technology. You also have a home life that may include caring for children, paying bills, shopping, and making home or car repairs. Little near-term relief is in sight. So what can you do?

Don't wait for a "big scare." A starting point is to realistically assess how much stress you are dealing with and, if it's excessive, to commit yourself to a plan of action.

SELF-ASSESSMENT

Start with a medical checkup. Then assess your stress level with a comprehensive, validated stress inventory such as the *Personal Stress Assessment Inventory* (PSAI) (Kindler, 1997), which has been used by thousands of trainees over the past eighteen years. The PSAI measures three key variables, as shown in Figure 1:

- *Predisposition* to react reflexively to stimuli in a self-harmful way;

- *Resilience* in the face of events that trigger upset; and

- *Stress sources* from work and non-work environments, both ongoing and episodic.

Predisposition

The predisposition scale focuses on Type A behavior in general and hostile reactions in particular. Type A behavior initially was defined as an unconscious drive to rush and to compete aggressively. Later, the more harmful criterion—in terms of undermining one's cardiovascular system—was identified as *hostility*. It's easy to imagine feeling hostile if you've been programmed to

Figure 1. Factors Related to Stress Symptoms

zip in and out of traffic and then are blocked during rush hour. Similarly, if it's all-important to keep winning, and you lose, hostile feelings may arise.

Unlike the questions that follow, answers to the actual PSAI questions are framed in terms of numerical magnitudes.

Sample Questions

During the past month:

- What was your level of irritation when things didn't go your way?
- How often did you become annoyed by people who were pushy or insensitive?

Resilience

The PSAI's resilience scale reflects the respondent's capacity to bounce back from adversity by checking for physical-mental-emotional-spiritual lifestyle balance.

Sample Questions

During the past month:

- How often did you engage in creative activities outside of work?
- How often did you spend time thinking about what is important to you?

Stress Sources

These scales measure upsetting aspects of life that drain energy.

Sample Questions

During the past month:

- Did you attend meetings that felt like a waste of time? If so, what was the level of emotional impact you experienced?
- Did you lack involvement in decisions that seriously affected you? If so, what was the level of emotional impact you experienced?

DESIGNING YOUR STRESS MANAGEMENT ACTION PROGRAM

Following are some elements to consider in your personal program design.

1. Address the Source.   Some sources of stress can be addressed directly between people of good will who are open-minded and non-defensive. Candid, respectful talk, coupled with patient, attentive listening can open the door to new possibilities through problem solving.

2. Reframe.   If you choose to accept a situation you cannot change, you may be able to reframe what's been bothering you. For example, when a theatrical producer lost his fortune on one show, a competitor chided: "How does it feel to be poor, Mike?" Mike's response reflected re-framing. He said, "I'm *not* poor. I just have a cash flow problem."

3. Practice Deep Relaxation.   Everyone has the capacity to relax. It's the natural way to moderate excessive stress by helping your endocrine and autonomic nervous systems reverse the fight-or-flight response. Practice some form of deep relaxation daily, such as meditation, prayer, yoga, progressive muscle relaxation, or autogenic training. These will decrease tension, increase energy, and improve health.

4. Manage Your Time.   Good time management is central to stress management. Contrary to conventional wisdom, time is not money; time is your *life*. Be clear about what matters most. Get your priorities straight. Consolidate, delegate, and eliminate everything that doesn't advance your priorities. Simplify. Make room in your life for play and laughter.

5. Be Here Now.   The present is all we have. Reliving the past (it's gone) and worrying about the future (it never arrives) clutters the space that is here to be lived now. Let go of past regrets and resentments; release future concerns and worry. Free yourself to experience this timeless moment.

6. Reach Out.   For many people, asking friends and associates for support—reaching out—is difficult. Receiving and giving are acts of human kindness that help us cope with stress and buffer the impact of crisis, isolation, and change. Support networks offer physical assistance, empathy, information, and fresh perspectives.

7. Honor Your Body. Keeping your body in good shape won't solve specific job-related problems, but it will help provide the vitality and self-esteem you need to resolve work and life dilemmas. With care, regular exercise, good nutrition, and adequate rest, your body will serve you well over a long lifetime.

New behavior takes time. Be patient and compassionate with yourself. If you start with only one new behavior, such as one fun activity or one quiet period each day, you will notice the quality of your life and the quality of your work improve. Why not start now?

References and Readings

Kindler, H.S.(1997). *Personal stress assessment inventory* (rev. ed.). Pacific Palisades, CA: Center for Management Effectiveness. (Available from Herb Kindler & Associates at 310–459–0585 or herbkindler@aol.com.)

Kindler, H.S., & Ginsburg, M.(1994). *Measure & manage stress.* Menlo Park, CA: Crisp.

Herbert S. Kindler, Ph.D., is a former CEO and professor of management. He graduated from M.I.T. and received his doctorate from UCLA. He is author of six books, trains trainers, and has conducted hundreds of workshops on stress management, managing change, risk taking, and managing disagreement.

Coaching the Superstars: Learning the Lessons of Hardship

Barbara Pate Glacel

Abstract: Executive coaches assist high-potential and high-performing superstars to make sense of the lessons of experience in order for them to make continuous improvements in their performance. Coaching superstars presents a particular challenge because these individuals have often not received negative feedback nor encountered hardships in their advance up the organizational ladder.

Research from the Center for Creative Leadership (McCall, Lombardo, & Morrison, 1988) describes the value of the lessons of experience, in particular from job assignments, other people, and hardships. Lessons learned from hardships are lessons not available to be learned elsewhere and add considerably to a leader's empathy, humility, sensitivity to others, and self-awareness.

When a superstar has not endured hardship, the coach must attempt to manufacture the lessons that are not available to be learned elsewhere. Suggestions for such opportunities are provided in this article.

EXECUTIVE COACHING

Executive coaches often are called on to work with "the good, the bad, and the ugly." Coaching "the ugly" is difficult and not very much fun. These are the people who just don't "get" it. They have probably received feedback over the years about ways they could improve, but the feedback is never really heard or believed. "The ugly" always find a reason to blame someone else for the situation, or they state boldly that they have been successful because of who they are and no one is going to change them. Coaching "the ugly" is often frustrating for the coach and nonproductive for both the client and the organization.

Coaching "the bad" can be rewarding because they often have a specific skill deficiency that can be targeted. Acknowledging that they have a deficiency allows "the bad" to become good through practice. The coach can provide skill-based training and then coach the client through practice and real-time sessions to improve the skill. A change in behavior often brings with it a questioning or distrust on the part of observers who do not realize why the behavior has changed. The coach can assist the client in how to make the change, how to communicate why the change has been made, and how to improve the interpersonal dynamics of using new, more productive behaviors. Coaching "the bad" is a good investment for the organization and motivating to the client and coach.

If coaching "the ugly" is difficult and coaching "the bad" is rewarding, coaching "the good" is surprisingly challenging. All persons have strengths and weaknesses, but "the good" perform so well that their weaknesses are more difficult to discover. "The good" are often eager to receive the feedback a coach has to offer. Their self-esteem is high enough to accept the constructive feedback and suggestions, and they soak up the new ideas like a sponge. Typically, however, they have not received much negative feedback in their stellar careers.

Coaching "the good" is akin to coaching an excellent baseball player to improve his batting average. If a baseball player gets three hits for every ten times at bat, he is above the norm in performance. If the coach can help that player to get just one more hit in ten times at bat, his performance increases by 10 percent. A .300 batting average increases to a .400 batting average, and the player becomes a superstar, the likes of which have not been seen for sixty years. Just one more hit in ten! This marginal increase is worth millions of dollars, and it inspires, motivates, and leads a team to higher productivity.

Coaching superstars in the business world allows the same kind of margin for improvement, like fine-tuning a Steinway or sharpening a Gerber knife. Coaching "the good" produces these incremental differences that reap incredible rewards for the person, the team, and the organization as a whole. The challenge for the coach is to find those areas for incremental improvement, often disguised behind excellent performance by organizational superstars and high-potential employees.

PAINTING A PORTRAIT OF HIGH PERFORMANCE

The performance of an organizational superstar can be assessed in a variety of ways, most effectively by combining several methods of observation.

360-Degree Surveys

A 360-degree survey instrument gathers written quantitative feedback from the person, as well as the individual's boss, peers, and subordinates. The results from such a written survey may alert the coach to behaviors for further observation and may suggest specific questions to ask. Usually, feedback from peers is most critical. This may be because peers see the person less often or because of the competition for promotion as the organizational pyramid narrows nearer to the top. Whether the feedback is accurate or perceptual, it provides necessary data for the superstar to consider in the quest for improvement.

Observation

A paper survey does not paint a three-dimensional picture of the subject, so it should only be used as a starting point. Using the preliminary data from a survey, the coach must construct a realistic model of the superstar's performance to determine what behaviors to address. To do this, the coach may shadow the superstar, observing real-time interactions, including behavior in meetings, procedures in decision-making situations, and interactions with peers, subordinates, the boss, customers, and clients. Not only does a shadow observation provide rich data for the coach, but it allows the superstar to receive real-time feedback about his or her performance in varied situations.

To help superstars learn from real-time observation, employ the EIAG technique: experience—identify—analyze—generalize. The coach observes the client having an "experience." Together, the coach and the superstar dissect the experience in order to "identify" what took place. What were the distinct behaviors and actions of the superstar individually and in relation to others during the course of the experience? Next, the coach and superstar "analyze" the impact of the behaviors identified. Because this action took place, what was the impact or result? Finally, based on this analysis, the superstar is able to "generalize" lessons learned. In similar circumstances, what behaviors should be consciously repeated? What behaviors should be changed? What behaviors should be omitted? Figure 1 further illustrates and explains the EIAG process.

A very simple case in point might be a staff meeting conducted by the superstar. The "experience" is the meeting. Each action within the meeting is "identified," such as the last arrival of one of the attendees. In fact, the per-

E **Experience:** Have an experience. Reflection on the value of the experience may take place in a formal feedback session, in after-action team critiques, or after planned experiential learning events.

I **Identify:** Consider the experience, and describe specifically what happened. What action, activity, or behavior has been identified from the experience? What was the sequence of events? Who did what, when, and how?

A **Analyze:** What were you and others thinking about during the experience? What were you feeling? Make observations or draw conclusions about the nature of what happened. How were the events and behaviors related to people's thoughts and feelings? How did the actions impact others? Was performance or progress on the task affected? What helped, and what got in the way of progress?

G **Generalize:** What general learnings are implied from the analysis? Generate guidelines for how to handle similar situations in the future. What might be done differently or the same? What advice would be given? Document the answers as learnings from this experience. When a similar experience occurs, reiterate the learnings in order to improve performance.

Figure 1. The EIAG Process

son who arrives last happens to be a cultural minority and a fairly new employee. The last arrival notes that the chairs around the table are full and she sits in a chair against the wall. The meeting convenes. In "analyzing" this action, the coach and superstar realize that the last arrival never participated in the meeting. She was in attendance, but did not add value. Is it possible that she felt excluded because of her physical separation from the meeting participants, in addition to her "difference," being new and a minority? The lesson that is "generalized" is that when someone arrives at a meeting, the leader should accept him or her into the group and encourage him or her to be included in the physical setup, as well as inviting the person's comments.

This lesson suggests a slight change in behavior that can reap tremendous rewards as the synergy of the group increases over time. This fine-tuning of behavior takes place immediately in real time, and the slight edge of improvement hones the superstar's skills.

Interviews

Finally, adding color and tone to the portrait, the coach may choose to interview the superstar's boss, subordinates, peers, and customers. Individual interviews focusing on the superstar's behavior would provide examples of specific behaviors and results that might otherwise not be known to the coach. During these interviews, the coach can use the "Stop, Start, Continue" model to frame questions:

- What is happening that should stop?
  - Which of the superstar's actions are impeding success in achieving the mission?
  - Is there a compelling reason for these actions?
  - Is the reason compelling enough to compensate for the negative effects of the action?
  - If the action is stopped, will the individual, team, or organization suffer?
- What is not happening that should start?
  - What behaviors should be initiated by the superstar to facilitate performance and learning?
  - What would create more success, more productivity, more quality, and more enjoyment in work?
  - Is there a compelling reason for not taking this new action?

- Is the reason compelling enough to compensate for the negative effects of not taking the action?
- If the action is started, will the individual, team, or organization suffer?
- What is happening that should continue?
    - What actions have been accomplished by the superstar that can be celebrated?
    - What actions are contributing to success?
    - How do these actions help achieve success?

Feedback from these interviews may provide explanations for other observations, perceptual or real. The data represents the opinions of others who work for, with, or around the superstar. Sometimes the data is even contradictory. Good ground rules to follow in conducting and analyzing the interview data include the following:

- All interviews are confidential. The superstar knows who is interviewed, and may even suggest the individuals, but will not know which person made which comments.
- Only collated data is fed back to the superstar, without attribution.
- A comment must be heard at least twice to be included in the feedback report to the superstar.

These rules invite candid comments and observations that contribute to the complete portrait of the superstar.

Putting It All Together

The task of putting together all the disparate data points into a portrait is akin to completing a one-thousand-piece jigsaw puzzle without the top of the box. The coach is not sure what the portrait will look like until it is completed. Often, however, the portrait of any superstar is similar to that of other superstars: The superstar is incredibly bright, is a high performer, has risen quickly in the organization, and is recognized by superiors as having unlimited potential. But the coach already knew that.

The weaknesses that give the portrait dimension are also strikingly similar. The superstar is considered arrogant, is aggressive in pursuing personal career success, often at the expense of others, and is not always to be trusted. The farther away that one works from the superstar, the more negative are the comments. So the coach wonders: Are these comments reality or perception? Are they based in fact or in rumor? Might they be attributable to jealousy and competition more than to actual behavior?

The question of reality or perception may be moot when one considers the potential detrimental effects of the superstar's suggested weaknesses. An organizational phenomenon, sometimes associated with high performers, is the "bloody chicken routine." In a barnyard, when a formerly healthy member of the flock becomes ill or injured, the rest of the flock pecks it to death. The superstar, protected by a mentor while climbing the corporate ladder with success and good results, is a prime target for the "bloody chicken routine" when a flaw becomes apparent.

The challenge for the coach, then, is to discover what might become a fatal flaw before the superstar succumbs to it.

LEARNING THE LESSONS OF EXPERIENCE

Twenty years ago, the Center for Creative Leadership (CCL) embarked on a research project to discover how successful executives learned the lessons necessary for them to reach their potential. In the course of this research, they also uncovered certain traits that led to involuntary derailment of executives. Derailment was defined as failure to reach the level that had been predicted for the superstars earlier in their careers. The authors said that their findings were not a prescription for developing successful executives, but were merely descriptive of what events in an executive's career journey taught what lessons. They cautioned that the lessons were not delivered with spellbinding clarity, but must be dug out of complex, confusing, and often ambiguous situations (McCall, Lombardo, & Morrison, 1988).

This seminal work has become a valuable model for assessing missing pieces in an executive's experience. Important lessons in executive development come from job experience, colleagues, hardships, and miscellaneous other events, including formal training programs. The lessons of hardship, however, are unique and not learned elsewhere, according to the CCL model. They may come from personal traumas, career setbacks, job changes, business mistakes, or subordinate performance problems. These situations require that the superstars turn inward and take long, hard looks at themselves.

The lessons of hardship are lessons of humility, empathy, and a sense of oneself. One learns to cope with situations beyond one's own control and to persevere through adversity. One may also learn about balance between work life and personal life. Personal limits and blind spots may become obvious. A thorough self-examination in the wake of hardship can reveal a sensitivity to the human side of management. Only through hardship does one learn the pain of failure and the depth of resources available within oneself to regroup and overcome adversity.

The superstar who has never experienced a hardship is unaware of the richness of the experience and the impact that pain has on one's relationships with others. The superstar without hardship appears arrogant and sometimes shallow. Through no fault of her own, she may lack humility and empathy for others. She may be unaware of the feeling of dread or the physical reaction in the pit of one's stomach when something goes terribly wrong and one feels both responsible and powerless. Her own success and high performance have shielded her from the lessons of hardship.

- The dilemma for the coach in this situation is how to facilitate learning the lessons of hardship without manufacturing a true hardship that might injure, endanger, or derail the superstar.

- The coach must help the superstar to absorb the suffering and learn from it, not distance himself from the event. Remember that this ability to absorb and learn, rather than to blame, delineated between "the good" and "the ugly."

The Superstar at Work

Imagine this portrait. Darren is twenty-seven years old, the youngest vice president in a Fortune 25 company. He began at the company five years ago as an entry-level administrator. His high performance was recognized immediately and he quickly rose through the ranks, soon supervising the person who had hired him. His subordinates generally like him, although they sometimes tire of his pushing when their plates are already full. They wonder if he has made vice president on their backs. Darren acknowledges his rapid ascent and loves his job. But he is also restless, believing that he can do his boss's job now. He knows that something is missing, but he does not believe that the "seasoning" gained through experience will make him any better. His boss tells him to make some mistakes, so that he does not appear perfect to others. His peers distrust him, believing he is only out for himself and the next rung on the ladder. And he asks, "Why don't I feel bad when I lay people off?"

Cynthia is thirty-two, a super-mom and superstar. She is a brilliant scientist in a high-tech research company who turns out results superior to all her peers. She is promoted quickly, sometimes twice within a year. She is the "golden girl" to the CEO and is named in his reports for her outstanding work. She is promoted to vice president ahead of many peers who have been at the company longer than she and who also do outstanding work. Her division grows rapidly and soon encompasses those she has passed by. She has beautiful children, access to excellent childcare, and a devoted husband. She believes that if she can work long hours and also be a mom that her people should be working long hours, too. When trouble arises in the ranks of her organization, she faces it directly and brings in an organizational consultant to address the problem. Her subordinates say, "She just doesn't get it. She hasn't been around organizations long enough to understand the different needs and competing priorities of her people." She asks, "What am I doing wrong?"

Darren and Cynthia are both victims of their own success. They are, as described, brilliant, high performers, aggressive, insightful, and results-oriented. But that may be the problem. In their focus on results, they have disregarded the lessons of experience that have to do with people, their individual personalities, and their own desires for success and fears of failure. Because Darren and Cynthia have not experienced their own hardships, they cannot empathize with the people around them. Darren and Cynthia are currently incapable of feeling the emotional depth of hardship.

Darren was asked, "What is your biggest regret or failure?" His response: "That I am not universally liked and respected by all." This naïve, yet idealistic response gave evidence of the lack of failure in Darren's life. As early as public school days, Darren had been a leader in his class and in extracurricular organizations. He had never lost an election to school office. He had gone on to state honors and had been recognized by his congressman. He was accepted at all the colleges to which he applied. He found an excellent job right out of college. He met and married a lovely and smart woman. On their first attempt, they succeeded in starting a family. His life was a bed of roses.

Cynthia was valedictorian of her class. She was very attractive and was elected homecoming queen. As a foreign exchange student, she had lived abroad with a wonderful family. On her return, she traveled the state giving speeches about her experience. She went to college on a merit scholarship that paid all of her fees. Because of her computer skills, she was offered several positions upon graduation. Her performance provided her with recognition, and headhunters called to lure her away to other companies. Her husband supported her career and their dual incomes allowed them to live well and enjoy the amenities of life.

The problem shared by Darren and Cynthia is that they do not know what they do not know. They do not know and understand humility and pain. They do not comprehend grief and loss. They do not show compassion. They cannot get into the shoes of another person to feel that person's pain. And they do not appreciate the depth of their own personal resources that could allow them to overcome adversity, because they have never been tested.

The fatal flaws that may trip up both Darren and Cynthia are lack of humility and a critical unawareness of themselves and how they would react to hardship. As one peer described the situation, "If we were in a true disaster, I would want Darren next to me to help solve the problem. But I would not want Darren to deal with a true disaster alone. He hasn't been proven in a failure situation."

Conceivably, both Darren and Cynthia are fully capable of learning the lessons of hardship. Conceivably, they are capable of showing compassion, empathy, humility, and patience. So how can the coach season them and give them opportunities to learn the lessons of hardship without truly endangering them?

THE COACH'S RESPONSE

Because Darren and Cynthia are bright and insightful, they can probably hear the message that there are lessons to be learned. The directness of the coach's feedback, based on observation and interviews, may be the necessary call to attention. After years of positive feedback and promotions, even this slightly alarming feedback may feel like being hit by a two-by-four that one did not see coming. If the coach can get Darren and Cynthia to slow down enough to listen to the feedback, there is hope that they will continue their rapid ascent in the organization and improve their performance along the way.

In order to accelerate the lessons of experience, the superstars must concentrate more on learning than on performance and results. The results are already well taken care of. Results come naturally. So raising their consciousness about learning allows superstars to increase their focus. The coach would have to work regularly with the superstars to analyze real-time situations. Using the EIAG model described above, lessons would be gleaned from seemingly insignificant occurrences that involved others, especially subordinates and peers. This would be an effort to fine-tune performance, increasing the batting average by just one more success in ten tries.

Seasoning can also be accelerated to some degree by learning from the experience of others. Reading about both success stories and failures, and analyzing the events surrounding each, would open up the superstars' minds to viewing the potential for different outcomes. While this is a somewhat academic approach, it would present the paradigm that the world is not always so perfect and that outcomes cannot always be predicted.

A more intense experience would be afforded if the superstar would become intimately involved with people and in situations that are uncomfortable. For example, Darren was never involved in sports because he did not think he was athletic enough to compete successfully. To learn humility and the lessons of failure in a safe environment, Darren could take up softball, tennis, or golf. Learning to perform at even a mediocre level would be a huge accomplishment, one that he avoided previously for fear of failing. He would learn that hard work, more than raw talent, can present admirable results.

Cynthia, enjoying the affluent life, could volunteer in a homeless shelter and take the time to get to know the people who are there. Listening to their stories and understanding that, "There but for the grace of God go I," would present to Cynthia an opportunity to learn the lessons of empathy and compassion. Another possibility would be to coach a Little League team in a poor community. Observing the conditions and challenges for poor families would provide lessons of hardship. It would also present opportunities to learn patience. Superstars often have the misfortune of grasping concepts so quickly that they do not give others time to "get it."

In a business setting, Cynthia and Darren could participate in task forces that were not focused on their strong suits. An engineer who designs the latest product to meet a customer need, Cynthia would not be a natural leader in a business meeting with the CFO where she had to discuss the financial implications of her decisions. A high-tech wizard opening up new applications of the worldwide web, Darren could learn humility from a task force in marketing a product advancement.

WHEN ALL IS SAID AND DONE

The lessons of hardship learned by superstars have wide applicability. Not only will results-based performance improve by their gaining a wider perspective, but the superstar will become a better manager and leader of people. The threat of the "bloody chicken routine" comes from other people. That is why the superstar must learn to relate to others, to "walk in their moccasins," to empathize, to show compassion, humility, and a self-deprecating sense of humor. The irony is that, by increasing one's focus beyond results to learning, the results actually improve over the long haul.

Learning the lessons of experience never ends. Sadly, there is no checklist that "the good," "the bad," or "the ugly" can complete to show that they have achieved success. As the researchers at CCL reported, there are times when serendipity works for or against us. By concentrating on the lessons of experience, the superstars may improve their chances for continuing success. However, the hardships may be welcomed as valuable lessons not learned elsewhere.

References

Dweck, C. (1999). Mastery oriented thinking. In C.R. Snyder (Ed.), *Coping: The psychology of what works*. New York: Oxford University Press.

Glacel, B.P., & Robert, E.A., Jr. (1996). *Light bulbs for leaders—A guide book for team learning*. New York: John Wiley & Sons.

Hyatt, C., & Gottlieb, L. (1987). *When smart people fail—Rebuilding yourself for success*. New York: Penguin.

McCall, M.W., Jr., Lombardo, M.M., & Morrison, A.M. (1988). *The lessons of experience: How successful executives develop on the job*. New York: The Free Press.

Barbara Pate Glacel, Ph.D., *is principal of The Glacel Group of Virginia. She is author of a business best-seller on teams. She works with individuals, teams, and organizations in the Fortune 500 and not-for-profit arenas. She has over thirty years' experience in coaching and teaching leaders at all levels of organizations. She is a well-known author and public speaker and has consulted in Europe, Asia, and South Africa.*

I HEAR AMERICA SPEAKING: LESSONS FOR LEADERS

Marlene Caroselli

Abstract: The events of September 11, 2001, inspired pride and patriotism in average citizens, courage and dedication in our fighting men and women, and some of the finest rhetoric the nation has ever known in our leaders. By studying the specific techniques employed by those who speak on our behalf, organizational leaders can learn much about motivation, optimism, and leadership itself. This article tells how.

One hundred and fifty years ago, poet Walt Whitman heard America singing—mechanics, carpenters, masons, boatmen, and deckhands—raising their voices in "strong, melodious songs." He heard individual Americans singing of their labor in a time of peace. Since September 11, 2001, we Americans have heard our leaders speaking with words characterized by the strength of our determination and our insistence on conquering evil. While the circumstances are rare, the stylistic devices employed by those who speak for us are *not* rare: They can be studied and successfully used by those seeking to lead within the corporate realm.

KEY-WORD TECHNIQUE

Shortly after the tragedy of September 11, George W. Bush flew to New York and, amid the rubble of Ground Zero, addressed an audience of rescue workers. Desperate to hear the President's words, one of the firefighters shouted, "We can't hear you!" Undaunted, the President replied, "I can hear *you*. The world hears you. And the people who knocked these buildings down will hear from all of us soon."

LESSONS FOR LEADERS

The key-word technique works best, in both formal and informal situations, when the speaker is able to engage in a verbal exchange with the audience. It requires the speaker to listen carefully, think quickly, and take a word just spoken and use it to fashion a response in which that word (or a related word) is key. George W. Bush did this masterfully when he took the word "hear" and made it the basis of his oft-quoted reply. Albeit unscripted, that reply remains among the most inspirational of the President's post-September 11 remarks.

PARALLELISM

In his remarks to Congress and, via television, to the entire world, President Bush addressed a fear-filled nation. "We will not tire," he promised. "We will not falter. We will not fail." By virtue of these deliberately repetitive phrases, he was able to assure us of the resolve that would destroy terrorism and terrorists. The words resonated with all who heard them that day.

LESSONS FOR LEADERS

The President's words were made more inspiring by virtue of the repeated syntax: "We will not. . . ." Repetition causes a momentum to build, a verbal crescendo that climaxes with the most powerful idea—in this case, the promise that assures the nation failure is not an option. Depending on the circumstances propelling your leadership, you'll need phrases that are worthy of repetition—ones that lift possibilities to the lofty realm of idealism becoming reality.

PLAYS ON WORDS

Circulating amid the cartoons and email chats in the days following the tragedy were observations that made us smile (designating George W. Bush as the "Turbanator") and those that bound us together in mutual admiration of our heroes. One of the most memorable, albeit anonymous, Internet lines paid tribute to New York City's fallen heroes: "Heroes come in many forms . . . but mostly, uniforms."

LESSONS FOR LEADERS

Plays on words seldom happen spontaneously. They are usually the result of much deliberate thought, much experimenting, much recollecting and rejecting and solidification of experience. When Colin Powell, for example, asserts, "Optimism is a force-multiplier," he no doubt bases his assertion on a lifetime of seeing how pessimism can destroy morale.

Reflect on your experiences. Record those that stand out the most. Then distill the essence of your experience into a clever, repeatable, perhaps even unforgettable comment about the business of life and/or the life of business.

SIMPLE WORDS

It was Winston Churchill who noted that "Big [wo]men use little words." We heard the power of little words in the battle cry of the doomed passengers on United Flight #93: "Let's roll!" We find that power again, the power of little words to convey big ideas, in these simple but decisive words of our President, spoken as he watched a plane strike the second tower: "We're at war."

Not only world leaders understand this power and optimize its use, but also organizational leaders who sound warnings and then rally followers to heed the warnings. Listen to Jack Welch, former CEO of General Electric (note the number of monosyllabic words): "When the rate of change outside the organization is greater than the rate of change inside the organization, we are looking at the beginning of the end."

LESSONS FOR LEADERS

Think about the most important messages you have to deliver. Write them down without worrying about the context. Then go back to the content and re-fashion your message until it rings with clarity, simplicity, and power.

JUXTAPOSED OPPOSITES

The stark clarity of two opposites—"dead or alive"—enables the reader or listener to grasp the speaker's message immediately. In reference to the aftermath of the terrorist attack, we find not only politicians, but pundits and poets alike using the juxtaposition of opposing terms to heighten the drama of their message or to bring into sharper focus the subject under consideration.

We heard, for example, Simon Schama, history professor at Columbia University, offer an "is not/is" perspective: "The best revenge is not bombing some desert in Afghanistan. The best revenge is life."

We also heard eleven-year-old Mattie Stepanek, best-selling poet, use a "not" construction: "We need to win the war on terrorism with words, not bombs." A variation is found in the "was/was not" syntax of historian Arthur Schlesinger, Jr.: "How like the movies it was. . . . Except it wasn't fiction."

LESSONS FOR LEADERS

It's been said that the leader's job is to keep hope alive, to serve as a bridge, to transform fear into faith. And it's the leader's words that make these things happen. Take the message you need to deliver in your own organization and try creating your own emphasis by juxtaposing opposite terms or fashioning your own connotation. This is what Lon Watters did with the word "school": "School is a building that has four walls with tomorrow inside" and what A.A. Latimer, did with his definition of a budget, "A budget is a mathematical confirmation of your suspicions."

CONCLUSION

Quality guru Joseph Juran is fond of pointing out that the best managers are polyglots—they can speak the language of money and the language of things as well. Today's leader must expand his or her lexicon to fit the various demands that come with the territory. There is a language of inspiration, a rhetoric of grief, a tongue of productivity, to name but a few. And within each lie stylistic devices that bridge the gap between events of the moment and needs of the future. No matter which language construct you use, you have the ability to unite others around a common cause in these uncommon times.

Marlene Caroselli, Ed.D., presents corporate training and keynote addresses on a variety of subjects. She also has written forty-nine books and curriculum guides to date.

LEARNER-DRIVEN TEACHING METHODS: DEVELOPING CRITICAL THINKING SKILLS

Elizabeth A. Smith

Abstract: Teaching and learning tools that use learner-driven, interactive methods and tacit knowledge, or "know how," are beginning to play prime roles in learner-centered classrooms. Learner-driven methods that recognize and reinforce students' efforts to think critically can also be used in the workplace.

In this article, the author stresses the importance of critical thinking skills and tacit knowledge and explains her method for teaching them using unstructured, learner-centered methods; scenarios; peer teaching; small-group discussions; and experiential learning exercises.

Critical thinking skills are keys to success in most professional and personal endeavors and achievements. These skills form the foundation for disciplinary understanding, empathy, ethics, multiculturalism, and professional judgment (Nelson, 2001). Critical thinking is a non-linear, unpredictable process that occurs in some situations and not in others. There are vast individual differences in critical thinking styles. Also, there is no one "best" way to teach or acquire critical thinking skills. Each person's critical thinking process is unique. Critical thinking processes are learned one small step at a time over relatively long periods. People will be motivated to think critically when each step of the critical thinking process and the results of critical thinking processes are acknowledged and appropriately rewarded.

INSTRUCTOR-CENTERED, ACADEMIC METHODS VS. LEARNER-DRIVEN, INTERACTIVE METHODS

Most academic teaching methods and practices revolve around instructors who transfer their knowledge to students. Many teaching contexts are competitive and individualistic (Cook & Cook, 1998). Most course content comes from textbooks, journals, and formal printed and electronic media. Students are required to recall or recognize specific facts, terminology, criteria, methods, principles, and theories and to use this knowledge to answer questions and write essays and papers. Relationships between students and instructors are often impersonal. Instructors often sort and classify students based on individual effort. Obviously, students want to pass tests and get good grades on assignments to please the instructor. Unfortunately, teachers who use traditional, linear thinking techniques emphasize known facts and dualistic thinking that imprison themselves and their students in very small boxes.

Academic models are gradually giving way to learner-enabled methods that share practical, action-oriented information based on experience and common sense (Cook & Cook, 1998). Non-linear, interactive methods are designed to foster and appropriately reward the expression and use of critical thinking skills. Relationships between students and teachers are focused on exchanges of data and information that gradually lead to understanding. Learners actively construct, discover, and transform their own knowledge. They use

The 2003 Annual: Volume 1, Training/© 2003 John Wiley & Sons, Inc.

open dialogue or discussions and question-and-answer sessions to help them interact with one another, process information, and think critically about what they are learning. Group-based, learner-centered methods use peer teaching and group problem solving. At work, learner-centered methods include internships, co-ops, and mentoring. Work skills are learned and used almost immediately in most learner-enabled methods (Smith, 1998).

Three major characteristics of learner-driven methods are described below:

1. *Student-centered learning breaks the bounds of traditional instructor-centered learning.* Methods designed to engage individuals in learning about what they are learning require the use of critical thinking skills. For instance, students who think about what they are learning see how their learning fits into the overall course objectives. They find that newly acquired knowledge is realistic and can be generalized or applied to other situations. Most students are reluctant or unprepared to answer "Why?" and "How?" Students who are intrigued by the opportunity broaden their perspectives and answer "Why?" "When?" and "How?" by using their common sense or practical intelligence.

2. *Learner-driven methods that encourage divergent thinking force students to compare a number of alternatives.* Before students make a decision or accept information as being reliable or consistent, they must evaluate the merit of various divergent opinions and information that comes from numerous sources.

3. *When learner-driven methods are used consistently, students' first small steps toward critical thinking must be appropriately recognized and reinforced by instructors and peers.* Otherwise, bursts of critical thinking will evaporate. Gradually, overwhelmed students will be intrigued and surprised by their newfound ability to competently evaluate various alternatives and think critically before making decisions.

STEPS IN THE CRITICAL THINKING PROCESS

Just switching to a learner-centered method of teaching may not be enough to encourage critical thinking. You must also understand the basic steps in the critical thinking process (Nelson, 2001). Steps do not necessarily occur in the order listed and may overlap.

Each individual engaging in critical thinking must:

- Question events, beliefs, or things usually considered to be true or personally believed to be true.

- Keep asking "Why?" until an acceptable or logical answer is given. (This step takes time. Accept the fact that questions may never be answered fully.)

- Gradually accept that events in our professional and personal worlds are uncertain. Nothing in life or science, for instance, is totally true. Truth can be relative and some things are true in some instances but not in others.

- Acknowledge that there are many ways to analyze and interpret the same data, event, opinion, or set of beliefs. Individuals make comparisons and decisions using their own mental frameworks, attitudes, beliefs, experiences, values, and templates.

- Make choices and take actions that involve uncertainty. Few things are clear-cut. Most people minimize their discomfort with uncertainty by dividing reality into correct and incorrect answers or possibilities. They use their feelings, opinions, and intuition to make choices that are comfortable.

- Use reason, common sense, and intuition to make choices or decisions. Critical thinking processes that have solid foundations can be expanded, reused, and gradually improved.

- Develop intellectual empathy by trying to understand the other person's viewpoint. Ask "Why?" and "How?" Then use empathic listening skills to learn what is really being said. (To illustrate, an empathic listener keeps repeating and clarifying what the speaker said until the speaker agrees that the listener completely understands what was said. It often takes several back-and-forth exchanges to ensure that the listener completely understood the speaker.)

- Keep asking "Why?" and "How?" questions to learn where and how people obtain their information and how strong their beliefs are.

- Watch for and question dualistic thinking—the tendency to divide issues into either/or scenarios, to see issues as black or white, with no gray or inconsistencies in their explanations and answers.

- Actively think about and then practice "thinking about what you are thinking" or "learning about what you are learning"(Argyris, 1994). Double-loop learning turns the question back on the questioner or digs more deeply into the question, like a follow-up to determine what *really* happened and *why* it happened. Double-loop learning reduces built-in barriers to self-understanding. It requires people to keep questioning themselves until they gain insights or become relatively satisfied with their thought processes.

- Reflect on and review the above critical thinking processes. The goal is to improve the speed and accuracy of decisions while minimizing risk. Jumping one decision-making hurdle at a time until it is time to make more decisions may be all we can expect.

EXPERIENTIAL LEARNING EXERCISES

To help the reader understand how to encourage critical thinking skills, the author offers the following exercises and activities that were used in her classroom.

Objectives and Methods for Teaching Critical Thinking Skills

The author, in teaching human and organizational behavior, determined that a main course objective was "to use critical thinking skills to improve the overall quality of ethical decision making and problem solving relative to human behavior in organizations and the prediction of possible outcomes." Methods used to achieve this objective have been incorporated into the following six examples, many of which can be adapted for workplace training. These examples balance the use of explicit knowledge—facts, logic, and information generally available obtained from the textbook, website searches, and other written material—with tacit knowledge—intuition, practical intelligence, and experience based on class discussions, question-and-answer sessions, peer teaching, and small-group discussions.

Students were encouraged to rely on their own knowledge, accept uncertainty, and give several answers to difficult questions. Students were discouraged from using dualistic thinking and making hasty decisions.

Use of Explicit Knowledge

Example 1—Recognize and Deal with Uncertainty:
Objective. To encourage students to recognize the main variables in a specific situation and deal more effectively with uncertainty and complexity.
Source Material. Newspapers, magazines, websites, TV and radio reports.
Method. Students were asked to verbally describe major pros and cons of the proposed AOL-Time Warner merger and view pros and cons in terms

of implications for customers, stockholders, and competitive advantage. The instructor captured students' responses. Students then gave their best numeric estimates of the level of uncertainty of outcomes and also estimated levels of complexity for each pro and con listed. The instructor discussed the first what-if scenario and provided a template for students' opinions and subsequent discussion. Each student carefully reviewed the problem and wrote down several possible scenarios and presented these scenarios to either the entire group or to his or her peer group. This process created an awareness of the need to consider risk and complexity from numerous viewpoints. Ongoing discussions reinforced the contribution of human and organizational variables that are hard to assess and relieved some concerns about making decisions under uncertain conditions.

Example 2—Recognize Transformational Leadership:

Objective: To apply information from the text to real-life situations.

Source Material. Textbook, videotape.

Method. Students read the textbook chapter on leadership, completed the skills bank exercise, and answered the discussion questions. The instructor led the class discussion on the various types of leadership, different leadership styles, the need to improve leadership, and so forth. Students used their own experience of a wide range of poor to excellent leadership styles to develop realistic criteria to evaluate leadership.

Next, students viewed a fifty-minute videotape featuring Herb Kelleher, former CEO of Southwest Airlines, an industry leader. Based on the video, they listed Kelleher's leadership skills and style and were asked to determine whether or not he was a transformational leader. Kelleher provided examples of ways to treat people, handle customers, and lead, not manage. He discussed current leadership qualities that are important now and in the future. After students shared their notes and discoveries about leadership with one another, all agreed that Kelleher was a true transformational leader. Their understanding of transformational leadership far exceeded material covered in the text.

Example 3—Creativity and Intrinsic Motivators:

Objective. Encourage students to ask "Why?" and "How?" and not just accept things that seem to be true. Help students feel comfortable questioning the logic and content of texts, journals, articles, websites, the media, and so on, and challenging the instructor.

Source Material. Article on creativity and intrinsic motivation.

Method. Students read the author's three-page article on creativity and intrinsic motivators. They wrote down ways to be more creative and how to reward creativity in their jobs. Next, they discussed their answers with group members. Individual differences naturally appeared due to different skills, personalities, knowledge, and personal preferences for intrinsic motivators. When the instructor assured students that individual differences were expected, they began to feel comfortable presenting their personal opinions. They learned that their views, attitudes, and values resulted in quite different answers. Gradually, they accepted the opinions of what a group member considered true at a specific point in time. Before a more controversial issue was introduced in subsequent classes, this non-threatening exercise was cited.

Use of Tacit Knowledge

It is hard to separate tacit and explicit knowledge into neat categories. Each of the three examples that follow uses primarily tacit knowledge, but explicit knowledge is interwoven. What people openly and eagerly talk about and share with others is really tacit knowledge. This knowledge is often acquired in direct or spontaneous conversations, in talking a person through problems, as in customer call centers, or in developing a novel way to solve a long-standing problem with a difficult employee.

Example 4—Disrupt the Status Quo:

Objective. Discourage students from selecting and supporting safe and/or acceptable opinions or what they think the instructor wants to hear.

Source Material. Websites.

Method. Students selected and reviewed ten websites of their own choosing and prepared a write-up for each that answered the question, "Would you like to work for this company?" The author reminded students that the write-ups were to focus on issues deemed important both now and in the future. Although some students reviewed the same websites, each student had slightly different opinions of the company's treatment of employees, benefits, financial status, future, and so forth. After reviewing several more websites, students became more comfortable with the array of different opinions influenced by personal interest, previous knowledge of the company, media reports, and other bits of fact and fiction.

Example 5—Avoid Dualistic Thinking:

Objective. To help students move away from rote memorization and dualistic thinking.

Source Material. A set of written scenarios.

Method. Three experiential learning exercises on solving common work-related problems (Sternberg, 1991) were used to show that people perceive and handle the same situation in quite different ways. Before beginning, students were reminded that there is rarely one best answer and that people can disagree constructively.

Each student read each of the scenarios and used a seven-point scale to rate each of the ten statements that described ways to handle the problem situations. Students then compared results for each statement for each of the three scenarios. Some students found that their rating differed by as much as six points (the maximum) from the ratings of their peer group. In general, students were extremely surprised to learn that their perceptions and actions differed significantly from those of their classmates. The author reminded students that individual differences in thoughts and behavior were expected and acceptable.

Example 6—Real-Life Experiences:

Objective. Encourage students to discuss and critique real-life, work-related experiences.

Source Material. Actual experiences.

Method. Each student described an actual situation, such as how he or she had disciplined an employee. Explicit knowledge (what happened and why it happened) and tacit knowledge (what people felt and said after the disciplining was over) provided valuable insights into the process of discipline and actual outcomes.

After hearing each story, group members suggested alternate ways that the storyteller could have handled the situation. Students often questioned their peers further to get more information or feedback. Most wanted verification that what they did was acceptable and that the outcome was satisfactory.

Peer teaching is invaluable, as students who described their experiences received peer feedback and also gave classmates and the author a spontaneous, valuable teaching moment.

PRACTICAL APPLICATIONS

First, by using these methods learners who lack explicit knowledge can use their tacit knowledge to solve problems they have not previously encountered. In the workplace, this skill is important for situations such as dealing with new scenarios, problem solving, and product development.

Second, students who have learned how to evaluate and work with risk and uncertainty effectively can apply this skill in the workplace in situations that require strategic planning, futurizing, and timely decision making.

CONCLUSION

Continuous upgrading of the growing array of technological innovations in the classroom, continual changes to the curriculum, distance learning, and better funding of education to improve results have not really increased the percentage of readily employable college graduates. Gaps between what students learn in traditional university classrooms and criteria for job success can be reduced by teaching students critical thinking skills. Of course, once they are hired, employees must continue to use their critical thinking skills and strive to improve them.

On the flip side, organizations must also do what they can to encourage critical thinking. Valuable information leaves an organization when people walk out, either at a shift change or permanently. Unless employees who use tacit knowledge are appropriately recognized and rewarded, organizations lose the benefit of their knowledge. Organizations that value critical thinking skills and that gradually build a reputation for hiring critical thinkers will have an enviable advantage in the marketplace of the future.

Organizations that mentor or provide co-ops, internships, and other on-the-job experiences for college students actively cultivate and use tacit knowledge. Students or employees who lack experience and training must rely on tacit knowledge and on their own abilities to generalize or apply what they know to new problems and situations. Unpredictable classroom and work environments require answers that explicit knowledge cannot provide. If current graduating students are to be employable, their ability to use tacit knowledge must be encouraged within and beyond the classroom (Smith, 2001).

References

Argyris, C. (1994, July/August). Good communication that blocks learning. *Harvard Business Review*, pp. 77–85.

Cook, J.S., & Cook, L.L. (1998, July). How technology enables the quality of student-centered learning. *Quality Progress*, pp. 59–63.

Nelson, C.E. (2001, April 20). Fostering critical thinking and mature valuing across the curriculum [workshop]. University of Houston Clear Lake, Texas.

Smith, E.A. (1998). Applying knowledge-enabled methods in the classroom and in the workplace. *Journal of Workplace Learning, 2*(6), 236–244.

Smith, E.A. (2001). The role of tacit and explicit knowledge in the workplace. *Journal of Knowledge Management, 5*(4), 311–321.

Sternberg, R.J. (1991). *Tacit knowledge inventory for managers.* San Antonio, TX: The Psychological Corporation.

Elizabeth A. Smith, Ph.D., *chief knowledge officer, CRG Medical, and adjunct professor, School of Business and Public Administration, University of Houston Clear Lake, Houston, Texas, teaches human and organizational behavior. Her books include* The Productivity Manual *(Butterworth Heinemann, 1995) and* Creating Productive Organizations *(St. Lucie/CRC Press, 1995). She has authored articles on productivity, creativity, motivation, and quality in health care. She belongs to Sigma Xi and the American Society for Quality and serves on editorial boards of several international journals.*

TRAINER SURVIVAL SKILLS

Susan Boyd

Abstract: This article addresses some frequently faced challenges by trainers: How to deal with negative or "know-it-all" learners; what to do when you don't know the answer, when a question or a discussion wanders off topic, or when people are not paying attention; and how to read a group to see if they're "getting it." It also presents a series of presentation and general training tips.

Dealing with negative or "know-it-all" learners, what to do if you don't know the answer to a question a learner asks, what happens when people aren't paying attention to what you have to say—these and many problems confront the experienced as well as the novice trainer. The ideas presented here can be of help. As you gain experience, you will likely come up with many other strategies to share with your fellow trainers.

DEALING WITH NEGATIVE LEARNERS

Negative learners are typically easy to recognize by their attitude. It is clear by their manner, tone, body language, and comments that they do not want to be trained in a new system or method. They may reject the trainer, the training class, or the content. This could be because they feel uncomfortable in a training situation where their level of competency (from their point of view) is being called into question or because they are faced with changing the way they work. The negative energy of one learner quickly infects a class if the trainer does not deal with this learner.

The following techniques can be used alone or in combination to help manage negative learners:

- Try to accentuate the positive, new aspects of this system or process over the old one;
- Recognize the person's reluctance to change;
- Relate your own feelings when first confronted with the system, in contrast with your feelings now;
- Empathize with the challenge of using new tools when under a deadline, but stress that the training will help with the transition;
- Don't embarrass a learner in front of the whole class;
- Talk to the individual privately and try to uncover other problems unrelated to the training; ask what you can do to help the class go more smoothly for that individual;

- Recognize that there could be factors totally outside of the class and system that are making the person so crabby and that he or she may just be taking the bad feelings out on you;

- If negativity is spreading, allow a minute for a "corporate whine" session to get all whining out of everyone's system;

- Determine whether the individual needs to attend a different class session instead;

- Reward people who have positive comments to say about the system or training (with verbal or tangible awards like candy, jumping frogs, stickers, etc.);

- Ignore the negativity unless it threatens to drown the whole class; and

- Be professional.

In summary, try to be open and empathic about the learning process. Assess how great a disturbance the negative individual is causing: ignore him or her if the rest of the class remains engaged, but speak with him or her privately if the negativity is impacting the training session.

DEALING WITH "KNOW-IT-ALL" LEARNERS

The "know-it-all" learner also presents a challenge to the trainer, especially to a novice instructor or one less experienced in the subject matter. This type of learner appears to have the skills, knowledge, and credibility to do the trainer's job. He or she usually doesn't resent being in the classroom, but rather is thrilled to show off his or her talents to the trainer and the other class members. The issue becomes one of control and who is really in charge of the class.

Rather than be intimidated by the "know-it-all" learner, try to keep the following in mind:

- Don't be threatened by their knowledge; we all can learn from each other;

- Don't set yourself up as an expert if you are not;

- Talk to the person privately if you feel he or she is affecting the class;

- Involve the person by eliciting comments, experiences, and so on. In an ongoing training program, these learners may be willing to do some further investigation and help other learners;

- Evaluate the person's skills to see whether he or she needs to take the class. Perhaps move the person to a more advanced class;

- Recognize that the person's learning pace may need to be faster; encourage the person to explore options such as computer-based training and online learning rather than classroom training;

- Identify what the person does need to learn and see whether you can help meet this learning need;

- Acknowledge the person if he or she comes up with alternate and better ways of doing something. However, only incorporate this method if it is not confusing to the other learners; and

- Build a rapport with the learner; don't treat him or her as your adversary.

The best way to deal with know-it-all learners is to try to use their knowledge to your advantage. Encourage them to share their knowledge and experiences with the group. Incorporate their ideas (if useful) into the training. However, as noted above, it's important that you not let the learner take over the class. Finally, if the know-it-all is too dominating or too knowledgeable, consider whether alternate situations—an advanced class, an online learning program—would be more appropriate.

Coping When You Don't Know the Answer

One of the biggest challenges a trainer faces is not knowing the answer to a question. Many trainers feel they must know everything about a course or subject they teach. In reality, no one can be an expert in every facet of a system or process. What is more important is knowing how to use the resources—and we also need to teach learners how to find the answers for themselves. Don't present yourself as an expert, as someone will certainly try to trip you up.

Try these techniques the next time you don't know the answer to a question:

- Admit you don't know the answer, but say you will investigate the issue and get back to the person (and be sure to do so);

- Ask whether anyone in the room knows the answer;

- Ask a learner to post the question on a whiteboard or flip chart (with a Post-it Note). Let the learner "own" the question and make sure you follow up after the session to find the answer;

- Let the group know that with new systems and processes, we are always learning and that no one knows all the answers;
- Check other resources (online help, frequently asked questions (FAQs) on the Internet, books, computer support staff, HR department, other trainers, etc.);
- Teach learners how to use the resources they will have back on the job to find answers to questions (online help, FAQs, reference cards and job aids, helpdesk, etc.);
- Try it! Many times, the question is about doing something a new way. Ask the person who posed the question to try it that way and let you know. Remember there are often many ways to do the same function.

The key to dealing with what you don't know is to recognize that you can't know everything, to not be afraid to admit that you don't know the answer, and to take advantage of all the resources available to you (including the learners).

PUTTING OFF TANGENTIAL QUESTIONS OR DISCUSSIONS

Tangential questions are those that are not directly related to the topic and typically require more information to answer. If the question is not directly relevant to the content, it can serve to detour the group, confuse the learners, and take time away from an already compressed teaching schedule.

Dealing with tangential questions and discussion requires some quick thinking on your part as to the best way to handle them with minimal impact on the learners and the time schedule. The following tips should help you deal with this issue:

- Answer the question if you can do so in less than three minutes;
- If the question is complicated, ask the learner to post it and tell him or her that you'll answer later if possible, or afterward;
- If the question will be answered later in the session, say this and ask the learner to hold the question until then;
- If the question and answer are beyond the scope of the class, say, "Good point—let's discuss it over break or after class";

- Be honest and let the person know that the question is beyond the scope of the workshop;

- Blow the whistle when discussions are getting out of hand and not advancing the class's needs. Try using a train whistle to keep everyone on track and on target. It quickly gets everyone's attention in a fun way and lets you move on; and

- Don't get bogged down in policy questions. Recognize that, while learners need to be heard when they have issues with policies, the classroom is not the place to solve this problem and you will need to cut short these discussions. Ask the learners to post such questions and tell them you can find answers after the session or have a guest speaker come in to address them.

Tangential questions and discussions can eat up a lot of training time, particularly if they are of interest to your learners. However, to preserve the training schedule, you should come up with a process for dealing with such questions. You can create a "parking lot" (a flip chart) where learners can list questions for attention during break or after class, offer to find the answers (or someone else who can provide them), or, when necessary, simply tell the learner that the question is beyond the scope of the session.

KNOWING WHAT TO DO WHEN PEOPLE ARE NOT PAYING ATTENTION

Probably one of the most frustrating situations a trainer faces is when learners are not paying attention. Sometimes the trainer feels like he or she is a substitute teacher in an elementary school and the learners are running amuck! Trying to gain and keep control and attention is also challenging when dealing with adult learners.

Next time you seem to be losing control, try some of these ideas:

- Stop and wait, as silence helps get everyone on the same track;

- Talking louder doesn't work, but often dropping your voice does;

- Do "musical name tags" to break up chatty pairs. Tell the class that you will rearrange seats during the next break so that everyone can view the flip chart or projection better;

- Keep talking, but move quietly to the talker's area;

- Tell the participants to do something when they have completed an activity, for example, wave their hands, put their hands on their heads, or clap. This usually gets the talkers' or day dreamers' attention;

- Recognize the signs that it's time for a break! Take a two-minute stretch or exercise break and let people move around;

- Change the pace by doing a quick team or partner exercise;

- Talk to the chatty or disruptive learners during break. Ask if there is a problem and be clear that it is affecting you and the other class members; and

- Don't rush to judge—a learner who is not paying attention might be so far behind that he or she has given up! Chatty learners might actually be helping each other learn the system.

In summary, gaining and keeping the group's attention for an entire training session is likely to be an ongoing issue. However, there are a number of non-disruptive steps you can take to keep learners on track.

READING A CLASS TO ASSESS LEARNING

Many times a novice trainer is so concerned about subject matter, classroom management, and control that it is easy to forget the learners! The purpose of training is not to present the material but to help the learners use and apply the concepts or skills back on the job. It is important to check both formally and informally with the learners throughout the class to see whether they are mastering the material.

Listed below are some ways to assess whether the learners understand the lessons:

- Look at faces for visual feedback;

- Eavesdrop over breaks to see what people are saying about the class pace and their comprehension;

- Check the comfort level. After teaching a lesson, ask the learners to write their names and comfort level on an index card (use ratings of 1 to 5, with 1 being least comfortable with their knowledge of the topic and 5 being very comfortable). Collect and quickly review these cards. Then adapt the pace and delivery as needed;

- Ask learners to write down three topics/skills they feel they know the most about and three topics/skills they know the least about. This is a good way to end/begin a day;

- Talk to facilitators or class aides to obtain their feedback;

- See how the learners do during the activities or exercises. Give positive feedback and encouragement;

- Talk to specific learners after class if you suspect a problem. Check whether they require some extra one-on-one help; and

- Recognize that the initial training session is the hardest and each day gets better for both the learners and you.

There are clearly many ways to assess the level of comprehension in the classroom. One of the keys, however, is to do an assessment early and often. Don't wait until the end of a full day's training to find out whether or not learners are "getting it."

OTHER TRAINING PRESENTATION TIPS

The following tips cover a multitude of common training situations.

General Tips

- Make sure content fits within the timeframe. List all topics and activities and estimate the time to be allotted. Identify sections to cut down or delete if there is insufficient time to cover all material.

- Take time to introduce yourself, the training objectives (what's in it for them), materials, and timeframe properly.

- Repeat questions or summarize comments from learners when training a large group.

- Set short times for team activities and use a timer.

- Post on the wall two flip-chart sheets marked "Parking Lot" and "System/Policy Questions & Enhancements." The Parking Lot is for questions learner have that will be answered later in class or after class. System/Policy Questions are those you need to get back to people on if you are unclear on the answer. Ask learners to write questions on Post-it Notes, include their names, and then post on the appropriate flip-chart sheet.

 The 2003 Annual: Volume 1, Training/© 2003 John Wiley & Sons, Inc.

- Be clear on activities and assignments before learners break into groups. Have the instructions in writing if there are more complicated steps.

- If using a ball toss (or any physical activity), explain how it works first, then call out the name of the first person you will toss the ball to so that he or she will be ready to catch it.

- Start and end on time. Shut the door when ready to begin. Stick to the time schedule, and start class when break time is up.

- Talk to learners before class and during breaks.

- Use learners' names to help them actively participate in discussions. Have name tags/cards to help you learn their names.

- Plan for ways to involve the learners throughout the training. Use partner/team activities, get them to do demos, encourage questions, use review games, ball toss for questions and answers, and so on.

- Leave ten to fifteen minutes at the end to wrap up the session, summarizing objectives, identifying next steps or resources, completing evaluations, and so on.

Room Setup/Lighting

- Arrive at least thirty minutes prior to the start of the training to set up equipment and supplies.

- Determine what room lighting choices are available and how dim the room needs to be to see the overhead screen or video monitor. The ideal is to be able to see the screen clearly, but still be light enough to see the materials and the presenter.

- Turn lights up for discussion and team activities if they needed to be dimmed for a presentation.

All Projected Material

- Use 36-point type for headings and 28 to 32-point type for text.

- Use the 7x7 rule. Try to have no more than seven bullet points and a maximum of seven words to a bullet.

- Avoid using all capital letters. Don't worry about complete sentences or ending punctuation.

Overhead Projectors

- Add color and graphics to transparencies, but don't get too carried away. Make sure all colors are dark enough to be seen easily.

- Use a pointer and move off to the side so you are not blocking the screen.

- If you don't have a pointer, you can use a paper arrow, pen, or coin right on the transparency to point to a section.

- Use a frame to block out extra light and help position overheads correctly.

- Place overhead transparencies in clear, protective, three-hole punched sleeves and insert in a binder to keep them in order.

- Give handouts of any detailed drawings, such as forms or charts, if these are too small to read on a transparency.

- Use wipe-off transparency markers if you need to add emphasis.

- Use the reveal technique (piece of paper covering part of the transparency) if you want learners to focus on a specific point, rather than the whole thing.

- Read directly from the transparency or have a hard copy of the presentation in front of you so you don't have to turn around to look.

- Turn off the overhead projector when not using.

Presentation Systems

- Use a dark colored background, with white or yellow letters.

- Add clip art, animation, and music to slides if appropriate.

- Arrive early to test all electrical connections.

- Have a backup copy of presentation on disk (saved in lower version of PowerPoint if necessary) and overhead transparencies in case of equipment failure.

- Position and prop up projector so it displays at the top of the screen.

- Use a pointer and move off to the side so you are not blocking the presentation.

- Have remote control to advance slides if possible.

- Have a hard copy of the presentation so you don't have to turn around to look at the slide.

- Put projection system on stand-by during longer discussions and group activities.

Slide Projector

- Add color and graphics to slides.
- Use dark colored background, with white or yellow letters.
- Position and prop up projector so it displays at the top of the screen.
- Use a pointer and move off to the side so you are not blocking the presentation.
- Have a hard copy in front of you so you don't have to turn around to look at the slide.

Whiteboard

- Write with dark colored dry-erase markers only. (Black, blue, and purple work best.) Use red or green for highlighting only, as these are more difficult to see.
- Don't talk while facing the board. Try to write on an angle so you can still face the group.
- If compiling a longer list, ask for two volunteers to write the responses on the board or flip chart. Help summarize/condense responses into a few words to simplify note taking.

Useful Trainer Supplies

- Timer
- Pointer
- Train whistle
- Soft foam ball
- Candy/paper cups
- Play money
- Inexpensive prizes
- Whiteboard markers
- Flip chart and overhead markers
- Power strip

- Highlighters
- Extra pens for learners
- Name tags and tent cards
- Case opener (to open boxes)
- Masking tape
- Post-it Notes in pads
- Extra bulbs for projector or batteries for laptop

CONCLUSION

Novice trainers (and experienced trainers as well) will undoubtedly face many of the issues reviewed in this article. While these situations may be intimidating or frustrating, trainers can learn to manage (and even learn from) these situations. Following the suggestions presented in this article will ensure a smoother training experience for all involved.

There is no "magic" formula to ensure a trainer's success with every learner. We wear many hats—from coach and director to cheerleader and psychoanalyst. Trainers will be faced with many challenges in the classroom, ranging from "problem" learners to "problem" computers. The best way to survive is to have a sense of humor, be able to empathize, deal with what you're able to change, be flexible, and think fast on your feet. Above all, keep the challenges in perspective and try not to take things personally!

Susan Boyd *is president of Susan Boyd Associates, a computer training firm that specializes in job-specific training programs. She is the author of* Accelerate Computer Learning with Analogies *and a contributor to the 1999, 2001, and 2002* Training & Performance Sourcebook. *Ms. Boyd has over twenty years' experience in the training and computer education field and is a member of the International Who's Who in Information Technology. Ms. Boyd is a national conference speaker and published author of over twenty training articles.*

GETTING THE MOST FROM A GOOD STORY

Lori L. Silverman and Mary B. Wacker

Abstract: Trainers often overlook the possibility of using stories they have collected in advance to enhance the training experience, even though many do use stories spontaneously in their presentations. This article delves into the use of stories in training, what makes a story effective, story selection, and their presentation. The authors explore the many places where stories can be found and how they can shape the design of a training session or be used to enhance or elaborate on specific content. Spontaneous stories, often told by participants, also have a role in training. The authors emphasize that no matter how they are generated, it is important that stories be appropriately introduced and debriefed.

$\mathbf{R}$emember when you were a child and your parents or grandparents used to read stories to you? These stories frequently left an indelible imprint on your memory and became a part of your conversations with your friends and family. Often, the same is true of stories that are told in training sessions. It is not unusual to find trainees retelling a story to their colleagues, rather than recounting specific content material, because the story made a lasting impression. Chances are also good that the participants may email or talk about the story to their family and friends, thus reinforcing the message the story was meant to communicate.

THE PURPOSE OF STORIES IN TRAINING

Good stories can serve many purposes in a training session. They can entertain or energize, educate, evaluate, engage, encourage, explore, and evoke. Each of these purposes has some type of relationship to the overall training: the training topic, the trainee, the trainer, and the design of the training material or the session in which they are being used.

Entertain/Energize

There are a variety of reasons for using stories that entertain or energize in a training session. They can help to humanize the trainer, thus increasing the person's credibility and rapport with the audience. This is especially true if the trainer shares a situation that makes him or her appear to be a bit vulnerable. Stories can also change the energy level in a room. Imagine being in a room where the energy is low, perhaps after lunch, and hearing an instructor recount a situation that brings belly laughs to all who hear it. This type of story can also release tension in the room. It might be appropriate to use it during a training session that helps individuals prepare to take a certification exam or address a serious organizational issue.

Stories that entertain can also be a way of remembering a concept that is to be applied in the workplace. In team-development sessions, one of the authors of this paper often uses a story about how three college students went about creating a large slingshot that was eventually located on the top deck of a fraternity house situated on a lake. The purpose of the slingshot was to provide "feedback" to the crew team that practiced on the lake very early in the morning, even on weekends. Unexpectedly, an unripe canta-loupe that was launched around 5:00 a.m. one day actually sank a crew boat (no one was hurt). What the story demonstrates is that the builders of the slingshot (the "team") had a goal, a plan, and defined roles, responsibilities, and ground rules.

Educate

Stories that educate are meant to introduce new knowledge or to build on al-ready existing knowledge. An example might be the types of stories used in new-employee orientation. Instead of presenting a list of the organization's core values, the trainer could elect to tell a series of stories that help partici-pants to identify the organization's values, their importance, and how these values might influence the decisions the participants will make in their fu-ture work. When introducing new concepts, such as the topic of variation, stories that educate can also be effective. Here a story might be about special and common cause variations involved in driving to work.

Evaluate

Evaluating the rightness/wrongness, goodness/badness, or appropriateness/inappropriateness of behaviors or options in a given situation is another pur-pose for using stories. These types of stories are effective when speaking of policies and procedures, industry regulations, work standards, customer re-quirements, and local, state, and federal guidelines. For example, consider telling a story about an employee in procurement who has been asked by a major customer to engage in a series of actions that have some ethical and legal implications. The trainees' task is to outline what the employee should do in the situation. Used in this way, the story provides a context for discussing appropriate and inappropriate behaviors.

Engage

Stories that engage participants capture their hearts and minds and help them move from being passive to being invested in the training. Imagine the following story being told to a healthcare audience and the type of impact it might have.

A five-year-old boy with severe asthma, who spent much of the first eighteen months of his life in the hospital, took his first camping trip. He discovered a nest of duck eggs at the edge of the campsite. By the end of the trip, he was able to watch the baby ducklings hatch. His excitement knew no limits. The boy was able to go on that trip because of the wonderful medical care he had received.

At this point in the story, imagine that the trainer thanks the participants for all that they do and asks them to remember how much of a difference they make.

Encourage

Stories can also be used to encourage participants to demonstrate behaviors or take some sort of action they might otherwise not take. In this way, the stories have a motivating effect on behavior. It could be a story about an individual who has overcome adversities similar to what participants are experiencing. Or the story might be one that offers realistic ways to approach a situation that is uncomfortable, such as confronting a colleague on a sensitive issue.

Explore

Stories whose purpose is to explore a topic, concept, or behavior in more depth serve to enhance or expand on knowledge participants already have. These types of stories may pick up on a nuance in a situation or explore it from a different angle. Consider the following story that might be told in an advanced coaching workshop: A new manager inherits a long-term employee with a history of significant performance problems. Unfortunately, the prior manager failed to coach this employee or document her poor performance. The employee has recently developed a serious health issue and is now claiming that as the reason for her work problems. After relaying this story, the trainer could have participants identify actions the new manager needs to take as well as actions the prior manager could have taken to prevent the situation from occurring. From there, the trainer might follow up with a discussion on implications for effective coaching within the organization.

Evoke

Finally, there are some stories that, when told, immediately evoke a response from trainees. These stories are wonderful lead-ins to large- and small-group discussions. Chances are this type of story also engages the emotions of the listener. For stories like these, it is advantageous to have participants put themselves in the shoes of the person who is having the "experience." For example, imagine being the daughter whose father has become gravely ill and is in the intensive care unit of a local hospital. You arrive at the hospital to visit your father and, on the elevator ride to his room, overhear two nurses talking about that "new case" in ICU, whom you assume to be your father. Apparently, the attending physician is going to have to break some tough news to the family. The nurses proceed to outline the issue in general terms as you continue to listen. No doubt, when the trainer tells this story, the participants will have a strong negative reaction. This energy can be used to fuel a discussion on what the participants would have done in the situation and what the nurses might do if confronted. This might also lead to a discussion of times that trainees have been embarrassed by some action they took and what they did to recover.

WHAT MAKES A STORY EFFECTIVE

It Is Memorable

Great stories are, first and foremost, memorable. What makes them memorable is that they engage both the heart and the intellect of listeners and create a visual image and/or short movie in the mind's eye. This often is accomplished through highly descriptive words and phrases and through the use of gestures, facial expressions, and vocal intonations on the part of the storyteller. Picture listening to a mountain climber who has been to the top of Mount Everest recount a portion of the climb that was grueling at the same time he is lying on the floor going through the same physical motions, with the same energy and the same emotional state that he experienced while on the mountainside. As a result, those who are present in the room vicariously become engaged in the story.

It Is Universal

Great stories are universal in nature. Each person who hears them can relate to what is being told. In addition, they are told in a manner that makes them relevant to that specific audience. The trainer might alter the level of language and the words that are used, perhaps using colloquialisms, to fit the demographics of the group. To this end, the same story can be told from different perspectives, depending on who is listening to it. Let's take a customer service story where, in a retail setting, the checkout clerk decides to uphold a company policy with a customer, which results in the customer being treated poorly. It could be told from the perspective of the employee to a group of managers who are responsible for policies that might conflict with providing good customer service. Then again, it could be presented from the perspective of the customer to a group of employees who are going through customer service training. In this scenario, employees could be asked what choice they would have made and why, which then could lead into a discussion of implications within their own jobs.

It Brings Realization

Great stories conclude with a compelling point or "aha" for the listener. Thus, they may motivate trainees in the direction of a particular action or set of behaviors or cause a shift in thinking or attitude. They may also bring about an increased level of sensitivity or appreciation for a situation that was previously misunderstood. For example, a major corporation in the chemical industry holds as one of its values the safety of its employees. During a new-employee orientation session, a participant raises a question about the stringency of the organization's safety policies, which she sees as unnecessary. The trainer relates a story about the inception of the company, the original purpose of which was to produce ammunition during the Civil War—a potentially catastrophic situation if not handled correctly. What the story points out is that the safety policies are not arbitrary—that they are an integral part of respecting the health and welfare of all who pass through the company's doors. This story grounds the current situation in the organization's history and provides a context for appreciating the care that the organization affords to its employees.

It Is Practiced

For a story to be truly powerful, it must be told in an effective manner (that is, with attention to facial expressions, eye contact, vocal inflections and intonations, body language, and the use of pauses) and at the appropriate point in the training session. In addition, it has to be long enough to make its point but not so long that listeners lose interest. All three of these items point to the importance of practicing telling stories out loud to others to gauge their reactions.

WHERE TO FIND STORIES TO USE IN TRAINING

Your Own Experiences

Stories are all around us. The easiest place to find them is within our own life experiences. Consider keeping a personal journal and logging situations in it or recording items on index cards, in your daily planner, or on Post-it Notes so that you are able to remember the details. These situations may be portions of conversations with family members or significant others, observations of children or pets, and positive or negative experiences you encounter throughout the day at work and other places. They might also include your experiences at special events, such as holiday gatherings, birthday parties, anniversaries, graduations, and the like. Often, these gatherings are places where others recount stories and tales from the past. Your own thoughts, insights, hopes and fears, dreams, and images are also wonderful sources of inspiration for creating stories.

Friends and Colleagues

Friends and colleagues can be great resources for stories. They may tell you about situations they or others have experienced or send you emails that trigger a story line. Recently, one of the authors received a series of daily emails from a colleague who was traveling on business through Bulgaria and Macedonia. Not only did these notes detail her travel and work experiences, but they also contained her observations and the stories she told her students. One email spoke to how she taught business planning by referencing different ways people obtain directions when they are seeking out a new location; another, entitled "The Thirteenth Fairy," explained how a fairy tale was related to a dinner meeting she attended. Both of these are examples of wonderful stories that can be used in specific types of training sessions. They can be saved in electronic files for future reference or printed and logged by topic.

Consider querying friends and colleagues for stories on particular topics. For example, let's say you have been asked to give a short presentation on "schmoozing" to a group of attorneys who are going to be entertaining a large group of clients at a company-wide social event. Email communication is an easy-to-use medium to send out notes to others asking for their most memorable or embarrassing "schmoozing" moments. Their responses can form the basis for determining specific topics to be included in the talk as well as provide examples of situations that stress key points.

Organizations and Professional Associations

Other places to find stories include community, civic, and religious organizations and professional associations on a local and national level. People you meet or overhear on bus, train, or airplane trips may have interesting life stories to share as well.

The Media

Print media—newspapers, magazines, industry trade journals, and the like—include a wealth of possibilities. Cut stories out and save them by topic area. If the story is one that is found online or is sent by email, keep electronic files organized either by topic or by relevant workshop. Radio talk shows and television news programs are another source. Because of their real-time nature, it is important to record notes immediately in order to recall facts and details accurately.

HOW TO USE STORIES IN TRAINING

Stories can be used to shape the design of a particular training session. To this end, they can become the focal point for the topic, as described earlier in the example about "schmoozing." In addition, they can be used:

- To introduce or wrap up a topic;
- To kick off a small-group activity or large-group discussion;
- To form the basis for a case study; or
- To transition between topics or key points.

More often, stories are inserted into training materials after the initial design of the workshop or session. When used in this manner, they can serve to enhance or elaborate on the content by:

- Providing an example of right versus wrong, good versus bad;
- Making a concept, theory, or principle more tangible;
- Detailing what can occur if a particular action does or does not take place;
- Moving people to take action;
- Delineating the steps that can or should (or should not) be taken if a specific situation occurs; or
- Refocusing or reframing a situation.

Here is an example of a story that can be used in a variety of ways. Consider the scenario where a large retail home-improvement chain operation enters a small town that currently has a similar, locally owned and operated store. While this new competitive situation may appear negative because it may put a local store out of business, it also has benefits associated with it. This challenge might cause the local retailer to find unique ways of providing value, such as through exceptional customer service. In a training setting where this story illustrates a situation the organization anticipates in the near future, the main purpose of the story could be tasking participants with brainstorming creative options for the local storeowner. It can then lead to options the organization and its employees could engage in within their own work situations. In addition, the story could serve to make the concept of creating value more concrete.

Stories grounded in the content of a training session need to be set up through an introduction and debriefed afterward. The set-up may include contextual information, such as when the story occurred, the geographic location, who was present, and its historical significance, as well as how the story was obtained. Since the story itself is used to make a point or raise an issue, the debriefing may be a large-group discussion, a small-group activity, or an exercise involving individual reflection.

Thought-provoking questions are a key technique for debriefing stories. Think about asking questions similar to the following:

- "What do you think she felt at this point?"
- "What would you do in this situation?"
- "What's at stake here?"
- "What are the implications for the company?"
- "How does this apply to your work setting?"

Don't assume that all participants have reached the same conclusion as a result of hearing the story. Some trainers poll their groups to check reactions before highlighting key learning points. The amount of reflection the story elicits is in direct proportion to the amount of time spent debriefing it.

Not all stories need to be planned, of course. You might spontaneously tell a story as a result of a question or comment or in reaction to what is happening in the room. In addition, participants can be asked to tell their own stories or they may volunteer to share them during the course of the session. For example, within a workshop that is addressing customer service, an activity could be designed to have participants provide a story of the best (or worst) service they have ever received. From here, they could outline what made that experience exceptional (or a disaster). From these points, the group can determine what sorts of behaviors are appropriate and inappropriate when working with their own customers. The benefit of participant-generated stories is that they have a vested interest. From the trainer's perspective, this is also an excellent way to pick up more stories for use in other training situations.

Be willing to debrief a participant's own story. It will provide additional learning for the group and acknowledge the trainee who took the risk to share a personal situation. Consider asking: "What was most difficult about that for you?" or "What did you learn from that experience?"

CONCLUSION

Stories are an integral part of the fabric of our lives and our work. Getting the most from them during training involves knowing the audience, ensuring the story is relevant, using a variety of sources and types of stories, and practice, practice, practice. Bring your own genuine enthusiasm to the telling of the story and you will carry your participants along with you. To avoid getting stale, incorporate new stories into your standard program topics. In addition to using stories in training programs, you might also use stories in one-on-one coaching, on sales calls, and with employees and co-workers during meetings. Regardless of how they are used, stories are a powerful tool for enhancing learning.

Lori L. Silverman is the co-author of Critical SHIFT: The Future of Quality in Organizational Performance *and the owner of Partners for Progress, a management consulting firm specializing in organizational change, strategic manage-*

ment, and performance improvement. Ms. Silverman holds a master's degree in counseling and guidance from the University of Wisconsin-Madison and an MBA from Edgewood College, Madison, Wisconsin. She is the co-author of a forthcoming Jossey-Bass/Pfeiffer book on storytelling in training.

Mary B. Wacker *is the president of M.B. Wacker Associates, a firm specializing in team building, leadership development, and customer service systems. She is the author of numerous manuals and training kits, including one on leading virtual teams. Ms. Wacker is a past president of the ASTD Southeastern Wisconsin Chapter and holds a master's degree in educational psychology from the University of Wisconsin-Milwaukee. She is the co-author of a forthcoming Jossey-Bass/Pfeiffer book on storytelling in training.*

Delivering Effective Presentations: A Review of Techniques for Enhancing Audience Involvement

Ira J. Morrow

Abstract: This paper examines various technology-independent techniques for helping presenters to be more audience-focused and to increase the impact and persuasiveness of oral presentations by enhancing the audience's involvement in the presentation. The author discusses several techniques to enhance the impact and interest of presentations. Attention is given to those steps that can be taken to heighten the audience's sense of involvement and participation. The rationale underlying the use of each technique is explained, and examples of the techniques are provided.

Effectiveness as a communicator is generally considered to be a critical skill for success as a manager, and studies that have examined how supervisors, managers, and senior-level executives actually spend their time universally support the finding that managers are essentially communicators.

One major component of being an effective communicator is one's ability, when called for, to deliver informative, interesting, and persuasive presentations to an audience. This type of communication typically becomes more important as one rises through the managerial ranks in an organization. However, presenters may sometimes find to their surprise and disappointment that their carefully prepared presentations have fallen short of the intended goal and have not had the desired impact on their audience. Often, this is due to the fact that presenters have carefully prepared their presentations in terms of the necessary background research, technical preparation, and content, but have forgotten to be adequately audience-focused. Presenters sometimes err in believing that if they distribute outlines or other handouts or if they make use of audiovisual technology to show either traditional overhead slides or more contemporary computer-mediated slides, such as is possible with PowerPoint, that they have done as much as is necessary to enhance audience involvement in their presentations. However, such audiovisual assistance often just makes it easier for the audience to follow what the speaker is saying. Some audience members may find the material being presented in this manner more interesting than they otherwise would.

However, in and of itself, the use of technology does not necessarily make presentations more involving or even more interesting for the audience. First of all, the use of such technologies has become so commonplace and taken for granted that it does not necessarily help get the attention or involvement of audience members. Secondly, slides presented with such technologies may still be poorly prepared. A common mistake, for example, is to show too much information on one's slides. These technologies can often make it just as likely to lose one's audience as to win them over.

It's Best to Ask

The easiest way to enhance audience involvement while delivering a presentation is simply to ask questions, not just to invite questions from the audience, but to throw questions at the audience. There are a number of ways to do this effectively, and these are discussed in increasing order of sophistication.

Asking Rhetorical Questions

It is often helpful for the speaker to ask rhetorical questions when raising or illustrating a point. There is something powerful and involving when a point is made in the form of a question, rather than as a declarative statement, even when no answer is actually being solicited from the audience. For example, let's assume that the topic under discussion is the stresses and hassles associated with commuting to work. The presenter could begin with a rhetorical question such as, "Have any of you ever had a frustrating morning like I recently had?" followed by the example. Certainly, if the example that follows is well-chosen and crafted, many members of the audience will be able to relate to certain parts of it and reject others. In effect, they are silently answering the rhetorical question by saying to themselves something like, "Yes, something just like that happened to me" or "No, I thought my commute to work was awful, but his is much worse than mine." The point is that your audience becomes more attentive and involved with the topic when you use rhetorical questions.

Asking Real Questions

Of course, there is no reason to limit one's use of questions to rhetorical questions. If rhetorical questions help to involve your audience, asking actual questions helps to do this even more effectively. There are a number of ways to ask actual questions. One easy technique is to ask your audience for a show of hands in response to questions that typically begin with phrases such as, "Who here feels that. . . ?" or "Who believes that. . . ?" or "Who wants to. . . ?" or "How many of you have or are. . . ?" or "How many of you agree that. . . ?" One can then count the hands corresponding to each category of answer, or the audience can roughly judge the count for themselves. The main reasons for asking these types of questions is to relate the general topic to the audience's own experience or views and to get a feel for how the audience stands on the issues at hand. A topic becomes less abstract and more relevant and meaningful for an audience when the presenter relates the topic to their experiences or solicits their views.

Presenters should make every effort, however, to vary the kinds of questions they ask. For example, overuse of simple questions requiring merely a yes/no or show-of-hands response is likely to wear thin. Often, the most interesting and provocative questions are open-ended questions that ask people to think about something and to respond in their own words. These are far more likely to encourage a true back-and-forth discussion between members of the audience. The ultimate indication that an audience is involved in a presentation is when they are discussing the issues on their own so that the presenter does not even have to say anything for a while. Of course, the presenter should never abandon his or her role as the leader and the controller of the presentation. If the discussion begins to get out-of-hand, off-the-track, or too time-consuming, the presenter will have to reassert control and end the discussion or redirect it with another provocative question.

Questioning Selected Audience Members

Another way to handle asking questions is to select certain individuals from the audience to respond to your question. The key here is that both the person being picked to respond and the other members of the audience who are witnessing this become more involved. Asking questions of specific individuals can bring out more information after you have asked a question of the entire audience with a request for a show of hands. For example, if you have just asked how many audience members have participated in a diversity workshop, you could then ask a follow-up question of one or more of the people who indicated that they have. A questions such as, "Could you tell us what was discussed at this workshop?" might be appropriate. Once other audience members hear what was said, they are likely to add to the discussion, describing both similar and different experiences. The main things to be cautious about when asking questions of particular individuals is not to ask anything that might be embarrassing to the respondent in any way and not to ask a question that is too difficult to answer.

Using Questions in Writing

A very effective way to ask questions of an audience is to do so in writing prior to the actual presentation. The presenter then prepares an analysis of the audience's data and uses the presentation session to provide the audience with the survey results. The rationale for this technique is that a more extensive set of questions can be asked than might otherwise be possible, the questions can be more comprehensive and systematic, and the data can be analyzed in greater depth than is possible by counting a show of hands. At the very least, the percentage of the audience indicating one response or another can be calculated and pie charts or bar graphs may be prepared.

Another rationale for gathering data from one's audience in this manner is that it allows the presenter to provide information to the audience that they are most likely to be interested in, namely information about themselves. Being audience-focused means realizing that audiences are egocentric and interested in learning more about themselves. Providing information to the audience about their own experiences, views, opinions, and feelings is interesting to them in and of itself. Moreover, this interest can be augmented by using data from the audience in contrast to data from society in general. For example, the presenter might report that, "Whereas X percent of working women were reported in a recent survey to be smokers, in this audience, only Y percent are." In order to utilize this technique, the presenter needs to know in advance who will be attending and how to contact the attendees.

Presenters should also make certain that the questionnaire they are planning to use contains clear, specific, and unambiguous questions, instructions, and ways to respond. Effective survey or questionnaire construction calls for certain skills and techniques, but a detailed discussion of these matters is beyond the scope of this paper. (For more information on questionnaire construction, see Westgaard, 1999.)

THE GREAT DEBATE

If the topic under discussion is a controversial one with two or more sides or points of view, the presenter could use a debate format to enhance involvement and participation. The presenter could use one of several techniques. One is to present one point of view on the controversial issue and then, at several strategic points, to stop and ask the audience for an opposing argument or point of view. To help keep the audience alert, the presenter could alternate the point of view that he or she presents, sometimes the pro and sometimes the con, and then ask the audience for the opposing viewpoint.

An alternate technique is to divide the audience into two teams, one to support and argue the pro side of the issue and the other the con side. The presenter would merely present the relevant issues related to the topic and at certain appropriate points stop and ask each of the opposing teams for its arguments. To make things even more interesting, a third group of audience members could be assigned to play the role of a panel of judges. They would not take part in the actual debate, but would render their judgment as to which of the two sides prevailed. The presenter could provide the panel of judges with scoring instructions, a scoring sheet, or a rating key in order to play the role as objectively and systematically as possible.

THE PLAY'S THE THING

Using Skits

Depending on the issue or topic, a powerful technique for enhancing audience involvement is to act something out. Clearly, certain topics or issues may lend themselves more readily to this dramatic treatment than others. For example, when delivering a presentation on such issues as "dealing with difficult employees," "managing your boss," "effective networking techniques," "dealing with discipline problems at the workplace," "effective negotiating strategies," or "providing performance feedback," one could make a strong case for the use of skits to demonstrate effective or ineffective techniques.

Skits might require more than one participant, so in many cases this technique could not be used by a solo presenter unless a volunteer from the audience took one of the roles. In this case, the skit could be planned in advance of the presentation or at the start, depending on whether one desires to prepare the volunteer to play the role in a certain manner or to just let the volunteer wing it.

The use of a volunteer in conjunction with the use of a dramatic skit is likely to be quite stimulating and involving for an audience. Not only is the power of drama utilized, but the audience can further identify with one of their own. Audience members are likely to feel a combination of relief that they are not up there, envy because they are not, and curiosity about how well the volunteer will perform. They may wonder, "What will he say next?" or "How would I have handled that?"

Even more benefit can be derived from the use of skits by combining them with the use of questions. At appropriate points, such as at the conclusion of a scene or perhaps at the conclusion of the skit, the audience could be asked such questions as, "What did the manager do that was effective/ineffective?" "What did the subordinate do that was effective/ineffective?" "What could have been done to make that meeting more productive?" "What important concepts that we mentioned earlier did you notice during the skit?"

or "What should the boss do next?" Between watching the skit and responding to questions, the audience is likely to become highly involved.

Using Cases and Exercises

Presenters can quickly involve their audience by distributing an appropriate case or exercise that pertains to the topic. Depending on time available, a case could be distributed for reading and analysis in advance of the presentation, allowing for the use of a lengthier case, or at the start or conclusion of the presentation, when a shorter case would probably be better. The presenter could lead a discussion of the case after it is read and thought about by the individuals in the audience or after subgroups from the audience review and discuss the case among themselves. The case could be used to initiate further treatment of the topic during the rest of the presentation or to summarize and review key points raised earlier. It is quite conceivable that one's entire presentation on a topic could be based on leading the audience through a discussion of a case with the use of thought-provoking, open-ended questions.

Similarly, either an individual exercise, such as a quiz, problem, or inventory, or a group-based activity, such as a conflict-resolution or negotiation activity, can be distributed to an audience at an appropriate time to illustrate concepts or procedures that will be discussed later or that were previously discussed. Audience members who participate in such activities will be interested in learning about the quality of their own or their group's analysis of a case or performance during a role play. They can learn about this from a presentation. Alternately, if such activities are used to conclude the session, this provides audience members with an opportunity to immediately apply the lessons, procedures, or concepts back on the job. In either case, heightened audience involvement and interest are likely.

CONCLUSION

The author has presented and discussed the use of several techniques for enhancing the quality and impact of presentations delivered before an audience. Emphasis has been given to techniques that are likely to heighten an audience's sense of involvement and participation. The procedures discussed result in a win-win outcome for the presenter and for the audience. Presenters will find that presentations can actually be enjoyable, rather than a dreaded and stressful chore. They will be gratified by the positive reactions and high energy level found in the audience. Audiences in turn will feel that the presentations are more interesting, exciting, and personally relevant. They are likely to appreciate the opportunity to become active and involved, rather than to sit passively and be lectured to. They will appreciate that the presenter is more audience-focused.

Reference

Westgaard, O. (1999). *Tests that work: Designing and delivering fair and practical measurement tools in the workplace.* San Francisco, CA: Jossey-Bass/Pfeiffer.

Ira J. Morrow has a Ph.D. degree in industrial-organizational psychology from New York University. He is currently associate professor of management at Pace University, working with M.B.A. students from around the world as part of a faculty team that designed and implemented a two-semester, skills- and theory-oriented graduate management course. He consults extensively in the field of human resources, with an emphasis on management assessment.

Designing Curricula for Learning Environments: Using a Facilitative Teaching Approach to Empower Learners

Sharon Drew Morgen

Abstract: In this article, the author differentiates between the traditional term "training environment" and the newer term "learning environment." The training environment is based on the traditional method of trainers imparting information to learners. The learning environment is derived from a different basis, that trainers should teach learners how to learn. The author explains how to use this method to help learners recognize and break down beliefs that are impeding effective learning. The author makes the point that once learners recognize an incongruity between their beliefs and actions, they are now open, even anxious, to learn new skills and behaviors that are in alignment with their beliefs.

Methods shift over time, but the trainer's essential job remains: to create change. Over time, we trainers have used various methodologies with differing beliefs as to the most effective approaches. We've used workbooks and exercises, repetition and experience, audio and video, interactive and solitary, sitting in classrooms and swinging from ropes. For as long as we can remember, we have trained by imparting information and having students learn it.

More recently, the term "learning environment" has taken its place in the field of training. Trainers define this in different ways, but it's generally taken to mean *the creation of an environment in which students learn by doing*—internal to external—rather than by having information given to them—external to internal.

To date, learning environments have been designed around exercises and role plays, activities and case studies, group discussions and projects—all created to give participants the experience of the topic. A sales course, for example, might include role plays to practice the different types of pitches being presented. Team building might include having team members define a problem and work together to solve it—and then breaking down the experience so that participants can replicate it in their actual work environment. Trainers often provide participants with follow-up work or activities to take back to their jobs to further integrate the learning.

This type of experiential training is based on the presentation of behavioral material at a skill level in order (one hopes) to have the new approaches and information touch the participants' at the belief level. We do this because we know participants will be unwilling to change their behavior unless and until the behavior becomes a part of their value and belief systems.

Let's use an example of teaching an information-gathering program to take a look at how this model of training is carried out.

Information-gathering skills are typically taught by having the trainer present the different types of questioning strategies that he or she believes to be the most effective (and the choice is quite subjective, leading to different models containing different sets of strategies with different aggregates of information, depending on the trainer). Therefore, Step 1 would be in the hands of the trainer: He or she would research the different types of questioning strategies and design a presentation based on the perceived needs of the clients.

Step 2 involves the trainer choosing or creating experiential models—such as case studies or role plays—that allow the participants to familiarize themselves with the information the trainer has chosen to promote. The results are then discussed in small groups, in which participants share, expand on, and explain their choices.

In Step 3, the group members take the responsibility for teaching one another the skills they've learned.

Step 4 brings the findings and learnings to a large-group discussion to install and expand the learning from the individual and small-group level. By this time, the participants should have successfully learned the questioning skills the trainer chose for them to learn and be able to take some of the new information or skills back to the workplace.

START WITH A BELIEF CHANGE

The Process

Another way to approach the issue of effecting permanent behavioral change is to start with a belief change, find the skills the participants already possess, add additional skills and information as necessary, and leave the behavioral change to the individual. The idea is

1. To gain group and individual agreement as to the beliefs the participants wish to model in the area of the subject taught;

2. To have participants evoke a memory of a skills-based experience in alignment with the subject taught;

3. To have participants examine the values and beliefs the experience brings forth and the commensurate skills needed for executing the experience;

4. To observe what personal behaviors best manifest the skills;

5. To compare the differences between the skills used during effective execution and those used during ineffective experiences;

6. To install conscious triggers that make the appropriate behaviors easy to choose at any point during an interaction; and

7. To have trainers replace skill and information deficiencies with necessary knowledge and expertise.

This process differs markedly from traditional methods in that participants are, in effect, being taught how to learn. The primary goal is to help learners to examine their belief systems to discover how those beliefs may assist or impede learning. Next, skills are reviewed in light of these beliefs. Most people assume their skills support their beliefs and judge themselves to be incongruent if they do not. When they discover disparities between the beliefs they hold and the operating skills they use, they are eager to self-correct. Thus, the trainer's job becomes one of facilitating the learning, rather than finding ways to instill information.

The Learning System

Once a decision is taken to create training based on learning through (1) recognizing beliefs, (2) transferring skills, and (3) choosing appropriate or effective behaviors, the learning system has to be designed.

First, a list of beliefs must be agreed on by the trainers and course designers. To continue with the previous example of creating a program to teach how to gather information, let's say that one of the beliefs is that people must take responsibility for shared communication. The course designers might use the following questions to address this issue:

- Do we want people to collaborate? What are the beliefs we hold around that?

- Do we want people to create a win-win environment with their clients? What are our beliefs around this?

- What would we gain by having our staff work in agreement with clients?

Sometimes managers want their people to learn skills that are not supported by the work environment. Thus, no matter how good the training, the participants will find it difficult to receive support at work for the continued use of any new skill sets. Although trainers are not typically in a position to impact the work environment, they can address this issue by asking participants near the end of the session: "What do you need to know or do differently to move forward with this learning in your current environment?" This question gives the participants an opportunity to consider how their new skills and behaviors will be perceived in their workplaces and challenges them to immediately put their new learnings to work to solve this problem.

Once the beliefs are agreed on, exercises need to be designed to help participants discover the skills that best support them, that is, to allow participants to access their inherent skills.

The main tool used in this approach is questioning. Through facilitative questions, we can access already existing information and lead the participants to the place where their own answers lie. This is the easiest way to support learning: Have people access their existing patterns, noting what works and what does not work, and let them choose consciously to support their own successful patterns and drop their unsuccessful ones. We are thus helping the participants set up a communication between their conscious and unconscious behaviors and patterns, thereby giving them choices around the best behaviors to use in any situation.

The technique involves using questions in a certain pattern: What does it look/sound/act/feel like when the behavior is effective? What does it look/sound/act/feel like when it's ineffective? This information can be gathered in several ways:

- Mental imaging can create pictures that most people can access and compare;

- Questionnaires designed by the curriculum designer can be self-administered;

- Dyad-based exercises can facilitate understanding one another; and

- Group-based exercises can require that each participant take responsibility for practicing one concept, thereby learning one piece of a puzzle and then sharing their learning.

A word of caution here. While trainers love to impart information, it's important to note that too much information offered prior to an exercise will bias the end result. Give the directions as to how to proceed in the exercise, find out how it turned out, and then put the information together with a pre-arranged lecture on the topic *after the participants have come to their own conclusions.* Then people can assess their own learning, where it fits into the overall course design and where it does not, and what they wish to use to supplement their already existing skills.

An Example

Let's illustrate this new model using our example of an information-gathering skills learning experience. In the new approach, the trainer or curriculum designer would begin by assuming the participants were capable of asking the most effective questions for any situation but did not always know how or why or when to ask. In Step 1, the curriculum designer and trainer would use their expertise to list a set of operating beliefs that would form a foundation for the program. In other words, they would determine what they thought participants needed to believe in order to facilitate learning. In the case of information gathering, for example, beliefs might include the following: "It is the responsibility of the information gatherer to facilitate an environment of discovery" or "Whoever wants to get something from an interaction is responsible for creating the communication environment in which to have his or her needs met."

The curriculum designer and trainer then create the course content. They assume that the learners have the skills with which to utilize any new information as well as those required to cull existing information and belief sets from their brain/thought processes.

The beliefs are brought to the participants. They are asked to agree with these beliefs or at least to accept them and be willing to take them on as their own over the time period of the program. Given these are the beliefs that the trainer has chosen, participants may not agree right away and may need to see in action just how the beliefs can support a skill set within their own behaviors.

In Step 2, participants are led through an exercise in which they recollect a previous time or times they used information-gathering skills. The trainer might tell the participants the following: "Think of two situations in which you were helping someone solve a problem—one in which you were successful and one in which you were not." The trainer then asks the participants to think about the components of each interaction, that is, what physical, mental, and spiritual behaviors either aided or impeded their success.

In Step 3, participants must deeply examine their experiences, with questions and support from the trainer, to discover the conscious or unconscious beliefs they have in place. Appropriate questions might include the following:

- What were the differences between the two experiences in terms of the beliefs you operated from? The goals you entered with? The outcomes?
- How did you decide which skill set to bring forth? (This decision is always based on beliefs.)
- What choice points did you notice during each interaction?
- What beliefs did you use to make each choice?

In Step 4, ask participants to consider their behaviors: "What were the differences, the similarities? What worked best? How did you do that? What worked less effectively? How did you do that?"

The 2003 Annual: Volume 1, Training/© *2003 John Wiley & Sons, Inc.*

In Step 5, ask participants to examine their skills: "What skills did you use in each experience? Listening? Questioning? Use of physiological options, such as voice, body language, or movement?"

In Step 6, participants develop triggers to help them recognize choice points about behaviors. The trainer should give the following instructions: "Go back through each experience. Notice the differences in your body stress. Stress is frequently a sign that your behaviors are not aligned with your beliefs. Go into the less effective experience, find the stress point(s), and decide what color it is. This color then becomes a trigger for you, letting you know that you've reached a point of dissonance and that you need to make a choice about your behavior."

The participants would be led through the workings of the exercise to understand that how they learned externally through the course—through the trainer's teaching and modeling of the questioning process—is the exact same model they must use internally to promote effective behaviors.

In Step 7, the trainer would work with the large group and request random input to help the participants understand:

- How questioning skills support the stated beliefs;

- What specific skills are already in place;

- Which skills work well, which do not;

- What additional behaviors are needed to improve questioning skills to enhance the information-gathering process; and

- How it felt to have the training process model the internal process.

The Results

Through this approach, once participants understand the benefits of the operating beliefs and can accept them into their own belief systems, they are usually willing to take on new behaviors and thus add to the skills they already have in place. They are also willing to learn any additional skills that would help their effectiveness, as these were already demonstrated to them during the exercise and found to be beneficial. The exercise would have brought the participants to the learning by:

- Having them consciously discern what they already knew; and

- Having them understand what they still needed to learn.

This makes the job of the trainer one of a learning facilitator. It's a bit like a Michelangelo chipping away at the stone and freeing up the figure, rather than a painter creating a figure on canvas where none existed before. This strategy solves many problems at once:

1. Resistance to learning is minimized because participants want to learn the skills to enhance their beliefs.

2. Behavioral integration doesn't have to be forced, as it is already within the person's system and needs only to be chosen, not relearned.

3. Follow-up is easy, as participants already have the skill sets and need only to use them at appropriate times, rather than having to learn new skills.

ALTERNATE THE APPROACHES

Because so much mental energy is required from the participants to discover their own patterns, they tire easily. Make sure there is an unstructured trainer-led discussion after each exercise and/or following each break. After a substantial break, such as lunch or the period in between multi-day sessions, the recommended discussion time is ninety minutes. The time to allot after exercises varies depending on the length of the exercise. For example, you might follow a one-hour exercise with a twenty-minute discussion or a two-hour exercise with a thirty-minute discussion. The biggest piece of the training goes on internally and requires the discussion and integration time. While this is a rather right-brained concept, it is imperative to process it well, or the participants' inherent confusion can result in an inordinate amount of discomfort, making it impossible for them to continue learning.

Make sure to alternate the types of learning activities, the number of people in each experience, and the amount of time the participant has at any moment to work internally.

Try to have one block of time open to lecture on the topic overview somewhere in the middle of the program, thereby giving participants time to let off some steam, get out of the limelight, kick back and relax, and ultimately to have the material being presented integrate with what they are learning internally. Do not put this lecture time at the beginning of the program, as it will presuppose what the participants will attend to it (either positively or negatively). Also, since the trainer is an automatic authority figure, this position must be used only when the participants already know what they know and how they do what they do. If the lecture comes before participants are aware of their unconscious behavior patterns, they will be picking and choosing what pieces they will listen to according to inaccurate notions about their skill sets and will not use the information well.

CONCLUSION

Facilitative teaching approaches are extremely powerful for ensuring that behavioral changes are integrated on a permanent basis because the participants' belief systems support the change. Not only do they learn around the particular course content, but they also have a system in place—through the internal learning models the training uses—that they can use to self-teach any future concepts.

The technique also respects and empowers the individual learner, giving the trainer less to do around imparting information and more to do around supporting individuals to be all they can be.

Sharon Drew Morgen *is the author of* The New York Times *bestseller,* Selling with Integrity: Sales on the Line, *and over one hundred articles on new paradigm sales and decision making. She develops decision-making systems that help people facilitate collaborative environments, such as buyer/seller, teacher/learner, and partnership relationships. With such clients as Intuit, IBM, and KPMG, Ms. Morgen has broadened the sales paradigm to include truly collaborative communication approaches and has created a unique type of question that supports learning and discovery.*

WHY LEARNING GAMES ARE IMPORTANT AND HOW TO CREATE YOUR OWN GAMES

Carolyn Nilson

Abstract: Games for learning have been a popular presence in training rooms for several decades. Professional book catalogs are full of learning games of various sorts, reflecting changes in emphasis to mirror current training trends. Games workshops, online templates and shells, board games, activity books, e-learning exercises, and survivor games have all entered the field in recent years. Games seem to be a useful training device with considerable staying power.

This article describes some of the reasons why games can be a trainer's best friend and how one can create learning games. This article is based on a solid foundation of thinking in systems and learning theory, but the academic jargon has been removed. From the point of view of an experience-based learner, the author illustrates why and how to make up your own games.

The operative word at the dawn of the millennium is *knowledge*. Everybody wants it, seeks it, values it, tries to categorize and codify it, build it, and share it. We also need both to maximize it and to minimize it. Our technologies demand immersion and breadth at the same time they allow and encourage us to focus on only what's relevant and to screen out what is not. As thinking beings, we have enormous knowledge challenges.

We also have expectations about what work should be. We want meaningful work, work that makes the most of a full range of diversity within the workforce, work that honors the increasingly more prevalent differences among us, and work that brings out the best of collaborative relationships within work groups. We want work that matters to us as individuals and that is connected to the success of others.

We also have seen big changes in the structures and supports of corporate America, and these changes are making a difference in how workplace learning is thought about and placed within companies. Trainers are alive with possibilities for designs for learning and for ways to convey the message of training experiences. Design and delivery are challenged to be flexible and on target.

Numerous important ideas in figuring out how people learn have been part of our dialogue for the last decade. Trainers have been immersed in learning styles, multiple intelligences, emotional intelligence, situated learning, action/reflection learning, on-the-job learning, coaching and mentoring, learning online, and in general a challenge to facilitate learning from one's own work in a self-directed way. Trainers are being asked to help individuals be all they can be on the job, through a variety of formal and informal learning setups.

Games are one kind of learning aid that trainers can devise to bring learners to the brink of new discovery, to help them experience a different way of learning, to practice enhanced communication, to take an objective perspective on a business problem, to see important concepts in a new light, and to get creative juices flowing. Games for learning can be useful in helping employees cope with tough situations as well as help them take charge of workplace change. Games can help people overcome inertia and stretch their ways of thinking.

The bottom line is that employees are required to be creative, to develop their skills of problem solving, and to find ways to work with others for both individual and mutual benefit. Creating games from the essence of work is a serious endeavor whose aim is to enable employees to function in today's complex workplace. To this end, games are useful in helping people organize and manage knowledge, see commonality through differences, and build mental and emotional flexibility.

KNOWLEDGE

How to Think About It

Some people believe that learning experiences have to be designed in order for efficient learning to take place, whereas others think that the only learning worth having is embedded in the trials and errors of experience. The images that come to mind are of the trainer as instructional designer or the trainer as facilitator. The truth is that the same trainer on the job is called on to be both designer and facilitator, instructor, coach, and manager, too. Trainers have to think about a variety of ways to help people learn at work. Knowledge often is simply seen as the results of learning, and trainers are generally seen as the people who are responsible for making those results happen.

It's helpful, therefore, to think about the learning process as a key component of each person's ability to build and manage knowledge. People at work need to engage in many kinds of learning tasks, including recognizing patterns, making sense of lists and categories, pegging relationships correctly, finding the facts they need, and organizing their time productively. These are some of the essentials of being a good learner and are the kinds of things that responsible trainers need to figure out how to teach or facilitate as people build knowledge.

Sample Game-Building Strategies

Games are devices that support learning. Games that help people organize and manage knowledge come in many forms that mirror the structure or the challenge of the knowledge work that people must do. When you choose to use a game as a learning tool to help people gain knowledge, first pay attention to the structure of the work task that must be done. Ask yourself questions like the following:

1. What kinds of rules govern the work task? Trial and error? Working backward? Responding to cues? Networking?

2. What kinds of processes pertain to the task required?

- Classifying? Analyzing? Hypothesizing?

- Extrapolating? Mapping? Explaining?

3. What kinds of relationships are suggested by the work task? Relationships with information? with colleagues? with superiors? with customers? with data? with machines or tools?

After answering questions like these and figuring out what knowledge work means to an employee, choose characteristics that can become the foundation for a short exercise. Such an exercise becomes a game, in that the exercise mimics reality and has a purposeful design that enables learners to come to a better understanding and experience of the reality on which the game is based. The game is a learning-to-learn exercise complete in itself.

For example, here are a few characteristics of knowledge work that could become the foundation for a game or short exercise:

- The characteristic of definition: no one has yet defined the problem;

- The characteristic of consistency: measures of productivity seem inconsistent across functions;

- The characteristic of direction: old timers' views of work based on company history clash with newcomers' future visions; and

- The characteristic of alignment: the way work is actually being done is not in synch with corporate mission statements and departmental goals.

Typical Game Sources and Structures

Following are some typical sources and structures for knowledge-building games: lists, tables, models, graphs, plans, systems, timelines, networks, stories, webs, and illustrations.

DIFFERENCES AND COMMONALITIES

How to Think About It

One of the most important things about becoming and staying employed these days is to internalize the meanings of difference and commonality. The strong American economy and work ethic have been built on the development of the individual, with a track record of historical and legal support for individual differences. The responsibility pendulum has swung back and forth throughout workforce history regarding how much the individual is responsible for in terms of career building and accumulation of courses, certificates, CEUs, diplomas, degrees, and other qualifiers of employability value. At the start of this millennium, that pendulum is at the high point of individual responsibility for one's own learning. American workplaces clearly value individuals who can make a contribution to corporate success, and American workplaces are structured and accountable to provide equal opportunity for all workers.

Individualism and difference are closely linked. At the same time, we are building and rebuilding our workplaces around the idea of commonality—new ways of working online with globally scattered colleagues and customers, new mandates for group and team decision making and accountability, new visions created by giant mergers and blending of corporate cultures. Workers today need to know how to deal with difference and commonality. Games can help.

Sample Game-Building Strategies

Games to help people deal with both differences and commonalities often require the most difficult kind of cognitive and emotional learning, which is best characterized by a need to "restructure" one's customary ways of looking at things. Such restructuring almost always involves self-analysis of one's biases and preferences, introspection, a stretching to learn new emotional skills, personal risk taking, and new dimensions of personal awareness. Being comfortable and productive in common endeavors—from simply communicating across time zones and cultures to being successful in high-level teams—is a typical challenge for today's workers.

When you choose to use a game for learning to deal with difference and commonality, think first about defining the work relationships that give meaning to what is valued at work. Ask yourself questions like the following:

1. What are the real communication patterns at this workplace? What are the expectations? What gets rewarded?

2. What are the person-to-person behavioral goals? Are these realistic? What can be changed to make improvements in practice?

3. Are systems and networks in place or being planned so that common endeavors can be productive? What are the obstacles to their effectiveness?

After answering questions like these, think beyond them to attitudes and behaviors that can be shaped in order for progress to occur in these areas. Keep in mind the instructional goal of enabling a learner to restructure his or her way of thinking about difference and commonality. Trainers can make a difference here, but only to the extent that individuals are enabled and rewarded for changing their behavior. Learning in this arena is vastly different from knowledge-based learning and the tasks it embodies. Exercises and games that are appropriate here go beyond the typical knowledge-based game that seeks to identify, define, match, list, categorize, and explain. Games dealing with difference and commonality will not work if they stay within the realm of data and information. These games must be built around attitudinal and emotional centers, using a variety of situations that approximate the attitudinal and emotional requirements of valuing and managing differences and commonalities.

It is instructive to think about what some of these attitudinal and emotional centers might be and to think of situations that help employees to benefit from the kinds of learning that address these debilitating challenges:

- The challenge of inadequacy: facilitate brainstorming and other equalizing activities designed to value each person's contribution equally;

- The challenge of exclusion: conduct exercises and games that define expectations and measure "who speaks to whom" in a controlled environment; allow team members to come to their own conclusions and see what the problems are, aiming for maximum and deliberate participation from each person in the group; and

- The personal fear of job-related risk taking: create safe zones for trial and error, learning from mistakes as creative endeavor, and creating a laboratory environment; provide obvious management support for learning on the job—recognition, rewards, sharing results, encouraging communities of practice, providing collaborative spaces.

Typical Game Sources and Structures

There are some typical sources and structures for games and exercises to facilitate dealing with differences and commonalities. Realize that these sources and structures are loaded with emotional content and that the range of emotions must be considered in order for individuals to be enabled to restructure their ways of thinking. Fear, for example, includes a range from mild anxiety to horrific terror; sadness can include both self-pity and dejection imposed by actions of others. Devise games around these concepts: beliefs, learning styles, trust, honesty, multitasking, sensory awareness, authenticity, variety, assertiveness, and inclusiveness.

FLEXIBILITY

How to Think About It

Flexibility is an important characteristic of problem solvers, good decision makers, and leaders. Leaders know that they need followers and therefore must be in tune with the fringes as well as the core of their enterprises; good decision makers know that variety and range of input fosters better results; and problem solvers work best when many options are defined and considered. All of these require flexibility.

Students of problem solving like to subdivide the concept into various types of mental activity, such as breaking a problem into subparts, differentiating problem finding from solution finding, seeing the whole in the parts, applying rules of thumb, identifying and satisfying constraints, sampling, chunking, predicting, and taking short cuts. There are a wide variety of approaches to defining and explaining what problem solving is all about. Cognitive flexibility is at the heart of most of these approaches.

Capacity building, a related practical component of competence, is also at the heart of flexibility—people developing "know-how" as opposed to "know-what." Important new movements in educational psychology and how people learn emphasize the context of learning tasks, the situation in which learning demands are made, the role of an individual's working environment, and the intrinsic and cumulative value of experience. People need to be flexible and tuned in to their environment in the broadest sense, including recognizing that their own experiences have made an impact in their lives and on their capacity to be competent learners and workers.

Sample Game-Building Strategies

Games to build capacity for flexibility can be seen as the most directly relevant to today's demand for creative workers and problem solvers in all walks of life. Perhaps it's the speed and discontinuity of change today; perhaps it's the demographics that show how the workforce is changing; perhaps it's the reality that global influences are having an impact on us as individuals; perhaps it's the deluge of information available to us—perhaps it's all these plus more that push us into needing to become more flexible in our outlook and in the way we work.

When you choose a game to help employees develop flexibility, think about the processes and procedures work. Think about what kinds of problem solving each process requires and about what corporate supports, structures, and actions enhance or inhibit problem solving. Think about what personal characteristics enhance or inhibit flexibility. Then ask yourself these questions:

1. Are people solving the right problems? Do people think innovatively enough so that the real problems are defined and addressed?

2. What do employees have to do in order to increase their capacity for flexibility? Where are solutions to inflexibility to be found: in systems? in individuals? in organizational structures? in perceptions? in communications? in rewards? in punishments? in motivational factors?

3. Do work processes illustrate and support the company's vision of itself and its future?

Answers to these questions can provide some ideas about creating a game that addresses various issues in flexibility. For example:

- Reach agreement on what the problem is, what several solutions might be (plan A, B, C), and then work backward from each of these solutions in a team or group meeting. Engage in "what if" exercises involving various steps in solution generation.

- Find some self-analysis exercises, use "mirror image" types of activities that define and verify one's own and others' perceptions, engage in "what I do best" types of facilitated exercises in group settings; focus on the self within the group.

- Engage in visioning exercises through metaphor from history, science, or Native American culture. Remove yourself from the typical corporate jargon. Give the creation of a vision more substance through interdisciplinary investigation and through metaphor.

Typical Game Sources and Structures

There are some typical sources and structures for games that encourage flexibility and its related competencies of creative thinking, decision making, problem solving, and leadership. When you devise these kinds of games, focus on the objective of helping employees to "tune" their understandings and behaviors with what the workplace and their own work require. Tuning demands flexibility. It demands that a person see reality and move beyond it to vision. It requires the ability to seek inputs from many sources; it requires the ability to scan and monitor, synthesize and evaluate, and generate options. Devise games to encourage flexibility around these actions: question, rearrange, modify, combine, simplify, restate, elaborate, simulate, play a role, and discover a pattern.

GAME CREATION PROCESS SUMMARY

Games appeal to our desire to be all that we can be, to contribute our own individual competencies so that organizations and groups can be more effective. Games allow us to become objective about a difficult situation, to experiment and save face, to experience new feelings or craft new procedures that can contribute to success on the job. Games can bring us to the brink of learning and can focus our attention on specific tasks in a way that is different from business as usual. Games can expand capacity for creative thinking, stretch our range of emotions, and point the way for accumulation and management of knowledge.

Games are created by intentional big-picture thinking about a work situation, coupled with an analysis of the parts and parameters of that situation. The elements that make up the work situation are defined according to their cognitive, behavioral, and emotional components. Analogies, illustrations, metaphors, and other representations from the broader work environment, home, or community environment are chosen for their ability to mirror the work situation and engage the learner in discovery. Elements of play are introduced, such as objectives, simple rules, and experience-based content. A game should have a single purpose and be clearly aimed at a particular learning style. Collections of games should present a variety of games appealing to many different learning styles.

Formula for Documenting a Game

- *Title:* describes the game and reflects the work situation;
- *Objective:* an objective for the learner, emphasizing the desired end state after having engaged in this game;

- *Procedure:* a step-by-step elaboration of what to do while playing this game; these steps often have parallels to what one needs to do on the job;

- *Discussion Questions or a Guide to Issues:* a teaching guide for the trainer or game facilitator to help bring the experience of the game to the issues of the workplace;

- *Materials:* what's needed to play the game; and

- *Time Required:* an indication of how much time is required for this game to be played, including the discussion time.

CHALLENGE TO TRAINERS

Trainers have an unprecedented opportunity to design learning experiences for today's complex workplace. Ideas, information, data, and accessibility all abound in great quantity.

Restructured organizations have delivered individuals to the training room door, complete with empowerment and motivation to manage their own careers. People are communicating with each other at speeds and in numbers unimagined only a decade ago.

Voices from historians, politicians, sociologists, educators, journalists, academics, and executives are telling us that organizations need people who can solve problems, make decisions, think creatively, amass and manage knowledge, lead organizations, and be high performers. Support from all corners is pouring into the learning enterprise, especially the workplace learning enterprise. Trainers and learning facilitators must seize the day. Learning games are one powerful tool to do just that.

Carolyn Nilson, Ed.D., *is the author of three best-selling games books published by McGraw-Hill:* Team Games for Trainers, Games That Drive Change, *and* More Team Games for Trainers. *She is also a collaborator with Ed Scannell and John Newstrom in* Complete Games Trainers Play II. *Her work with learning games has been featured in* Fortune, Entrepreneur, Successful Meetings, Training, *and* Training & Development *magazines. She is the author of seventeen additional training systems books. Four of her training books are among Amazon.com's* "50 Best-Selling Training Books," *including three of her games books.*

DELIVERING EFFECTIVE TRAINING PRESENTATIONS

Julie A. Furst-Bowe

Abstract: Trainers who are confident and competent presenters are more likely to achieve both personal and organizational goals (Engleberg, 1994). In this article, written primarily for those new to the training field, a six-step plan for preparing and delivering effective training presentations is described. This plan includes analyzing trainee characteristics, developing a content outline, creating presentation graphics, preparing the learning environment, delivering the presentation, and evaluating the results. Within each part of the plan, the underlying concepts and principles of effective teaching and learning are presented. In addition, the article contains numerous strategies and specific techniques that may be valuable for experienced trainers who are interested in improving their presentation and training skills.

Trainers who are confident and competent presenters are more likely to achieve both personal and organizational goals (Engleberg, 1994). Information that is conveyed by an effective presenter is often perceived as more important, more meaningful, and more interesting by trainees. Skilled presenters are also better able to motivate trainees to apply the information they have learned in the workplace.

Although subject-matter expertise is important for training success, the ability to communicate information clearly to others is equally important. Presentation skills are essential for instructor-led training. Currently, 77 percent of all formal training takes place in classrooms with live instructors (Industry Report, 2001). Effective communication skills are also critical in many technology-based training environments, such as training via satellite or interactive videoconferencing. In a recent survey, more than 5 percent of all organizations reported that they use some type of technology-based system where the instructor is in a remote location to deliver training programs (Industry Report, 2001).

In this article, the six basic steps in preparing and delivering an instructional presentation will be summarized. These steps include (1) analyzing trainees, (2) developing the content, (3) creating visual materials, (4) preparing the learning environment, (5) delivering the presentation, and (6) evaluating the results.

ANALYZING TRAINEES

To give an effective instructional presentation, you must first know who your trainees are. You need to know their general characteristics, such as age, gender, job title, and educational background. You also need to know the size of the group you will be training. While these general characteristics are not directly related to the content or subject matter, knowing this information in advance will help you in determining the level of the information presented and assist you in selecting contexts and examples that are meaningful to your learners (Heinich, Molenda, Russell, & Smaldino, 1996).

Ideally, it is most beneficial to obtain this information well in advance of the training session. However, if this is not possible, the trainer is advised to open the presentation with a short icebreaker in which participants share their backgrounds with the instructor and the other participants. Even this superficial analysis of learner characteristics can provide the trainer with useful information to help make the training session more relevant to the trainees.

Trainees are not simply passive receivers waiting to be supplied with the correct information; they come to class with their own experiences and expectations (Robbins, 1996). In addition to the demographic characteristics of learners, it is important for the trainer to have an understanding of the knowledge, prerequisite skills, attitudes, and learning styles of the trainees (Heinich, Molenda, Russell, & Smaldino, 1996). If the trainer underestimates or overestimates the knowledge or skill levels of a group of trainees, valuable training time will be wasted covering inappropriate content. Methods of assessment can be very formal, such as written pre-tests, skills assessments, or learning style inventories completed in advance of the training session. However, in some situations, the assessment may be as informal as having the trainees identify what they know about the topic and what they want to know about the topic (Robbins, 1996).

DEVELOPING THE CONTENT

Once you have identified who your trainees are and what they need to learn, you can begin to design your training session. The first step is to establish your objectives or intended outcomes for the session. Typical objectives may read: "Following the training session, each participant will be able to describe ten techniques for more effective time management" or "After the training session, each trainee will be able to design a personal web page." Objectives can deal with knowledge, skills, or attitudes.

With the end results in mind, you then need to identify the key points or major steps involved in accomplishing each objective (Heinich, Molenda, Russell, & Smaldino, 1996). For some content areas, you will work with subject-matter specialists to determine the key steps and appropriate information to be included.

Once the content has been identified, you need to make decisions on how best to present the content. You will develop a content outline that indicates the desired sequence in which to present the material. Content should be sequenced in a logical manner that will facilitate the trainees' understanding of the subject.

You then need to review the content outline and determine what media and materials will accompany each key point or each section of the outline. Options may include presentation graphics, handouts, training manuals, CD-ROMs, videotapes, or other learning materials. A typical training session may begin with a short presentation, followed by a videotaped demonstration, followed by a question-and-answer session, and ending with a period in which the trainees practice their new skills. To ensure that you will have adequate time during the session, you should anticipate the length of each learning activity and note it on the content outline.

To combat trainee passivity, particularly in televised training sessions, design sessions so that trainees are consistently engaged in the learning process (Poppell, 1998). Avoid the "talking head" approach in which trainees simply listen to your presentation. Don't lecture for more than fifteen or twenty minutes at a time; instead, provide participants opportunities to apply what they are learning. Supplement lecture materials with activities such as role plays, case studies, games, quizzes, and group problem solving (Popell, 1998). There are numerous resources, including this handbook, that can provide you with examples of appropriate learning activities.

The level of preparation and amount of time that you spend preparing the session depends somewhat on your expertise and comfort level as a presenter. Some trainers are comfortable with a basic outline and list of accompanying media and materials. Others will expand the outline and prepare detailed instructor manuals that include "scripts" to be used in each training session. These detailed lesson plans may be useful if more than one individual will be responsible for conducting the training.

CREATING VISUAL MATERIALS

According to studies, presenters who use visuals are perceived as better organized, better prepared, and more interesting than their counterparts who choose not to use visual aids (Engleberg, 1994). Currently, there are a wide variety of user-friendly presentation graphics software programs that can help you create attractive and effective visuals in a relatively short time.

All visual aids should be designed to augment the learning process. Research has indicated that retention increases when trainees are provided with both verbal and visual cues (Heinich, Molenda, Russell, & Smaldino, 1996). In instructional presentations, visuals should be concise and functional; they may be used to highlight or reinforce key concepts, clarify complex information, condense information, illustrate comparisons and contrasts, and help reach trainees with varying learning styles (Furst-Bowe, 1998).

Whether you are designing presentation graphics to be shown in your training room or to trainees across the country via satellite, it is important that your visuals adhere to the following principles: simplicity, legibility, appropriateness, and consistency. With these principles in mind, here are some techniques to create effective visuals:

Designing the Presentation

- Keep it simple—introduce one concept per visual. Complex concepts can be broken down into a sequence of visuals.

- Use graphics instead of words whenever possible. Charts, graphs, diagrams, illustrations, and photographs are more effective than tables of numbers or lengthy text descriptions.

- Use the same background for all visuals—avoid background templates that contain grids or graphics.

- Information on visuals should be consistent with other learning materials used by trainees, such as technical manuals, videotapes, or CD-ROMs.

Organizing Text

- When using text, limit yourself to key words and phrases—not entire sentences and paragraphs. Include a maximum of forty words per screen.

- Separate key points with bullets or numbers.

- Use the "build" feature of the software to show key points one at a time.

- Develop printed handouts to accompany visuals that contain large amounts of text.

Increasing Legibility

- Use a type size of 30 points or larger for all projected visuals.

- Use simple, sans-serif fonts, such as Helvetica or Universe, for all projected visuals. Use the same font throughout the entire presentation.

- Use highly contrasting colors for text and background.

- Avoid using uppercase letters or excessive underlining—use bold or italic type for emphasis (Lamb, 1992).

- Proofread all visuals at least twice. It often helps to have another person read through the presentation as well.

Adding Graphic Elements

- Use lines and boxes to highlight and separate sections of information.

- Use "clip art" sparingly. Graphic elements should be used to enhance learning—not to decorate or "fill the space."

- Use color sparingly—limit yourself to between two and five colors per screen. Use the same color combinations throughout the entire presentation.

- Use cartoons with caution—humor can be very effective as long as none of the trainees is offended.

PREPARING THE LEARNING ENVIRONMENT

Prior to the presentation, review your outline and determine the best physical environment for your session. Items to consider include room arrangements, placement of media equipment, and lighting. Arrive in the room well in advance so you can preview your visuals and any other media you plan to use. Walk around the room to ensure that your projection equipment is operating correctly and that trainees will be able to see your visuals from any location. Adjust seating or image size if necessary. Check color contrast, as colors may be different on a large screen than they appeared on your personal computer monitor. Experiment with the lighting. Ideally, the room should be as light as possible while still allowing the trainees to be able to view the visuals clearly.

If you are presenting to multiple sites via technology, check to see that all connections have been established and that participants will be able to see and hear you at all sites. Verify that the correct number of handouts or other instructional materials are available at all of the sites. Although taking the time to prepare the environment may be difficult if you are on a tight time schedule or training in a remote location, it is well worth the additional effort. A training session that begins with numerous technical difficulties will affect your confidence as a presenter and immediately damage your credibility with the trainees.

In terms of personal preparation, you should always remember to dress neatly, appropriately, and professionally (Brody, 1998). Become familiar with the dress code of the trainees' organization. Avoid bright colors, distracting patterns, or flashy jewelry; this is particularly true if your presentation is to be televised or videotaped. Remember that participants will be forming their initial impression of you within the first two minutes of your session. You should pay as much attention to your appearance in a training session as you would when preparing for a job interview (Engleberg, 1994).

Individual preparation or rehearsal strategies may vary based on the trainer's confidence level and experience. Some individuals will choose to "visualize" or mentally review the presentation. Others will actually rehearse the presentation by themselves, in front of a video camera or in front of one or more colleagues. In general, as trainers become more experienced and their anxiety level decreases, they will spend less time "rehearsing" presentation material.

DELIVERING THE PRESENTATION

If you have analyzed your trainees and carefully prepared your presentation and your learning environment, you have already significantly increased your chances of delivering a successful training session. When you arrive at the session early and take care of any equipment problems, you can use the last few minutes before the session to greet trainees and introduce yourself to new participants.

Even if the trainees have met before or work together on a regular basis, it is a good idea to begin the session with the short icebreaker or warm-up activity. This allows both you and the participants to relax and focus on the forthcoming training session. If the session is being delivered via some type of distance learning technology, familiarize the participants with the equipment at the beginning of the session (Poppell, 1998). Following any introductory activities, you will want to provide the trainees with an overview of the training session and the objectives to be accomplished.

During the presentation, there are a number of techniques you can utilize to make your presentation more interesting and effective:

- Use names of participants whenever possible—if you are unfamiliar with all trainees, have place cards or name tags available.

- Don't read your presentation from your note cards or from your visuals.

- Talk with, not at, your trainees (Jeary, 1998). Use a conversational tone throughout the session.

- Speak loudly enough so you can be heard by everyone in the room and at all remote sites.

- Maintain contact with trainees—use nonverbal cues from trainees to adjust the pace of your presentation.

- Incorporate short pauses when you want to emphasize a point or simply give the trainees time to formulate responses to your questions.

- Avoid excessive use of filler phrases such as "um," "uh," "you know," and "okay?"

- Move around the room if possible—in a televised presentation, you may change camera angles to provide visual variety.

- Use natural gestures—avoid nervous habits, such as wringing your hands, tapping your feet, or fiddling with your hair or objects in your pockets.

- Tell personal anecdotes and stories if appropriate—they give your trainees something to relate to and make the training more personal (Jeary, 1998).

- Don't apologize or make excuses during your presentation. Apologizing calls attention to problems most trainees would not have noticed and undermines your credibility.

An instructional presentation typically ends with some type of a review or synopsis of the information presented during the session. You may summarize the information for the trainees or allow them to assist you in developing a summary of the key concepts learned.

EVALUATING THE RESULTS

There are numerous methods of obtaining feedback on your presentation skills, including trainee evaluation, supervisor/peer evaluation, and self-evaluation. If you request that trainees evaluate your skills at the end of the session, design the evaluation instrument to obtain the information you need. The form should include specific items regarding the trainer's ability to communicate information, the trainer's capacity to relate to the trainees, and the quality of the visuals used. Allow space for the trainees to elaborate on their ratings or provide additional comments and suggestions. In addition, keep in mind that how well your trainees perform on written tests and the degree to which they use the knowledge and skills presented back on the job may also be a reflection of your training skills.

As part of your professional development process, you may invite a supervisor or a peer to observe your training sessions on a periodic basis. Before each observed session, meet with the observer to determine what type of feedback you are most interested in receiving. After each session, debrief with the observer to discuss the strengths of the presentation and to identify areas for improvement.

Self-evaluation can also be extremely valuable in helping you to continually refine and improve your presentation skills and teaching techniques. Arrange to have your training sessions videotaped. By reviewing the tape, you can see your actual appearance and hear how your voice sounds to trainees. Often this evaluation technique allows you to observe problems in your presentation style of which you were totally unaware, including nervous habits and overuse of filler phrases. Once you are aware of these problems, you can make a conscious effort to refine and improve your presentation and training skills.

CONCLUSION

In this article, a six-step plan for preparing and delivering effective training presentations was described. This plan includes analyzing trainee characteristics, developing a content outline, creating presentation graphics, preparing the learning environment, delivering the presentation, and evaluating the results. Although you may not have adequate time or resources to follow all of the steps every time you prepare a training presentation, the more work you are able to do in advance of the presentation, the more effective you will be as a trainer. As you go through the preparation process numerous times, you will find your skills and confidence increase with each training session. Your trainees will appreciate your efforts, and their skills and abilities will increase as well.

References

Brody, M. (1998). *Speaking is an audience-centered sport.* Elkins Park, PA: Career Skills Press.

Engleberg, I.N. (1994). *The principles of public presentation.* New York: HarperCollins.

Furst-Bowe, J.A. (1998, August). *Creating effective visual learning aids.* Presentation at the Training Skills for Technical Instructors Workshop. University of Wisconsin-Stout, Menomonie, Wisconsin.

Heinich, R., Molenda, M., Russell, J., & Smaldino, S. (1996). *Instructional media and technologies for learning* (5th ed.). Englewood Cliffs, NJ: Merrill.

Industry Report. (2001). *Training, 38*(10), 66–80.

Jeary, T. (1998). Establishing the proper tone ensures speaking success. *Presentations, 12*(1), 26.

Lamb, A. (1992). *Powerful presentations.* Orange, CA: Career Publishing.

Poppell, T. (1998). Training via videoconferencing. *Training & Development, 52*(7), 15–17.

Robbins, P. (1996). *Interactive training for enhanced learning and performance improvement.* Satellite videoconference sponsored by the American Society for Training and Development, Alexandria, Virginia.

Julie A. Furst-Bowe, Ed.D., *is an associate professor and chair of the Communications, Education, and Training Department at the University of Wisconsin-Stout. She teaches courses in training systems, instructional design, and multimedia applications. She has presented at several state, regional, and national conferences and is the author of several articles and book chapters on the use of instructional technology in education and training.*

Training for Leadership Development: Three Process Keys

Marshall Sashkin

Abstract: When organizations want to develop their leaders, they frequently call in consultants or coaches to work directly with the leaders. While this approach may be effective, it has drawbacks in terms of cost and the number of people who can participate at any given time. An alternative to one-on-one coaching is leader development training programs. There is some question, however, as to the effectiveness of such programs. In this article, the author reviews three different studies of leadership development training. From these studies, he proposes three elements—time, context, and reflection—that are key to effective leadership development training.

$\mathbf{I}$s leadership development possible in a training context? Surely it is possible to do meaningful leadership development in a one-on-one coaching framework, and executive coaching has become one of the most visible growth fields in the realm of management and organizational consulting. Yet this approach, so costly in time and dollars, seems impractical as a general approach to leadership development. What, then, are the best options? Can a workshop format—be it two days or two weeks—be successful? Are off-site intensive sessions most effective? Very little research has been done that directly addresses these and other questions surrounding leadership development. My aim in this piece is to report some of the results of research my students and I have conducted over the past few years and to share the key lessons we've learned, not so much about leadership as about the *process* of leadership development.

WHAT THE RESEARCH TELLS US

Much research on the effects and effectiveness of training and development is sadly limited to "smiley face" assessments—end-of-seminar ratings by participants of their degree of satisfaction or happiness with the training. While acceptance of training is certainly a relevant concern, such evaluations are of relatively little value for determining the real effects of training. Over several years I have worked with various doctoral students to obtain more meaningful and valid assessments of the outcomes of leadership development training. The results of three of these efforts do, I believe, tell us some useful things about this work. Two of our studies examined change in individuals' leadership assessments over the course of relatively long training programs. One was a ten-month residential course and the other a year-long weekend course supplemented by extended start-up and wrap-up seminars, along with a week-long session in the middle. The third was a true field experiment focused on identifying the effects of multi-source leadership feedback. I'll describe each, briefly.

A Ten-Month Residential Program

The first study was conducted as part of Brad Lafferty's (1998) doctoral dissertation. He was interested in the effect of a new program developed for the Air Command Staff College, a unit of Air University in Montgomery, Alabama. The new program was developed around the latest concepts of "transformational" leadership first described by James McGregor Burns (1978). No officer has ever been promoted to the Air Force general staff without completing the earlier versions of this program, which very selectively admits several hundred candidates each year.

Prior to the start of the ten-month term, each participant completed *The Leadership Profile (TLP)* (Sashkin & Rosenbach, 1998), a leadership assessment based on the leadership theory developed by me and my colleagues (Sashkin, 1988; Sashkin & Rosenbach, 2001). The participants filled out the same questionnaire after completing the course and also one and two years later. This process was repeated for each new class over several years.

Although we could only obtain self-assessments, by having the questionnaire filled out annually after the training course was over we were able to form what is known in the research literature as a "quasi-experimental" design. In this case, each subsequent administration served as a "control" group for a new pre-training group. That is, we looked not only at the pre- and post-training scores to see whether scores improved after training, but we also made sure that subsequent pre-training scores of subsequent groups were comparable to those of earlier groups. That way we could be sure that the trained groups' changes (if there were any) could not be due to some outside factor (which also would have raised pre-training scores of the incoming participants).

Lafferty determined that the training course did, in fact, produce statistically significant improvements in leadership assessment scores. A wide range of research studies in banks, retail stores, schools, and other organizations has shown that higher *TLP* scores are associated with higher levels of performance as measured by such criteria as supervisors' performance ratings, goal attainment, sales, and achievement test scores. Thus, it is not unreasonable to suggest that a training program that produces incremental changes in *TLP* scores may also result in performance increases.

While Lafferty's study was not a true experiment, it provided evidence that is much stronger than the usual sort of pre- to post-training ratings by participants. The results showed that a long-term intensive training course can, in fact, produce substantial improvements in leadership.

A Year-Long Weekend Program

From 1990 through 1994 I was involved in a program aimed at developing young leaders in the field of vocational education. The Ohio Vocational Education Leadership Institute (OVELI) competitively selected twenty to twenty-five "high flyers"—young people judged to have substantial leadership potential—to participate in a year-long program of workshops. The group met once a month throughout the year, with extended sessions at the January kickoff and the December final meeting and with a ten-day session in the summer that involved a week in Washington, DC, to learn the ins and outs of vocational education funding at the federal level. Unlike the ACSC program evaluated by Lafferty, the institute covered a wider range of content with a lesser focus on leadership. And also unlike ACSC, the OVELI fellows received "360-degree" assessments, both prior to and at the end of the year's training. As was the case for the ACSC study, it became possible to analyze the data we obtained in terms of a quasi-experimental design. That is, we were again able to use prior years as experimental controls for subsequent years, so that if we did find consistent improvements we could legitimately conclude that they were caused by the training and not some other factor.

A graduate student, Ruth Axelrod, and I analyzed the data. We found that not only were there significant improvements in self-perceptions, but that those improvements were also seen when we looked at the perceptions others had of the participants as leaders (Axelrod & Sashkin, 2000). Most interesting of all was our finding that participants who had initially disagreed with the way others saw them changed in that, at the end of the program, their self-perceptions were in substantially and significantly greater agreement with the perceptions others had of them. Leadership researchers generally consider such agreement an indicator of self-awareness, and self-awareness is one of the most important elements of what has come to be called "emotional intelligence."

In summary, we were able to empirically demonstrate not only that the training program had a significant effect in improving leadership but that the effect was not merely a general increase in leadership scores but a clear increase in participants' capacity for self-reflection.

A True Field Experiment in the Effects of 360-Degree Feedback

Both of the programs described previously incorporated a focus on transformational leadership and specifically involved the use of my "visionary leadership theory" in the assessments conducted, as well as in the content that was covered. Could it be that this theory and assessment approach was so powerful in and of itself that the training was secondary? Would it be possible to obtain an effect by simply providing trainees with the assessment information or, perhaps, with only a brief workshop to focus and clarify that information? This was what my student Jim Stryker (2001) asked. To answer that question, he designed and conducted a true experiment. With access to the entire group of about 120 managerial personnel in a small organization, he randomly subdivided the group into three equal subgroups. Everyone took part in a 360-degree assessment process. The first group, one third of the managers selected at random, received a packet of feedback information with a step-by-step explanation and directions for using the information to plan their own development. The second group of one-third of the managers not only received the same feedback packets but received them in the context of a half-day workshop that included a brief one-on-one planning session. The final third received no feedback at all; they were told that it was not possible to get back to everyone right away but that they would receive their feedback in three months.

Three months later Stryker re-administered *The Leadership Profile* to everyone. He then conducted the promised feedback workshop for the third and final group. He expected to find the most change in the group of managers who had taken the earlier workshop, no change among those in the group that received no feedback at all until after the experiment was over, and, perhaps, some change in the group that did receive feedback but had no workshop. He was disappointed. None of the three groups showed any changes, except for a few very small positive changes in the group that was excluded, that is, those who had received no feedback. I would love to say that it was my theory and assessment that was behind it all, that it was now a proven and certain remedy for inadequate leadership. It would have been nice to say that my approach is so good it works even with only a short workshop, instead of months of intensive development work. But none of that is true.

I still believe that my leadership approach, "visionary leadership theory," is one of the best approaches for understanding and developing leadership. Nevertheless, I must admit that a key to effective leadership training may not be whether one applies my approach, the well-known approach developed by Jim Kouzes and Barry Posner (1996), or some other less-recognized leadership theory or model. The real keys may very well be those evident in— or missing from—the leadership development efforts I've just described.

THREE PROCESS KEYS

Reviewing the three experimental and quasi-experimental studies described above, I looked for lessons that might be drawn. I saw three elements were common to one or both of the successful efforts and absent from the one that failed.

Long-Term Learning

Few would argue that leadership is a simple skill easily learned in a two- or three-day workshop, much less developable after a four-hour briefing session. Despite this, we still find that most leadership training consists of short seminars ranging from a day to a week. Stryker's study most clearly demonstrated the folly of trying to develop leadership on a short-term one-shot basis. The results of the three efforts I've described show that, just as there will be but minimal effects from leadership training that consists of short seminars, there can be substantial outcomes from long-term learning.

Work-Context Linkage

One of the common characteristics of the two successful programs that I've described was their intense focus on the organization of the work itself. Rather than being focused on abstract concepts or general skills, these programs were content-focused. Yes, they had a strong leadership element, but the aim was not simply to become a better leader but to become a better *Air Force* leader or a better *vocational education* leader. The program that failed had so little contact time between trainers and participants that most of the training was focused on the basic concepts and measures rather than on what they meant in the context of the participants' own work and organization. The lesson seems clear: Effective leadership training requires a strong focus on the context and content of the leader's work and organization.

A Reflective Focus

The OVELI study most clearly displays what I consider the third key to effective leadership training: a focus on increasing participants' capacity to reflect on their own leadership learning. It is no surprise that Jay Conger, when he examined a variety of executive leadership development programs, concluded that the best ones involved participants in "back home" assignments

The 2003 Annual: Volume 1, Training/© 2003 John Wiley & Sons, Inc.

followed by additional seminars (Conger, 1994). Such reflective learning happens in at least two ways. It occurs, first, in terms of how participants see themselves in comparison with how others see them. Second, it happens as participants have an opportunity, in the connection between the training and the work context, to plan, act, observe the consequences, reflect, learn, and then repeat this cycle again and again. Leadership assessment feedback from others is an essential part of the reflective learning process, as is a link between leadership learning and the work context. And the time it takes to obtain such information, from actions and from others, and to reflect and learn from it, is not short.

WHAT RESEARCH TEACHES FOR PRACTICE

The three keys I can extract from my own experience in directing and assessing leadership training and development are intimately intertwined. The three keys—(1) a realistically long development timeline, (2) a strong connection between the training and one's actual work context, and (3) an emphasis on reflective learning—may not all be present in every learning opportunity and may not need to be. However, I doubt that a leadership training program from which one or more of these keys is totally absent is likely to have much of an effect, if it has any at all.

This report has been focused on my own learnings about what is required for an effective leadership training and development process. I have strong views as to what content must be part of an effective leadership training and development process, but my purpose here has not been to present and convince the reader of the merit of my own leadership theory and its application. I have shared what I have learned, usually with considerable effort—and sometimes to my dismay—about how to do successful leadership training and development.

References

Axelrod, R.H., & Sashkin, M. (2000, August). *Outcome measurement in a leadership development program.* Paper presented at the annual meeting of the Academy of Management, Toronto.

Conger, J. (1994). *Learning to lead: The art of transforming managers into leaders.* San Francisco, CA: Jossey-Bass.

Kouzes, J.M., & Posner, B.Z. (1996). *The leadership challenge* (2nd ed.). San Francisco, CA: Jossey-Bass.

Lafferty, B. (1998). *An empirical investigation of a leadership development program.* Unpublished doctoral dissertation. The George Washington University, Washington, DC.

McGregor Burns, J. (1978). *Leadership.* New York: The Free Press.

Sashkin, M. (1988). The visionary leader: A new theory of organizational leadership. In J. Conger & R. Kanungo (Eds.), *Charismatic leadership: The elusive factor in organizational effectiveness.* San Francisco, CA: Jossey-Bass.

Sashkin, M., & Rosenbach, W.E. (1998). *The leadership profile.* Seabrook, MD: Ducochon Press.

Sashkin, M., & Rosenbach, W.E. (2001). A new vision of leadership. In W.E. Rosenbach & R.L. Taylor (Eds.), *Contemporary issues in leadership* (5th ed.). Boulder, CO: Westview Press.

Stryker, J. (2001). *The effects of 360 degree feedback: A field experiment.* Unpublished doctoral dissertation. The George Washington University, Washington, DC.

Marshall Sashkin, Ph.D., *is a principal in Marshall Sashkin & Associates and professor of human resource development in the program in human resource development at the Graduate School of Education and Human Development, George Washington University, Washington, DC. He received a Ph.D. from the University of Michigan and taught there and at the University of Maryland prior to his current appointment. Dr. Sashkin has been active in HRD as a researcher, teacher, and consultant for over thirty years. He was associate editor of the* Annual Handbook for Group Facilitators *from 1979 to 1983. He has worked with organizations such as GE Capital, American Express (Corporate), and the World Bank. His latest book,* Leadership That Matters, *will be published by Berrett-Koehler in 2002.*

Contributors

Lynne Andia
1800 Chautauqua Trail
Malvern, PA 19355
  (610) 983–9603
  fax: (610) 983–9604
  email: FogelmanAndia@msn.com

Kristin J. Arnold, MBA, CPCM
Quality Process Consultants, Inc.
48 West Queens Way
Hampton, VA 23669
  (757) 728–0191 or (800) 589–4733
  fax: (757) 728–0192
  email: karnold@qpcteam.com
  URL: www.qpcteam.com

Teri-E Belf, M.A., C.A.G.S., M.C.C.
Founder and Executive Director
Success Unlimited Network
2016 Lakebreeze Way
Reston, VA 20191
  (703) 716–8374
  fax: (703) 264–7867
  email: belf@erols.com
  URL: www.erols.com/belf
  URL: www.successunlimitednet.com

Robert Alan Black, Ph.D.
Cre8ng People, Places & Possibilities
P.O. Box 5805
Athens, GA 30604–5805
  (706) 353–3387
  email: alan@cre8ng.com
  URL: www.cre8ng.com

Susan Boyd
Susan Boyd Associates, Computer
  Training Specialists
270 Mather Road
Jenkintown, PA 19046–3129
  (215) 886–2669
  fax: (215) 886–7931
  email: susan@susan-boyd.com
  URL: www.susan-boyd.com

Marlene Caroselli, Ed.D.
Director
Center for Professional Development
324 Latona Road, Suite 1600
Rochester, NY 14626
  (716) 227–6512
  fax: (509) 696–5405
  email: mccpd@aol.com

Richard Chang
President and CEO
Richard Chang Associates, Inc.
15265 Alton Parkway, Suite 300
Irvine, CA 92618
  (800) 756–8096
  fax: (949) 727–7007
  email: rchang@rca4results.com

Phyliss Cooke, Ph.D.
1935 Harton Road
San Diego, CA 92123–3819
  (858) 569–5144
  fax: (858) 569–7318
  email: phyliss6@earthlink.net

Teresa Torres Coronas, Ph.D.
Rovira i Virgili University
Av. Universitat, s/n
43204 Reus (Tarragona)
Spain
    email: mttc@fcee.urv.es

Julie A. Furst-Bowe, Ed.D.
303 Administration Building
University of Wisconsin-Stout
Menomonie, WI 54751
    (715) 232-2421
    fax: (715) 232-1699
    email: bowej@uwstout.edu

Peter R. Garber
Manager, Teamwork Development
PPG Industries, Inc.
One PPG Place
Pittsburgh, PA 15272
    (412) 434-3417

Barbara Pate Glacel, Ph.D.
12103 Richland Lane
Oak Hill, VA 20171
    (703) 262-9120
    fax: (703) 264-5314
    email: BPGlacel@glacel.com
    URL: www.glacel.com

Donna L. Goldstein, Ed.D.
Development Associates International
3389 Sheridan Street #309
Hollywood, FL 33021
    (954) 893-0123
    email: devasscint@aol.com

Lois B. Hart, Ed.D.
President, Leadership Dynamics
Director, Women's Leadership
    Institute
11256 WCR 23
Ft. Lupton, CO 80621
    (970) 785-2716
    fax: (970) 785-2717
    email: lhart@seqnet.net

Mila Gascó Hernández, Ph.D.
International Institute on Governance
C/Córcega 255, 5º 1ª
08036 Barcelona
Spain
    email: mila.gasco@iigov.org

Cher Holton, Ph.D.
The Holton Consulting Group, Inc.
4704 Little Falls Drive, Suite 300
Raleigh, NC 27609
    (919) 783-7088 or (800) 336-3940
    fax: (919) 781-2218
    email: cher@holtonconsulting.com

Herbert S. Kindler, Ph.D.
Herb Kindler & Associates
427 Beirut Avenue
Pacific Palisades, CA 90272
    (310) 459-0585
    email: herbkindler@aol.com

Chuck Kormanski, Jr.
133 East Beaver Street
Bellefonte, PA 16823
    (814) 353-0638
    email: CLKeducation@aol.com

Chuck Kormanski, Sr., Ed.D.
Kormanski Consulting
25 Bedford Street, R.D. #1
Hollidaysburg, PA 16648
  (814) 695–2935
  email: Kormanskiconsult@aol.com

Tara L. Kuther, Ph.D.
Department of Psychology
Western Connecticut State University
181 White Street
Danbury, CT 06810
  (203) 837–8694
  fax: (646) 349–4262
  email: TKuther@aol.com

David J. Maier, MS
8452 Appleton
Dearborn Heights, MI 48127
  (313) 277–2940
  email: david@dmaier.net

Sharon Drew Morgen
411 Brazos #220
Austin, TX 78701
  (512) 457–0246
  email: sdm@austin.rr.com
  URL: www.newsalesparadigm.com

Ira J. Morrow, Ph.D.
Department of Management
The Lubin School of Business
Pace University
1 Pace Plaza
New York, NY 10038
  (212) 346–1846
  email: imorrow@pace.edu

James L. Moseley, Ed.D.
Wayne State University
School of Medicine
Department of Community Medicine
University Health Center, Suite 9D
4201 St. Antoine Avenue
Detroit, MI 48201
  (313) 577–7948
  email: jmosele@med.wayne.edu

Carolyn Nilson, Ed.D.
38 Rood Hill Road
Sandisfield, MA 01255
  (413) 258–3369
  email: ttc13672@taconic.net

Marshall Sashkin
The George Washington University
2134 G Street, NW
Washington, DC 20052
  (202) 994–8649
  email: sashkin@gwu.edu

Bob Shaver
University of Wisconsin-Madison
Fluno Center for Executive Education
601 University Avenue
Madison, WI 53715–1035
  (800) 292–8964
  email: bshaver@bus.wisc.edu

Lori L. Silverman
Partners for Progress
1218 Carpenter Street
Madison, WI 53704–4304
  (800) 253–6398
  email:
  lori@partnersforprogress.com
  URL: www.partnersforprogress.com

Elizabeth A. Smith, Ph.D.
Summit Resources
1015 Ashford Parkway
Houston, TX 77077–2403
　(281) 497–8876
　fax: (713) 785–4818
　email: smithce@flash.net

Steve Sphar
2870 Third Avenue
Sacramento, CA 95818
　(916) 731–4851
　fax: (916) 739–8057
　email: sphar@pacbell.net

Sivasailam "Thiagi" Thiagarajan
QB International
4423 East Trailridge Road
Bloomington, IN 47408
　(812) 332–1478
　email: Thiagi@thiagi.com

Chih-Hsiung Tu, Ph.D.
2134 G Street, NW
Washington, DC 20052
　(202) 994–2676
　fax: (202) 994–2145
　email: ctu@gwu.edu

Lorraine Ukens
Team-ing With Success
4302 Starview Court
Glen Arm, MD 21057–9745
　(410) 592–6050
　fax: (410) 592–8263
　email: ukens@team-ing.com

Mary B. Wacker
M.B. Wacker Associates
3175 N. 79th Street
Milwaukee, WI 53222–3930
　(414) 875–9876
　fax:(414) 875–9874
　email: mbwacker@wi.rr.com

Ryan Watkins, Ph.D.
Assistant Professor
Educational Technology Leadership
George Washington University
2134 G Street, NW #103
Washington, DC 20052
　(202) 994–2263
　email: rwatkins@gwu.edu

CONTENTS OF THE COMPANION VOLUME, THE 2003 ANNUAL: VOLUME 2, CONSULTING

*See Experiential Learning Activities Categories, p. 6, for an explanation of the numbering system.

**Topic is "cutting edge."